The Reputation and Writings of Alexander Pope

Also by James Reeves

Collected Poems 1929–1974
The Questioning Tiger
Subsong
Poems and Paraphrases

ANTHOLOGIES
The Poets' World
The Modern Poets' World
A Vein of Mockery

EDITIONS IN THE POETRY BOOKSHELF SERIES
Chaucer: Lyric and Allegory
John Donne
Andrew Marvell (with Martin Seymour-Smith)
Jonathan Swift
S. T. Coleridge
John Clare
Five Late Romantic Poets
Robert Browning
Emily Dickinson
Gerard Manley Hopkins
D. H. Lawrence

ABOUT POETRY
A Short History of English Poetry
The Critical Sense
Understanding Poetry
Teaching Poetry
Inside Poetry (with Martin Seymour-Smith)
How to Write Poems for Children

The Reputation and Writings of Alexander Pope

by

JAMES REEVES

Le vers se sent toujours les bassesses du cœur.
BOILEAU: *L'Art Poétique*

. . . No man is demolished but by himself.
RICHARD BENTLEY: *Letter to Pope, 1735*

The life of a Wit is a warfare upon earth.
ALEXANDER POPE: *Preface, 1717*

HEINEMANN
LONDON
BARNES & NOBLE
NEW YORK

Heinemann Educational Books

LONDON   EDINBURGH   MELBOURNE   AUCKLAND
TORONTO   HONG KONG   SINGAPORE   KUALA LUMPUR
IBADAN   NAIROBI   JOHANNESBURG
NEW DELHI   LUSAKA

ISBN (U.K.) 0 435 18774 0
ISBN (U.S.A.) 0-06-495820-5
© James Reeves 1976
First published 1976

Published in Great Britain by
Heinemann Educational Books Ltd
48 Charles Street, London W1X 8AH
Published in the U.S.A. 1976 by
Harper & Row Publishers, Inc.
Barnes & Noble Import Division
Printed in Great Britain by
Cox & Wyman Ltd
London, Fakenham and Reading

Acknowledgements

The writing of this book over the past ten years has been accomplished with increasing difficulty. I am therefore all the more grateful to the many friends who have helped me, especially in the final preparation of the text for the printer. I am particularly indebted to: Peter Dixon of the University of London, Susan Hibbert of the Society of Indexers, Greta Hodges, Michael Irwin, F. R. Lockhart and Keith Thomas. I am of course solely responsible for any errors of fact or interpretation which remain.

J. R.

The engraving of Pope reproduced on the back of the jacket is by P. Condé, after a portrait by William Hoare, included in the Warton edition of Pope's works, 1797. It is reproduced by kind permission of the Trustees of the National Portrait Gallery.

Contents

Preface

Pope was the late-born only son of a retired London linen draper. His intellectual precocity was heightened by the physical handicap which early made him almost a cripple and an enforced valetudinarian. A spinal infection in childhood turned him into a hunchback of diminutive stature and made him an object of pity to his well-wishers and ridicule to his enemies. It has been maintained that the restrictions to which Roman Catholics were subjected after the Revolution, and during the period in which the Protestant establishment was in constant fear of Jacobite reaction, added to Pope's sense of deprivation. There is no evidence of this. On the contrary, Pope turned his religion to good advantage, since it prevented him from succumbing to the temptation of accepting public office and made it impossible for him to excel in any direction except the one he chose – that of literary distinction. For excel he must as compensation for his physical disadvantages combined with intellectual talent unregulated by any conventional scheme of education. He was the paradigm of the deprived child clamouring for attention. It need hardly be said that other handicapped people have come to terms with their problem in different ways, especially in the direction of maturity and resignation. Pope remained in some degree all his life a spoilt child who never fully matured.

The literary world in which, as an adolescent, he sought to make an impression was, he soon discovered, a hard and competitive one. Pope was prepared to compete by the same methods as others. 'The life of a Wit,' he wrote in 1717, 'is a warfare upon earth; and the present spirit of the learned world is such, that to attempt to serve it (any way) one must have the constancy of a martyr, and a resolution to suffer for its sake.' This is the key to an important aspect of his writings. It was not enough, he discovered, to publish his poems and let them and the critics speak for him. He must speak for his poems. Most of his work, whether in verse or prose, contains this built-in element of self-advertisement. Pope's later verse is always searching for a proclaimable *raison d'être* – the exposure of fools and pretenders, the reform of public morals, care for cultural standards. The real motive behind everything he wrote was the establishment and maintenance of his own position of authority among poets and wits, his acceptance by the arbiters of taste and fashion among men of rank and position. For it may have been that a consciousness of his own humble, though respectable and in no way discreditable origin, was an added spur to his ambitions. The system of patronage on which literature depended at the close of the seventeenth century was still in effective operation. However talented a writer, there was no independent readership which he could appeal to without the approval of some at least of the great. If there is any validity in the theory of the 'ruling passion' or, as we might say, central instinctual drive which fascinated Pope, it is abundantly clear that in Pope's own case this was the instinct of emulation, the passion to be perpetually noticed and commended. That this often entailed controversy and abuse, even violent abuse, did not trouble him much: indeed, he reckoned it part of the 'warfare upon earth'. He had the wit to discover very early that it is more profitable for a writer to be abused than ignored. He may indeed have been the first publicist of any note to discover this fact, which has been a notable feature in the careers of some of our contemporary stars of the media.

Given Pope's early psychological make-up and the life-style it initiated, it is not difficult to admire, as many of his admirers do, the dogged, even courageous, single-mindedness with which Pope fought his battles. In an age of hard and ruthless competition in which the *esprit de dépassement* was so much in evidence, the career of Pope could be applauded as little less than a triumph. But it was a triumph achieved not without some cost. The cost must be counted in terms of poetic achievement.

The poetry was, as I have said, never allowed to speak for itself. I believe that ultimately all poetry speaks for itself. A reputation inflated during the life of the poet usually adjusts itself in time; the same is true of poetry not adequately recognized during the poet's lifetime. This is true of the poetry of Swift no less than of Coleridge, of Marvell no less than of Clare, of Smart no less than of Emily Dickinson. What, it may be asked, has this to do with Pope, whose reputation, in some quarters at least, has always stood high? It is this problem which led me to undertake a detailed study of Pope's reputation and writings. My study began, not from a feeling of antipathy to the man, but from a conviction that his poems have been over-valued in the present century. It seemed to me, therefore, more interesting to begin this book with a close study of Pope's reputation from its beginnings, through the crucial period when the adult Pope was alive to foster it, then onward until the present time. There never has been a time since Pope's middle years when his writings have not been the subject of controversy. The Pope industry in literary criticism, as it may be called, had its beginnings in the writings of the founder, continued in what may be called an unprofessionalized way until it was adopted by English academic circles early in the present century after the establishment of schools of English literature in the universities. The great American take-over has injected into the industry new capital in the form of research and critical enthusiasm evident in the many exhaustive studies by American academics.

What, then, of the poetry which is the concern of this impressive industry? This is the subject of the second part of my book. It may be asked why a writer evidently as unsympathetic as I should undertake such a study. Why spend so much trouble on a work which, after all, may be characterized as purely negative? The answer, I think, must be that it is the obverse of the positively critical and appreciative work on other poets which has occupied most of my time as a writer on poetry. I have found some evidence in academic quarters that an admiration of Pope is in some degree a *sine qua non* of critical respectability. I use the word 'academic' in a purely descriptive and not in any way pejorative sense. Indeed, since the serious study of literature, especially in America, is becoming increasingly reserved to the universities, it is all the more necessary to come to terms with academic attitudes and, if it is not presumptuous to say so, to influence them in right directions. I have met academics who do not share their more vociferous colleagues' infatuation with Pope. The tone of much of the criticism quoted in this book, especially in its later pages has a touch of stridency, of protesting too much, of proclaiming the tenets of a religion rather than inculcating a spirit of rational and objective appraisal. Does the hardline Pope admirer, one is inclined to wonder, really want his students to judge for themselves? If not, he will deprecate the reading of my dangerous thoughts. But I write less for the uncritical devotee than for the reader concerned with poetic values, anxious to test his reactions for himself.

I cannot say to him 'You must enjoy this or that': all I can do, if I may anticipate what I say at the conclusion to Part i, 'is to try to show you what you enjoy'.

J. R.

Lewes, 1964–1975

I

POPE'S POSTHUMOUS REPUTATION

1 Warton

Almost everyone who has written on Pope has remarked on the fluctuations of his reputation and on the violence of those fluctuations. John Dennis, for instance (not Pope's contemporary but the author of a handbook on *The Age of Pope* published in 1894), writes:

> Pope's standing among his country's poets has been the source of much controversy. There have been critics who deny to him the name of a poet, while others place him in the first rank. In his own century there was comparatively little difference of opinion with regard to his merits. Chesterfield gave him the warmest praise; Swift, Addison, and Warburton ranked him with the peers of song; Johnson, whose discriminative criticism reaches perhaps its highest level in his Life of Pope, in reply to the question which had been asked, even in his day, whether Pope was a poet? asks in return, 'If Pope be not a poet, where is poetry to be found?' and adds that 'to circumscribe poetry by a definition will only show the narrowness of the definer, though a definition which shall exclude Pope will not readily be made'.

This typifies not only the view of Pope's reputation which obtained at the end of the nineteenth century, but also the half-truths and partial misrepresentations which have always been involved in this subject. Pope's status during the two and a half centuries since his appearance on the English literary scene cannot be represented by the idea of a critical pendulum. The truth is that there have always been two opposed views, both more or less active, and there have always been discriminating readers on either side. It is important both for the understanding of Pope and for the discussion of larger issues that this critical dichotomy should be illustrated in some detail.

In 1745, the year after Pope's death, it was possible to conclude his biography in these terms:

> It must be confessed, that not only of this Age, but speaking of all former Ages, in our Language, he was THE GREATEST POET.

This biography, *Memoirs of the Life and Writings of Alexander Pope Esq.*, published by Pope's old enemy, the bookseller Curll, was a piece of hackwork, and of its author, William Ayre, nothing is certainly known. The hyperbolical praise of Pope has of course no critical status; it merely demonstrates a view which would be perfectly acceptable among some of Pope's contemporaries, perhaps the majority of them. That it was not the only view is proved by Ayre himself, who quotes in his biography a number of hostile opinions, no more to be discounted because they came from Pope's enemies than some of the favourable opinions because they came from his friends.

The notion that Pope was supreme, in the sense implied by Ayre, throughout the latter half of the eighteenth century, and was only dethroned with the triumph of Romanticism has so often been repeated that it is still regarded as a truism. It is all the more necessary, therefore, to examine with some care the view expressed by Joseph Warton. It is usual among modern critics either to neglect or to misrepresent this 'pre-Romantic', as he has been called. Both as a poet of the 1740s and as a critic, he was before his time, and his achievement is not generally recognized. W. L. Macdonald[1] does little justice to Warton's account of Pope when he accuses him of imprecision and timidity.

> By reiterating in many forms what he said in the Dedication of his *Essay on Pope* he assumed the role of a revolutionary; but by failing to say anything of a specific nature in support of his bold pronouncement he has left the impression of playing the revolutionary without conviction.

This is not the impression Warton leaves on me. He is as precise as most critics of his time (Johnson for instance) and he writes of Pope with firm conviction, though without dogmatism. Nor does Macdonald give Warton full credit for the earliness of his views. The first volume of his *Essay on the Genius and Writings of Pope* appeared as early as 1756.

Joseph Warton writes as a sincere, often enthusiastic, admirer of Pope, and he makes it clear that his cool and dispassionate appraisal of Pope's limitations as a man and a poet is based, not on prejudice or personal animosity, but on his own convictions and judgement as a poet and a reader of discernment. Claiming a pioneer impartiality, he writes:

> We have never yet seen a fair and candid criticism on the character and merits of our last great poet, Mr. Pope.

[1] W. L. Macdonald: *Pope and his Critics*, London, 1951.

He praises the 'mellifluous' language of the *Pastorals* but censures their lack of originality:

> It is somewhat strange, that in the pastorals of a young poet there should not be found a single rural image that is new: but this, I am afraid, is the case of the Pastorals before us. The ideas of Theocritus, Virgil, and Spenser, are indeed here exhibited in language equally mellifluous and pure; but the descriptions and sentiments are trite and common.... Complaints of immoderate heat, and wishes to be conveyed to cooling caverns, when uttered by the inhabitants of Greece, have a decorum and a consistency, which they totally lose in the character of a British shepherd.

He censures, too, the lack of particularity in the descriptions of *Windsor Forest*, but praises Pope for introducing moral sentiments into descriptive verse. In this matter he notes Pope's debt to Denham. Warton is also very particular in his illustrations of Pope's debt to Flatman in his translation of Hadrian's farewell to his soul. In an interesting comment on this and other verbal echoes he makes a distinction between plagiarism and unconscious borrowing. Commenting on the plagiarism from Flatman, Warton remarks:

> There is a close and surprising resemblance . . . to one of an obscure and forgotten rhymer . . . . namely Thomas Flatman, from whose dunghill as well as from the dregs of Crashaw, of Carew, of Herbert, and others, (for it is well known he was a great reader of all those poets) Pope has very judiciously collected gold.

It was not till sixty years after Warton's *Essay* that Coleridge, in the high tide of Romanticism, referred to Pope and his followers as 'that school of French poetry, condensed and invigorated by English understanding'. It is to Warton's credit to have seen so early the bad effects on English poetry of French precept and example:

> Correctness is a vague term, frequently used without meaning and precision. It is perpetually the nauseous cant of the French critics, and of their advocates and pupils, that the English writers are generally incorrect . . . In no polished nation, after criticism has been much studied, and the rules of writing established, has any very extraordinary work ever appeared. This has visibly been the case, in Greece, in Rome, and in France; after Aristotle, Horace and Boileau had written their Arts of Poetry. In our own country, the rules of the drama, for instance, were never more completely understood than at present: yet what uninteresting, though faultless, tragedies, have we lately seen? So much better is our judgment than our execution . . . Whether or no, the natural powers be not confined and debilitated by that timidity and caution

which is occasioned by a rigid regard to the dictates of art; or whether
that philosophical, that geometrical, and systematical spirit so much in
vogue, which has spread itself in the sciences even into polite literature,
by consulting only reason has not diminished and destroyed sentiment;
and made our poets write from and to the head rather than the heart: or
whether, lastly, when just models, from which the rules have necessarily
been drawn, have once appeared, succeeding writers, by vainly and am-
bitiously striving to surpass those just models, and to shine and surprise,
do not become stiff, and forced, and affected in their thoughts and
diction.

It is perhaps not surprising that some academic critics of today
choose to ignore Warton. Passages such as this surely call in question
the picture of him as a timid revolutionary.

Warton was also in advance of the Romantics in his whole-hearted
admiration for *The Rape of the Lock*. While admitting Pope's debt to
Abbé Villars' *Le Comte de Gabalis* for the idea of the sylphs, and to
The Tempest and *A Midsummer Night's Dream* in the matter of their
various employments, Warton considers that Pope had improved on
Shakespeare. The *Rape* was admired for 'politeness, poignancy and
poetry'; it is 'the best satire extant', and Pope's highest title to rank as a
poet of imagination.

Warton's comments on this and other poems display a spirit of
critical objectivity almost entirely absent from critical comment appearing while Pope was alive. Of *Eloïsa to Abelard* he says that 'Pope was a
most excellent improver, if no great original inventor'. *An Essay on Man*
is described as argumentative and dry, but Pope 'has relied chiefly on
the poetry of his style for the purpose of interesting his readers' – a comment which contains the germ of much later criticism of the *Essay*.
Warton is also at pains in discussing the *Essay* and the *Epistles to Several
Persons* to point out the sources of Pope's thought in the French
moralists from Montaigne to Pascal.

His account of *The Dunciad* is cool and dispassionate. It too laid the
foundations for later critical comment. Warton did not admire Theobald and was more or less content with the three-book *Dunciad
Variorum* of 1729.

> Thus far all was clear, consistent, and of a piece; and was delivered in
> such nervous and spirited versification, that the delighted reader had
> only to lament that so many poetical beauties were thrown away on such
> dirty and despicable subjects, as were the scribblers here proscribed . . .

But the addition of Book IV is an unmitigated disaster, and the sub-
stitution of Cibber for Theobald is wholly inappropriate:

. . . the subject of this fourth book was foreign and heterogeneous, and the addition of it injudicious, ill-placed, and incongruous . . . With a great stock of levity, vanity, and affectation [Cibber] had sense, and wit, and humour.

There is some cogency in Warton's condemnation of the account of the education of young men on the ground that these methods had produced many of the gentlemen whom Pope praised, such as Wyndham, Talbot, and Pulteney. Warton also anticipates the psychological and moral interest in Pope as a man which featured so largely in the controversy of the early nineteenth century, and which has never quite died out. He perceives the connection between poet and man, and aptly quotes Bacon on this subject:

Whosoever hath anything fixed in his person that doth induce contempt, hath also a perpetual spur in himself, to rescue and deliver himself from scorn.

Warton was clearly right in taking note of the element of compensation for physical deformity in Pope's feverish literary and social life. He repeats the phrase which had been applied to Pope allegedly by Atterbury: *Mens curva in corpore curvo*, adding the dry comment:

This sentiment seems utterly inconsistent with the warm friendship supposed to subsist between these two celebrated men.

In his remarks on the *Epistle to Dr. Arbuthnot* he shows himself uneasy about the 'Sporus' portrait: 'Yet who would wish to be the author of such an invective?' Writing of *The Dunciad*, Warton censures 'the filthiness of the images' in Book II as 'extremely offensive and disgusting'. It is often said that in such contexts Pope merely panders to the taste of his time, and that it is only 'Victorian' prudery which condemns him on that account. Warton was neither a Victorian nor a prude.

It must be insisted that Warton's reservations about Pope and his poetry are those of a judicious and balanced commentator who was at the same time, as has been said, a sincere admirer. It is for this reason that they are to be respected. Almost all admirers of Pope until the present century have had serious reservations, and in his inability to reconcile admiration and revulsion Warton anticipates a century and a half of later criticism. There is no ambiguity in the words of the dedication of his *Essay on the Genius and Writings of Pope* to the poet Young:

I revere the memory of Pope, I respect and honour his abilities; but I do not think him at the head of his profession. In other words, in that species of poetry wherein Pope excelled, he is superior to all mankind:

and I only say, that this species of poetry is not the most excellent one of the art. We do not, it should seem, sufficiently attend to the difference there is, betwixt a Man of Wit, a Man of Sense, and a True Poet . . . A clear head, and acute understanding are not sufficient, alone, to make a poet; the most solid observations on human life, expressed with the utmost elegance and brevity, are Morality, and not Poetry; the epistles of Boileau in rhyme, are no more poetical, than the characters of La Bruyère in Prose; it is a creative and glowing Imagination, 'acer spiritus ac vis', and that alone, that can stamp a writer with this exalted and very common character which so few possess, and of which so few can properly judge.

In the conclusion to his *Essay* Warton expands some of the ideas suggested in the dedication. Justice has never, so far as I know, been done to Warton, who is dismissed as a somewhat ineffectual pioneer of Romanticism, 'a revolutionary without conviction', in Macdonald's phrase. Romanticism is at best a vague term, useful enough in literary history, but with little application to any of Warton's conscious aims. It was not Romanticism he was concerned with, it was what he called true poetry. In this context modern critics are inclined to put the word 'true' in quotation-marks, as if the notion of any such category made them uncomfortable. But neither Warton nor his contemporaries – Pope included – felt the necessity for the quotation-marks. When Pope writes of 'true wit', he is not writing of Augustan wit; when Warton writes of 'true poetry', he is thinking, not of poetry as judged by pre-Romantic canons but of poetic standards from Homer onwards. It is only necessary to keep in mind the distinctions and reservations of the following passage to realize how early after Pope's death the main lines of the later controversies about him were laid down.

> . . . the largest proportion of them [Pope's poems] is of the didactic, moral, and satiric kind; and consequently, not of the most poetic species of poetry; whence it is manifest, that good sense and judgment were his characteristical excellencies, rather than fancy and invention; . . . this turn of mind led him to admire French models; he studied Boileau attentively; formed himself upon him . . . He gradually became one of the most correct, even, and exact poets that ever wrote; polishing his pieces with a care and assiduity, that no business or avocation ever interrupted: so that, if he does not frequently ravish and transport his reader, yet he does not disgust him with unexpected inequalities, and absurd improprieties. Whatever poetical enthusiasm he actually possessed, he withheld and stifled. The perusal of him affects not our minds with such strong emotions as we feel from Homer and Milton; so that no man of a true poetical spirit, is master of himself while he reads them.

Hence, he is a writer fit for universal perusal; adapted to all ages and stations; for the old and for the young; the man of business and the scholar. He who would think *Palamon and Arcite, The Tempest* or *Comus,* childish and romantic, might relish Pope. Surely it is no narrow and niggardly encomium to say he is the great Poet of Reason, the first of ethical authors in verse. And this species of writing is, after all, the surest road to an extensive reputation. It lies more level to the general capacities of men, than the higher flights of more genuine poetry. We all remember when even a Churchill was more in vogue than a Gray. He that treats of fashionable follies, and the topics of the day, that describes present persons and recent events, finds many readers, whose understandings and whose passions he gratifies. The name of Chesterfield on one hand, and of Walpole on the other, failed not to make a poem bought and talked off . . .

Warton then concludes by assigning a place to Pope after Spenser, Shakespeare, and Milton, but just above Dryden.

2 Johnson

Dr Johnson, whose prefaces to the poets, later known as the *Lives*, appeared a quarter of a century after the first volume of Warton's *Essay*, is as much quoted as Warton is overlooked. Any critic can cite Johnson to his purpose, and it is difficult not to misrepresent him by quotation. I think it is true to say that the general view is that Johnson is extremely favourable to Pope. Geoffrey Tillotson, for instance, in his book *On the Poetry of Pope*, quotes what he calls a 'magnificent tribute, a paean' from Johnson, but when the passage is read in the context of the *Life* as a whole, it is doubtful if Johnson himself would have regarded the passage in question as unqualified praise. He commends Pope for his intellectual curiosity, which transcends mere good sense, regarded by Johnson as 'the constituent and fundamental principle' of Pope's 'intellectual character'. He commends Pope's diligence, comparing Dryden unfavourably with him in this respect. However, he makes it clear that he considers Dryden Pope's superior in intellectual energy and poetic fire. He awards Pope second place among poets since Milton.

There is in much of Johnson's outwardly favourable comment a note of irony, or at least of ambiguity, which perhaps conceals a certain coolness. This may deceive an unwary reader. It is as if Johnson were saying, 'This is an introduction to the most celebrated poet of the century. You must take my praise at its face value, but the discerning will see that I have reservations'. What, for instance, are we to make of the famous comment on Pope's technical achievement? –

> to attempt any further improvement of versification will be dangerous

What kind of brinkmanship is Pope supposed to have been practising? Again, the passage of Johnson cited above (page 1) in the quotation from John Dennis (1894), and quoted by many others before and since, is surely more equivocal than is realized by admirers of Pope who put their thumb into the Johnson pie and pull it out with such an air of triumph. Johnson wrote:

> After all this, it is surely superfluous to answer the question that has once been asked, Whether Pope was a poet? otherwise than by asking in return, If Pope be not a poet, where is poetry to be found? To cir-

cumscribe poetry by a definition will only show the narrowness of the definer, though a definition which should exclude Pope will not easily be made.

Reference to Johnson's dictionary shows that he was far too cautious to expose any such narrowness on his own part. *Poem* is defined as 'the work of a poet; a metrical composition'. *Poet* is given 'an inventor; an author of fiction; a writer of poems; one who writes in measure'. A poet would need to be endowed with a very indifferent talent to be sure of exclusion from this definition. Johnson seems to have been without any general theory of the nature of poetry, and to have been content with pragmatic assessments of poets and poems according to either subjective reactions or the taste of his time. This is not to disparage him as a critic; it does imply, however, that allowances must frequently be made for his judgements on temperamental or historical grounds. His strictures on Gray, for instance, tell us little about Gray but something about Johnson and about neo-classical standards. The fact is that Johnson did not admire Pope as a man, and was content to leave the assessment of his poetic status to the reading public. He goes on to say that Pope cannot be excluded from any canon of poets 'to whom the voice of mankind has decreed the wreath of poetry'. Johnson here abdicates the poet's and critic's function in favour of the *vox populi*. Writing in 1934, Sherburn considered that Johnson's *Life of Pope* was the best so far written. It is a sustained piece of bio-criticism in which, though Johnson ostensibly kept the man and the poet apart, it is clear that in his mind they were inextricably bound up together. Moral judgements, here as elsewhere in his criticism, spill over into aesthetic judgements, and colour them. He admires the *Essay on Criticism*, no doubt because, unlike Warton, he is himself a neo-classic; but his objection to the inconsistency of Pope's moral attitude in the *Elegy on the Memory of an Unfortunate Lady* is shrewd and well-grounded, gaining something of its effect from Johnson's ingrained antipathy to aristocracy.

> History relates that she [the Lady] was about to disparage herself by a marriage with an inferior; Pope praises her for the dignity of ambition, and yet condemns the unkle [*sic*] to detestation for his pride . . . on such an occasion a poet may be allowed to be obscure, but inconsistency can never be right.

Johnson and Warton agree in censuring the 'Sporus' passage as 'mean'; his analysis of the *Essay on Man* is also based on what he regards as defects in Pope's character. It is, he says, a very ambitious work, and

> Having exalted himself into the chair of wisdom, [Pope] tells us much
> that every man knows and much that he does not know himself . . .
> Never was penury of knowledge and vulgarity of sentiment so happily
> disguised. The reader feels his mind full, though he learns nothing.

Johnson's bitterest contempt is reserved for his account of the malice
which inspired the *Dunciad* and for the stratagems employed in writing
it and getting it known. He condemns Pope's hypocrisy in claiming a
moral purpose for what began as an act of revenge against Theobald.
Johnson seems to have admired, or at any rate enjoyed, the *Dunciad*,
and Boswell records that he recited the conclusion in his 'forcible
melodious manner'. But as a humane man he cannot conceal his contempt for what he regards as the poem's injustice towards lesser men.

Johnson expresses approval of the admirable character displayed in
Pope's letters ('there is nothing but liberality, gratitude, constancy, and
tenderness') without apparently knowing that the letters had been
doctored, and without betraying any sign that he thought them inconsistent with Pope's character as revealed by his friend Richard Savage,
who had known Pope intimately. He writes of Pope's love of stratagem
for its own sake; his deviousness, quoting Lady Bolingbroke's comment
that 'he played the politician about cabbages and turnips'. He describes
Pope as parsimonious, malignant, and a poor talker. He condemns
Pope's love of money –

> He seems to be of an opinion not very uncommon in the world, that
> to want money is to want everything.

his snobbery –

> Next to the pleasure of contemplating his possessions, seems to be that of
> enumerating the men of high rank with whom he was acquainted . . .
> He can derive little honour from the notice of Cobham, Burlington, or
> Bolingbroke.

Johnson further writes of Pope's 'voracity of fame', as one of his leading
characteristics, and of the personal motives behind much of his writing
in which a tone of moral rectitude is expressed. Writing of the failure of
Pope's edition of Shakespeare, he says:

> From this time Pope became an enemy to editors, collators, commenta-
> tors, and verbal criticks; and hoped to persuade the world, that he mis-
> carried in this undertaking only by having a mind too great for such
> minute employments.

As one would expect, Johnson is most repelled by what he regards as
Pope's hypocrisy and affectation. The temperamental differences

between the two men were too strong, and Johnson's nature on the whole too downright and straightforward for this antipathy not to reveal itself in outspoken terms.

> He very frequently professes contempt of the world . . . How could he despise those whom he lived by pleasing, and on whose approbation his esteem of himself was superstructed? Why should he hate those to whose favour he owed his honour and his ease? . . . His scorn of the Great is repeated too often to be real; no man thinks much of that which he despises . . . Some part of this pretended discontent he learned from Swift, and expresses it, I think, most frequently in his correspondence with him. Swift's resentment was unreasonable, but it was sincere; Pope's was the mere mimicry of his friend, a fictitious part which he began to play before it became him.

It is impossible to sum up in any simple phrase or formula the final impression left by Johnson's account of Pope. It is clear that there was much in Pope's life and character of which he could not approve. It is as if he were trying to reconcile his personal antipathy for the man with his critical endorsement of the received view of the poet. The cataloguing method, formerly employed by Warton, of going through the principal poems and awarding them certificates of varying merit has the disadvantage that it conveys in the end no final impression of a consistent critical standard. Johnson praises where he can the man and the poet. He writes very coolly of Pope's friendships with Wycherley, whom he evidently did not admire, and with Cromwell; but he commends his constancy in friendship:

> . . . it does not appear that he lost a single friend by coldness or by injury; those who loved him once, continued their kindness.

Similarly, Johnson shows evident pleasure in being able to pay a handsome compliment to *The Rape of the Lock*, which he calls 'the most airy, the most ingenious, and the most delightful of all his compositions', and he considers that Pope never surpassed it. Again, he refers to *The Rape* as 'the most exquisite example of ludicrous poetry'. He considers that *Eloïsa to Abelard* surpassed all other compositions of the same kind; Pope's *Iliad* is 'the noblest version [translation] of poetry which the world has ever seen'. There is thus about all Johnson's praise of Pope's poems a note of reservation. The *Iliad* is a great *translation*, not a great poem; *The Rape* is the best thing *Pope* ever did; *Eloïsa* is better than anything else *of its kind*. As the voice of critical authority in the later eighteenth century, there is a noticeable element of inconsistency, of hesitation about Johnson's pronouncements on Pope. He never wishes to appear eccentric in his judgements; he rarely speaks slightingly of the opinions of the man in the street; he therefore appears to be relieved when he can endorse the popular verdict and confirm Pope's immense prestige. But as a fundamentally modest and humble man who dislikes vanity, affectation and snobbery in others, he finds more in Pope's character to disapprove than to approve. Since he has never made up his mind how far biographical considerations ought to be allowed to weigh, he is all the more anxious to do justice to Pope's poetry; he is, however, far from being the unequivocal, rapturous admirer he is usually taken to be. It is clear that the modern notion that disapproval of Pope was a Romantic, or even a Victorian, aberration will not stand up to a close examination of either Warton's *Essay* or Johnson's *Life*.

3 The Early Nineteenth Century

What has come to be called the Bowles–Byron controversy represents a climax in the history of Pope's posthumous reputation. It raged during the first quarter of the nineteenth century and effectively divided the Romantics from the neo-classics. The Romantics won the argument, but did not extinguish Pope. In the reaction in favour of Pope which has taken place in the twentieth century Bowles has become something of a critical casualty, so it may be worth while to examine what he actually wrote.

The Bowles–Byron controversy is not merely a matter of literary history. Tillotson, in a footnote to his book, *On the Poetry of Pope*, justly says:

> The controversy is a muddle of vituperation, pedantry, and vital aesthetics, and represents the nearest thing English literature can show to a battle of poetic principles such as that which waged round Victor Hugo. Though Pope is the stated subject, the real question at issue is the nature of the true poet.

Not all modern Pope specialists show themselves to be seriously interested in 'poetic principles'; but so long as 'vital aesthetics' and 'the nature of the true poet' are matters of more than historical concern, the controversy will be worth some attention.

The Rev. William Lisle Bowles's edition of Pope appeared in 1806. In his preface he repeats the high praise of *The Rape of the Lock* which Johnson and others had already expressed, and calls it wholly original. His was only one of many voices by which Romanticism took this poem to itself. Bowles expresses moral disapproval of the *Dunciad* as revealing a hypocritical streak in Pope:

> What was dictated by private spleen, he persuaded himself was the language of general virtue; and there is no persuasion that wounded self-love more easily admits.

He considers that the *Essay on Criticism* was motivated by spite against Dennis, 'the most accurate critic of the age', for having ignored his *Pastorals*. Bowles's attitude to Pope is more strongly bio-critical than Johnson's, and reveals the growing tendency by which literary criticism was finding it impossible to detach the poet from the man. Indeed, Bowles's importance lies in his having made the first sustained attempt to understand Pope in the light of biographical and psychological influences. He finds that Pope was motivated largely by vanity, which he attributes to childhood influences. As the sickly child of middle-aged parents, Pope demanded incessant attention and had been spoilt. He did badly at school through lack of adulation, and would have been a happier man had he enjoyed a more regular education.

> Let it be remembered, Pope, from being tenderly brought up, was through life impatient of contradiction, scarcely brooked a dissenting voice, and having been fostered by early patronage, lived afterwards in the sunshine of flattery.

Bowles is not, however, unsympathetic in recognizing the loneliness of Pope's situation.

> He was never indifferent to female society, and though his good sense prevented him, conscious of so many personal infirmities, from marrying, yet he felt the want of that sort of reciprocal tenderness and confidence in a female . . . on whom, in sickness and infirmity, he could rely.

In further analysing Pope's character, Bowles reinforces what Johnson says of his duplicity, vanity, lust for praise, and hypocrisy. He detects also an element of paranoia. He took to himself criticisms not intended for him. This was the cause of his lifelong hostility to Welsted.

Writing in 1818, Hazlitt adopts a more aesthetic, less moralistic standpoint. On the whole he approves of Pope. Certainly there is no evidence of a strong Romantic reaction against him. Having relegated him to top place among poets of the second order, masters of 'the artificial style', Hazlitt allows himself to be enthusiastic. (Chaucer, Spenser, Shakespeare, and Milton are the poets of the 'natural style', superior in breadth of understanding and imaginative power.)

> . . . he was a wit, and a critic, a man of sense, of observation, and the world, with a keen relish for the elegances of art, or of nature when embellished by art, a quick tact for propriety of thought and manners as established by the forms and customs of society, a refined sympathy with the sentiments and habitudes of human life, as he felt them within the little circle of his family and friends.

Hazlitt's image of Pope is of one circumscribed within narrow limits ('Pope's Muse never wandered with safety, but from his library to his grotto, or from his grotto into his library back again'), but within those limits an exquisite verbal miniaturist. He does not admire the *Essay on*

Man ('All that he says . . . would prove just as well that whatever is, is *wrong*, as that whatever is, is *right*') or the *Dunciad*, which 'has splendid passages, but in general is dull, heavy, and mechanical'. His highest praise is bestowed on the *Essay on Criticism* and on *The Rape of the Lock*. As a literary critic, Hazlitt is an impressionist, gaining his effects by broad, general statements and subjective judgements not closely related to their object.

> *The Rape of the Lock* is the best or most ingenious of Pope's works. . . . It is the most exquisite specimen of *fillagree* work ever invented . . . the atmosphere is perfumed with affectation.

But when Hazlitt comes to illustrate this exquisite delicacy, it is clear that he is not the first, nor the last, to have been dazzled by the gold and jewels of Pope's filigree. The first of the two passages he singles out for commendation describes Belinda's twin locks:

> This Nymph, to the Destruction of Mankind,
> Nourish'd two Locks, which graceful hung behind
> In equal Curls, and well conspir'd to deck
> With shining Ringlets the smooth Iv'ry Neck.

In other words, the *locks* hung in *curls* and conspired to deck the neck with *ringlets*. Unless it is claimed that there is an element of parody here (and no one, so far as I know, has made such a claim), the tautology is evident. No wonder Hazlitt admits that Pope has faults of syntax, and concludes that 'the praise of his versification must be confined to its uniform smoothness and harmony'. On the question of Pope's status, Hazlitt echoes Johnson:

> The question, whether Pope was a poet, has hardly yet been settled, it is hardly worth settling; for if he was not a great poet, he must have been a great prose writer, that is, he was a great writer of some sort. He was a man of exquisite faculties, and of the most refined taste . . .

Yet for all his manifest desire to do his subject justice, it is difficult to believe that in the last analysis Hazlitt really considers Pope a poet:

> His mind was the antithesis of strength and grandeur; its power was the power of indifference. He had none of the enthusiasm of poetry; he was in poetry what the sceptic is in religion.

That Byron's championship of Pope is of more than historical interest is indicated by the fact that it is still quoted by modern writers, and by the fact that Byron is the only considerable poet ever to have whole-heartedly admired Pope. Writing in 1930, Edith Sitwell, taking an anti-moralistic view of poetry, quotes Byron; and more recently G. Wilson Knight takes the opposite view and finds in him a powerful ally. His argument is that Byron admired Pope because both were moralists and believed that life matters more than art. If the terms in which Byron writes of Pope still shock us with their extravagance, we must remember that he was engaged in a hard-hitting controversy in the press.

> That this is the age of the decline of English poetry will be doubted by few who have calmly considered the subject. . . . That there are men of genius among the present poets makes little against the fact, because it has been well said, that 'next to him who forms the taste of his country, the greatest genius is he who corrupts it'.[1] . . . The great cause of the present deplorable state of English poetry is to be attributed to that absurd and systematic depreciation of Pope, in which, for the last few years, there has been a kind of epidemical concurrence.

Made in 1820, as nearly as possible an *annus mirabilis* in English poetry, this must be one of the most idiotic literary judgements on record. Writing in 1832, Henry Crabb Robinson expresses his belief that 'Byron's strange judgement about Pope was merely given to the world out of spite and affectation. It is, I think, impossible that his love for Pope could have been genuine. It would have produced fruits . . .' Without pronouncing on the difficult question of sincerity in Byron, I think it is possible to regard his admiration of Pope as genuine, at least in part. Of this admiration may not his later satires be considered to some extent the fruit? In his diaries Byron records, in 1817, his mortification on comparing passages in contemporary poetry, including his own, with the poems of Pope, and finding the latter superior 'in point of sense, learning, effect, and even imagination, passion, and invention . . .' He declares that only Rogers and Crabbe are free from 'the wrong revolutionary poetical system' now in operation. This sounds like bad judgement, but not insincerity. It is amusing to reflect that if Byron had followed the example of Rogers, and even of Crabbe, his posthumous reputation would have been of small concern.

The emotional tone of Byron's later polemic writings about Pope

---

[1] No doubt Byron wanted his readers to think of Wordsworth as the corrupting genius of modern poetry. He does not give the origin of the observation, but it is amusing to note that he could have borrowed it from Coleridge for the purpose of fraudulent conversion. Coleridge, whose *Biographia Literaria* had appeared three years before Byron's remarks, attributed the quotation to Reynolds and used it to illustrate what he considered the corrupting influence of Pope's Homer on eighteenth-century verse.

reveals that he at least thought himself sincere in attacking those who
had 'degraded' Pope, though surely no one would deny that his motives
were personal rather than aesthetic. He hated the 'Lake' school and the
'Cockney' school of Romanticism, and used Pope as a stick to beat them
with. But it is more than likely that he felt a certain affinity with the
'little Queen Anne's man' on account of his deformity, his snobbery, and
his affectation of misanthropy. He attacks Wordsworth and Keats for
their criticism of Pope, making fun of the *Lyrical Ballads* manifesto and
of *Sleep and Poetry.* He maintains that the depreciation is due to envy
of Pope's reputation and despair at not being able to equal the poet
'who harmonized our poetical language'. It is on this question of what
has variously been called 'harmony', 'correctness', 'smoothness', and
'texture', that Byron takes his stand.

> I will say nothing of the harmony of Pope and Dryden, for there is not
> a living poet (except Rogers, Gifford, Campbell, and Crabbe) who can
> write an heroic couplet. The fact is, that the exquisite beauty of their
> versification has withdrawn the public attention from their other ex-
> cellences, as the vulgar eye will rest more upon the splendour of the
> uniform than the quality of the troops.

We can understand that Byron should want to put in a word for his
friends, but we are bound to take note of the logical sleight of hand by
which he slides from the subject of 'harmony' to that of the claim for
Pope as a moral and philosophical poet.

> It is this very harmony, particularly in Pope, which has raised the vulgar
> and atrocious cant against him: – because his versification is perfect,
> it is assumed that it is his only perfection; because his truths are so clear,
> it is asserted that he has no invention; and because he is always intelli-
> gible, it is taken for granted that he has no genius. We are sneeringly
> told that he is the 'Poet of Reason', as if this were a reason for his
> being no poet. Taking passage for passage, I will undertake to cite more
> lines teeming with *imagination* from Pope than from any *two* living
> poets, be they who they may.

And this is the man who encouraged Coleridge to publish *Kubla
Khan!* More is said elsewhere about Pope's 'perfect versification' and
about his intelligibility. Meanwhile, the word 'vulgar' gives a clue to the
social motive of the old Harrovian, who, however, has temporarily forgotten his hero's own education and his views on education.

> The attorney's clerks, and other self-educated genii, found it easier to
> distort themselves to the new models than to toil after the symmetry of
> him who had enchanted their fathers.

This has something of the air of an old-fashioned Royal Academician at his favourite sport of knocking experimental painters.[1] Byron goes on to recommend Pope to 'some of my old classical friends who have still enough of Cambridge about them . . . to recollect that their earliest English poetical pleasures were drawn from the "little nightingale" of Twickenham'. Byron attacks Keats's *Sleep and Poetry* as an inferior *Essay on Criticism*, as if Keats had succeeded only in doing worse what Pope had done supremely well at the same age. He might have coupled with Keats's poem his own *English Bards and Scotch Reviewers*. Both poems perhaps illustrate Johnson's enigmatic warning that 'to attempt any further improvement of versification will be dangerous'. But neither Keats's nor Byron's reputation depends much on these works. If Byron had read his Johnson more carefully, he might have taken the warning on versification as justifying poets who recognized the futility of going on with the heroic couplet. But he repeats what he evidently regards as the cogent argument that it was despair of equalling Pope's couplets that had sent the Romantics astray – an argument which even Byron enthusiasts have scarcely thought it worth while to recall. He next invites the reader to make a 'fair comparison' of passages from Pope with the poems of any living writer, a process which will immediately convince him of Pope's superiority, 'even in *descriptive* poetry, the *lowest* department of the art'. This is the kind of puerile question-begging which is bound to throw doubts either on Byron's sincerity or on his sensibility. It is significant that Byron selects for special commendation the 'Sporus' passage from the *Epistle to Arbuthnot*, which had previously received the moral disapproval of Warton and Johnson, and interesting to note the variation of critical approval or disapproval for this passage, as for other key passages (such as the conclusion of *Dunciad* IV), during the last two centuries. It is, indeed, impossible to remain neutral about such passages, which must be regarded as something like touchstones of critical attitudes on more planes than one. It is clear that Byron's emotional allegiances were involved in his advocacy of the cause of Pope, something at once shallower and deeper than pure

[1] The day after I wrote this sentence the 74-year-old retiring President of the Royal Academy told the annual dinner of the Academy that the philosophy of Freud 'has not been beneficial to art . . . We are told that painters who are inspired by psychotics, anonymous wall-scribblers, lunatics and criminals are geniuses. And we swallow it whole instead of spewing it out as clear-minded and honest people should. Fortunately the ephemeral stuff which has recently appeared all over the world will disappear. Fortunately, too, the deep river of tradition has not dried up, nor will it, and I take comfort in the thought.' (*The Times*, 5 May 1966.)

aesthetics. He has, he says, always adhered to Pope, but has 'shamefully deviated in practice'. He has 'ever loved and honoured Pope's poetry with [his] whole soul', and hopes to do so till his dying day:

> I would rather see all I have ever written lining the same trunk in which I actually read the eleventh book of a modern epic poem at Malta, in 1811 . . . than sacrifice what I firmly believe in as the Christianity[1] of English poetry, the poetry of Pope.

Even allowing for Byron's histrionics, it has to be admitted that phrases like these confirm the presence of a new specifically nineteenth-century element in Pope criticism since his death – the element of emotional involvement. Johnson's censure of Pope the man I would call moralistic rather than emotional. Byron raises the temperature of the discussion. The element of loyalty, as it may be called, is something we shall hear more of. It is not unimportant, and can never be wholly discounted, even though its later appearances may be in more sophisticated guise. Byron evidently loved Pope, and his bio-critical championship of the poems got mixed up with his disdain for his contemporaries and their poems. His observations, crude as they now seem, may be wrong. His motivation is understandable.

A point worth noting about the Bowles–Byron controversy is that, from this time on, there is a defensive tone about all writing on Pope, with the exception of specialist academic studies. The shadow of the controversy hangs over all popular discussions, even comparatively scholarly treatments such as those by Tillotson, Sherburn, and Dobrée. The voice of advocacy is never silent for long. Younger academics are inclined to discount this defensive tone, and write as if the argument were settled once and for all. But however decisively the tide appears to have turned in Pope's favour, arguments for and against will be heard again, if only because discussions of poetic principle are never settled decisively. It is the nature of tides to turn.

Thomas Campbell's contribution to the controversy, published in 1819, is in much quieter and more moderate terms than Byron's. He says that Pope's 'peculiar rhythm and manner' are not necessarily the finest in all English poetry; the ear has been wearied of them by repetition, but if we could forget the work of Pope's imitators, we would readily appreciate the delight with which his style had struck his first readers. Campbell does not make it clear whether he has made a serious

---

[1] Byron is possibly replying here to Hazlitt's characterization of Pope as a 'sceptic' in poetry (quoted above, p. 15).

comparative study of the heroic couplets of other Augustan poets. He defends Pope against the charge of being too 'antithetic' and 'sententious', and claims that he had passion as well as wit.

Campbell argues persuasively in favour of a wider interpretation of the term 'nature'. To depict human nature, even in satirical vein, requires as much skill as to describe 'rocks and leaves'.

> Nature, in the wide and proper sense of the word, means life in all its circumstances – nature moral as well as external ...

He avoids, however, the larger issues raised by this distinction; he avoids also the subject of Pope's own moral character –

> The Vindictive personality of his satire is a fault of the man, and not of the poet –

a subject which was to be raised with increasing frequency as the century proceeded.

No sustained contribution to Pope criticism was made by Coleridge; the passing references in his letters and notebooks are on the whole antipathetic – not to the man as such, but to the high priest of the artificial style in poetry. Above all, Coleridge is concerned to assert the superiority of the English Renaissance over the Augustans with their disastrous dependence on French models. As we should expect, his comments show a far keener penetration into the nature of English poetry than those of most of his contemporaries – his comment, for instance, in a lecture of 1818, on meaning and harmony in Massinger and Pope:

> In Massinger, as in all our poets before Dryden, in order to make harmonious verse in the reading, it is absolutely necessary that the meaning should be understood – when the meaning is once seen, then the harmony is perfect. Whereas in Pope and in most of the writers who followed in his school, it is the mechanical metre which determines the sense ...

In the *Biographia* he had already expressed the idea, developed by Wordsworth, that Pope and his school wrote, not poetry, but prose 'thoughts translated into the language of poetry'. This state of affairs, he says, 'had been kept up by, if it did not wholly arise from, the custom of writing Latin verses, and the great importance attached to these exercises in our public schools'.

Charles Lloyd, the friend of Lamb and Coleridge, published in 1821 *A Poetical Essay on the Character of Pope, as a Poet and Moralist*, which is of interest partly because it must be the fruit of Coleridge's seminal influence. The epistle itself is composed in the kind of heroic couplets which undoubtedly made people feel that this form had had its day, but the prose notes are worthy of attention. In line with Romantic critics generally, Lloyd considers Pope deficient in feeling and imagination, but he shows a lively and liberal appreciation of what he regards as Pope's true qualities. This is the kind of thing which is overlooked by modern defenders of Pope when they write as if the nineteenth century had been wholly hostile:

> Though we see in Pope,
> Wit the most keen, of sense the amplest scope,
> Though he can be, if it so chance he please,
> Mighty from energy, and gay from ease;
> Though in a dialect perspicuous, terse,
> He sense can marry to immortal verse;
> And, with consummate elegance combine
> Force intellectual, through each nervous line;
> Though in the antithetic he can charm,
> With wit perplex us, and with splendour warm;
> Though his that playful malice, which, with grace,
> Can strip pretension of its grave grimace;
> Though he in numbers, tuneful as the spheres,
> Can make e'en crabbed themes enchant our ears;
> Though he can charm us to a pleasing trance,
> With quick meteorous lights, which love to dance
> To Fancy's eye; – though, eloquently bland,
> For him refinement all her stores expand;
> Yes, though thus opulent in many a dower;
> In feeling, in imagination's power,
> He is deficient; in each glorious gift,
> 'Bove earth, which doth the ravish'd spirit lift.

The chief power possessed by Pope, according to Lloyd, is 'sense', which must be preferred to mere 'euphony', the Spenserian and Keatsian quality. However, what Pope lacks is the power to explore human nature to its inmost recesses. Lloyd grants Campbell's point that it is as poetic to write of humanity as to write of inanimate nature, but maintains that Pope's knowledge of humanity is superficial. In ascribing this superficiality to deep-seated psychological causes Lloyd is before his time. In a prose note he penetratingly comments:

When we say that Pope has not sensibility, we mean in the comprehensive sense of the word, as implying sympathy with others, as well as the capacity for strong feeling ourselves. Sensibility, divested of a power of comprehensive sympathy, should rather be called sensitiveness; or, to

make the matter more clear, we would call feeling associated with dis-
interested affections, sensibility; feeling associated with self-love, sensitiveness.

At this point, however, Lloyd seems to stand his argument on its head,
for he says that Pope's sympathy with vicious qualities in others must
arise from the instinctive recognition of these qualities in himself.

> But do we not gratuitously affirm that Pope has only the latter quality?
> No. He always rather delights to analyse vice, than to suppose virtue.
> No man ever had a tact for the perception of passions, which did not
> primarily exist in himself; and he who could read that *Satire on Women*,
> and indeed most of Pope's ethical writings, and not feel that he gained
> his knowledge of human weaknesses from their prototypes in his own
> breast, may be a very good man, but certainly is not a very acute one.
> No man, that was not selfish himself, could have so acutely seen in
> others, the selfish aspect of even passions ordinarily supposed to be
> remote from considerations of self.

There is here, despite the apparent contradiction, a tentative step
further into the bio-critical field than had been taken previously. Lloyd
is making a hesitant, not fully conscious attempt to see the man and the
poems as an organic whole.

4 The Victorians I

With the reign of Victoria, Pope criticism took on a more overtly moralistic tone. Macaulay, writing on Addison in 1843, describes the character of Pope with unconcealed contempt. He sees things in strongly contrasted tones of light and dark, right and wrong: Macaulay is the Whig historian militant, but he is not the first or the last to find some aspects of Pope's character despicable. He is not a subtle psychologist, but he detects an element of paranoia in Pope. Maintaining that there is no evidence other than Pope's word for thinking that Addison conspired with Tickell to discredit Pope's *Iliad*, he writes:

> We do not accuse Pope of bringing an accusation which he knew to be false. We have not the smallest doubt that he believed it to be true; and the evidence on which he believed it he found in his own bad heart. His own life was one long series of tricks, as mean and as malicious as that of which he suspected Addison and Tickell. He was all stiletto and mask. To injure, to insult, and to save himself from the consequences of injury and insult by lying and equivocating, was the habit of his life. He published a lampoon on the Duke of Chandos; he was taxed with it; and he lied and equivocated. He published a lampoon on Aaron Hill; he was taxed with it; and he lied and equivocated. He published a still fouler lampoon on Lady Mary Wortley Montagu; he was taxed with it, and he lied with more than usual effrontery and vehemence. He puffed himself and abused his enemies under feigned names. He robbed himself of his own letters, and then raised a hue and cry after them. Besides his frauds of malignity, of fear, of interest, and of vanity, there were frauds which he seemed to have committed from love of fraud alone. He had a habit of stratagem, a pleasure in outwitting all who came near him. Whatever his object might be, the indirect road to it was that which he preferred . . .
>
> Nothing was more natural than that such a man as this should attribute to others that which he felt within himself. A plain, probable, coherent explanation is frankly given to him. He is certain that it is all a romance. A line of conduct scrupulously fair, and even friendly, is pursued towards him. He is convinced that it is merely a cover for a vile intrigue by which he is to be disgraced and ruined . . .

Macaulay goes on to vindicate Addison and attribute to him considerable magnanimity in not revenging himself on Pope. Some of Macaulay's charges against Pope have been mitigated by later researches, but none wholly refuted. Modern biographers have satisfied themselves that the 'lampoon on the Duke of Chandos' (the 'Timon's villa' passage towards the end of the *Epistle to Burlington*) was in fact not directed against Chandos, but against a composite, half-imaginary parvenu nobleman with illusions of grandeur. This is not wholly to the point, for in extricating himself from the awkward situation caused by the popular identification of Timon as Chandos (Pope and Chandos had mutual friends, and Chandos had been a generous subscriber to Pope's Homer), Pope never publicly denied it in so many words. He could scarcely do so without either saying who Timon really was or admitting that he was purely imaginary. Half the attraction of Pope's satire for the polite world lay in its interest as scandal, and it did not suit Pope that his readers should think there was no basis in fact for the scandal. Whether or not he really had Chandos in mind is unimportant: the point is, he had to be thought to have *someone* in mind. Accordingly, as Macaulay says, when the outcry in favour of Chandos became too indignant, Pope equivocated. He told Aaron Hill that since there were points of dissimilarity between 'Timon's villa' and Chandos's seat at Edgeware, Chandos could not possibly have been intended. The ball was back in the reader's court, and it was up to him to decide whom Pope *had* intended.

Writing about the same time as Macaulay, Thomas De Quincey applies to the study of Pope a fine analytical intelligence, a sense of humour, psychological insight, and a refusal, almost too resolute, to be deceived by appearances. Like Warton, he gives Pope first place among writers of light verse, but finds it hard to take him seriously as a serious poet. He attacks him on several of the grounds where previous critics had praised him. As a philosophical poet he lacked the capacity for sustained thought:

> All his thinking proceeded by insulated and discontinued jets.

Pope's aphorisms were like a string of pearls, with no relation but that of contiguity. This criticism was to be echoed a generation later by Leslie Stephen. Writing of the *Essay on Man*, De Quincey concedes that many passages, 'viewed in the light of fragments and brilliant aphorisms', have 'a mode of truth', though the poem as a whole lacks 'truth central and coherent'. This failure of intellect on Pope's part, somewhat surprisingly, De Quincey attributes to indolence of mind. Pope was a mere butterfly in the garden of books and ideas, a 'dilettante'.

De Quincey will have nothing to do with the view expressed by earlier critics of Pope as the indefatigable polisher of his own verses. Far from endorsing Byron's judgement that Pope is always transparently lucid, De Quincey finds his meaning often obscure :

> . . . but rare is the man amongst classical writers in any language who has disfigured his meaning more remarkably than Pope by imperfect expression.

His grammar is often 'vicious' and his meaning obscured by faulty and unnatural syntax.

> . . . Pope's defect in language was almost peculiar to himself. It lay in an inability, nursed doubtless by indolence, to carry out and perfect the expression of the thought he wishes to communicate.

De Quincey quotes from the *Essay on Man* an admirable example of the kind of obscure writing that he has in mind:

> Know, God and Nature only are the same:
> In man the judgement shoots at flying game.

The reader, he says, may misunderstand the first of these two lines; the second he *must* misunderstand. Pope is trying to contrast the fixity of God and Nature on the one hand with the ephemeral, the transitory character of man on the other. But the meaning is far from clear and has to be inferred from its context. At first it would appear as if God and Nature are the same as *each other*. What Pope means is that they are alone in being always the same as *themselves*. In the second line Pope is trying to say that man (unlike God and Nature) is as flying game to the marksman. But the marksman (the man who 'judges') can only be man himself; so we have the odd image of man judging himself as a moving object. This kind of illogicality is not uncommon when Pope is philosophizing and has been taken too little notice of by modern critics. I do not know if De Quincey is the first to have been upset by it.

De Quincey finds Pope's satires even more unsatisfactory than the *Essay on Man*. This was because Pope had no compelling satiric motive.

> They arose in a sense of talent for caustic effects, unsupported by any satiric heart; Pope had neither the malice (except in the most fugitive form), which thirsts for leaving wounds, nor, on the other hand, the deep moral indignation which burns in men whom Providence has from time to time armed with scourges for cleansing the sanctuaries of truth or justice.

Pope was no Juvenal; neither was he, De Quincey might have added, a Swift. If his *saeva indignatio* was synthetic, this was because

He was contented enough with society as he found it: bad it might be, but it was good enough for *him* . . .

If Pope thought he had a real satiric mission, it was 'merest self-delusion'. In his conviction that there was thus a built-in hypocrisy in Pope's position as a satirist, De Quincey was no doubt influenced by Johnson. We are reminded of Johnson's grave words:

How could he despise those whom he lived by pleasing, and on whose approbation his esteem of himself was superstructed? Why should he hate those to whose favour he owed his honour and his ease?

De Quincey's tone is lighter, perhaps more effectively deflatory. Contrasting Pope with Juvenal, he says:

Pope having no such internal principle of wrath boiling in his breast, being really (if one must speak the truth) in the most pacific and charitable frame of mind towards all scoundrels whatever, except such as might take it into their heads to injure a particular Twickenham grotto, was unavoidably a hypocrite of the first magnitude when he affected (or sometimes really conceited himself) to be in a dreadful passion with offenders as a body . . . Sudden collapses of the manufactured wrath, sudden oblivion of the criminal, announce Pope's [passion] as *always* counterfeit . . .

Some of Pope's modern admirers, while they must shake their heads at the levity of this, might be prepared to admit that it makes a point which needs to be met, and it makes it the more effectively for being light-hearted. The charge that as a satirist Pope was basically insincere is one we shall have to take account of. It is to be regretted that De Quincey, like Johnson before him, did not feel impelled to pursue his charge, so to speak, into the textual actuality of Pope's satires. Nevertheless he added a certain sharpness of definition to the bio-critical problem.

Thackeray delivered his lecture on Prior, Gay, and Pope in 1851. At the age of forty he wrote with vigour and authority, declaring boldly that Pope was 'the greatest literary *artist* that England has seen'. It is interesting to note that Crabb Robinson read the lecture on its publication in 1853 and did not admire it, although he was interested in its subject. This is to be expected from a staunch Wordsworthian, but we know that Robinson read and enjoyed Pope's poems.

Thackeray adopts Byron's adulatory standards, but sympathetic pity for Pope as a man degenerates into enraptured sentimentality. Thackeray is the precursor of Edith Sitwell and G. Wilson Knight. True, he admits Pope's imperfections of character, especially in the matter of his relations with women. He advises readers of Pope's letters to pass over those addressed to women:

> . . . there is a tone of not pleasant gallantry and, amidst a profusion of compliments and politenesses, a something which makes one distrust the little pert, prurient bard. There is very little indeed to say about his loves, and that little not edifying.

He censures Pope for his attitude to Lady Mary Wortley Montagu, for whom his hatred is more fervent than his love had been. He also condemns the attack on Dennis in the Robert Norris pamphlet – 'a vulgar and mean satire'. But such imperfections are to be overlooked in the life of a hero. With Carlyle in full vogue, it was reasonable, no doubt, to compare Pope with Bonaparte and Nelson:

> In their common life you will find frailties and meannesses, as great as the vices and follies of the meanest men. But in the presence of the great occasion, the great soul flashes out, and conquers transcendant.

Although Thackeray's account of Pope's life is adulatory to the point of hysteria, he is not very clear as to what these 'great occasions' were. He sees Pope as a 'gallant little cripple' of delicate, almost feminine sensibility doing battle in the robust male world of the coffee-houses. Pope was almost the only wit of the day who was not fat; even this seems to enhance his heroism. Thackeray is not an accurate biographer, and he seems unaware that Pope himself provoked the attacks of the 'Dunces' which he braved with such gallantry.

> . . . however much he protested that he disregarded their abuse, the coarse ridicule of his opponents stung and tore him.

This has been so often repeated that it must be insisted that the evidence for it is almost non-existent. If Pope writhed under abuse, his pain was masochistic and in part self-inflicted. We need not of course withhold our sympathy on that account, though we may have reservations as to the degree of heroism to be found in masochism. It does not occur to Thackeray that coarseness is the essential constituent of some of the letters to women and of the Robert Norris attack on Dennis which he himself condemns. As to Thackeray's contention that 'the delicate little creature sickened at habits and company which were quite tolerable to robuster men' – this is pure rubbish. Almost from boyhood his habits and company were of his own choosing, and there is no evidence that he did not enjoy coarseness as much as anyone of his time.

More difficult to understand is Thackeray's complacency in being willing to overlook what he regarded as the damage Pope did to the profession of letters.

> It was Pope, I fear, who contributed, more than any man who ever lived, to depreciate the literary calling. . . . The profession of letters was ruined by that libel of the *Dunciad*.

It is difficult to reconcile the condonation by one man of letters of such action by another except by the canons of Bonapartist ethics. Pope's influence on the literary profession, it is only fair to add, is regarded by some critics, notably Leslie Stephen, as on the whole good. The question as to what the status of a writer in Thackeray's time would have been had Pope never lived is one of those historical hypotheses that are more interesting than useful.

Thackeray leaves little doubt as to the real source of his gushing adulation of Pope. Thackeray was fascinated by snobbery and, like other middle-class English novelists, very ready to equate greatness with social importance. In the writings of Pope you rub shoulders with important people. What had been for Johnson almost a matter for disapproval was to Thackeray a source of delight.

> You are in the society of men who have filled the greatest parts in the world's story – you are with St John the statesman; Peterborough the conqueror; Swift, the greatest wit of all times; Gay, the kindliest laugher – it is a privilege to sit in that company. . . . I know nothing in any story more gallant and cheering than the love and friendship which this company of famous men bore towards one another. Who dares quarrel with Mr Pope, great and famous himself, for liking the society of men great and famous? To name his friends is to name the best men of his time.

That Pope's relations with the great and famous had been falsified in his published correspondence could hardly have been known to Thackeray, who takes at its face value almost everything Pope says of himself. It is significant that 'great' and 'famous' become 'best'. Even discounting this transition, however, I cannot help wondering where Thackeray placed such men as Defoe, whom Pope slighted, and Hogarth, whom he intrigued against. But the legend of Pope's friendships is something we must take account of elsewhere. We should have been grateful to Thackeray if he had considered in more detail the extent to which a friendship with St John was to Pope's credit. What we find in Thackeray, then, is an expression of the Victorian admiration of 'greatness' for its own sake: Pope was a 'great' man – or at any rate the friend of great men – and that is what matters.

Thackeray is nowhere precise in stating his grounds for believing that Pope is also 'the greatest literary *artist* that England has seen'.

> In speaking of a work of consummate art one does not try to show what it actually is, for that were vain; but what it is like, and what are the sensations produced in the mind of him who views it.

The sensations produced in Thackeray's mind are akin to those produced by the actions of Bonaparte and Nelson. This is subjective criticism at its crudest. The work that occasions it is the fourth book of the *Dunciad*. Thackeray's comments are worth quoting, if only to show what a mid-nineteenth-century literary audience was prepared to swallow. After repeating the final twenty-four lines – those lines which Pope himself was said to have been unable to read without emotion, and which Johnson intoned for the benefit of his circle – Thackeray goes on:

> It is heroic courage speaking: a splendid declaration of righteous wrath and war. It is the gage flung down, and the silver trumpet ringing defiance to falsehood and tyranny, deceit, dullness, superstition. It is Truth, the champion, shining and intrepid, and fronting the great world-tyrant with armies of slaves at his back. It is a wonderful and victorious single combat, in that great battle, which has always been waging since society began.

Shorn of its embarrassing rhetoric, this view of the closing lines of the *Dunciad* is echoed by Pope's most recent admirers.

Ruskin, in one of his *Oxford Lectures on Art*, 1870, seems to be echoing Thackeray. Both were prose men and may be allowed their rhapsodies when writing of poetry. The art-moralist, rousing the British public to noble deeds, is even more ecstatic than Thackeray, and certainly more influential. Those who think that anti-Pope criticism is a Victorian lapse forget that Ruskin placed Pope higher than anyone would now, except possibly G. Wilson Knight. '. . . every beauty possessed by the language of a nation is significant of the innermost laws of its being'. If a people is noble, manly and just, Ruskin continues, '. . . their tongue must needs be a grand one'. If a tongue is a noble one, the words are 'trumpet-calls to action. All great languages invariably utter great things, and command them . . . the breath of them is inspiration because it is not only vocal, but vital; and you can only learn to speak as these men spoke, by becoming what these men were'.

This is the sort of high-minded aesthetico-moralistic rhetoric which helped to make Victorian England what it liked to think it was, and at whose self-confidence we of a century later can only look back with nostalgia. Where does it lead to in the field of literary criticism?

Now for direct confirmation of this, I want you to think over the relation of expression to character in two great masters of the absolute art of language, Virgil and Pope. You are perhaps surprised at the last named; and indeed you have in English much higher grasp and melody of language from more passionate minds, but you have nothing else, in its range, so perfect. I name, therefore, these two men, because they are the most accomplished *Artists*, merely as such, whom I know in literature; and because I think you will be afterwards interested in investigating how the infinite grace in the words of one, the severity in those of the other, and the precision in those of both, arise wholly out of the moral elements of their minds: – out of the deep tenderness in Virgil ... and the serene and just benevolence which placed Pope, in his theology, two centuries in advance of his time, and enabled him to sum the law of noble life in two lines which, so far as I know, are the most complete, the most concise, and the most lofty expression of moral temper existing in English words:–

> 'Never elated, while one man's oppress'd;
> Never dejected, while another's bless'd.'

I wish you also to remember these lines of Pope, and to make yourselves entirely masters of his system of ethics; because, putting Shakespeare aside as rather the world's than ours, I hold Pope to be the most perfect representative we have, since Chaucer, of the true English mind; and I think the Dunciad is the most absolutely chiselled and monumental work 'exacted' in our country. You will find, as you study Pope, that he has expressed for you, in the strictest language and within the briefest limits every law of art, of criticism, of economy, of policy, and, finally, of a benevolence, humble, rational, and resigned, contented with its allotted share of life, and trusting the problem of its salvation to Him in whose hand lies that of the universe.

Once the merely emotive effect of this verbal orgasm has been discounted, it can be seen that Ruskin's influence was seminal. There is nothing in his claims for Pope which has not been echoed, in more measured language, by non-poets of later times. Ruskin believes that, apart from Shakespeare, neatly eliminated by a verbal trick (if one great English poet is the world's, why not another?) – Pope is our noblest poet. He is so on two accounts: he is our greatest artist in words, achieving a unique chiselled perfection, and he gives expression to the noblest moral sentiments. The case for Pope's 'character' as the source of this nobility of utterance goes by default. It will have to be considered elsewhere. It is when we examine Ruskin's quotation from the *Essay on Man* (IV, 323–4) that we are entitled to question his qualifications as a literary critic. Undoubtedly he finds in Pope, as others do, what he wants. The neatly packaged ethics of this and similar couplets have appealed to many readers more interested in ethics than in poetry. Yet the claim for them is also made that the moral element is not so much in their sentiment as in their art, their formal 'perfection'. Ruskin's position is a little ambiguous, but I think that here it is the lofty altruism of the sentiment that particularly attracts him. At all events he makes no attempt to see the couplet as a direct expression of Pope's own character; he is concerned, not with Pope's 'benevolence', so much as with the benevolence of his sentiments; this benevolence, indeed, derives not from Pope but from St Paul:

> And whether one member suffer, all the members suffer with it; or one member be honoured, all the members rejoice with it. (I Cor. xii, 26.)

The Twickenham editor also points out the parallel in a sermon on charity by Thomas Whincoop preached in 1701:

> According to this Description then, [of charity], we are obliged to all mutal Offices of tender concern for another's good, and endeavouring to promote it always, in being heartily compassionate towards all the Evils another suffers, and rejoycing in the good things He is partaker of . . .

Whether Pope had read Whincoop or was recalling his Douai bible, it is clear that his morality was not original, and that the claim for his being 'two centuries in advance of his time' is a strange one. It is not easy to see why Ruskin prefers Pope to St Paul.

Hard on the heels of Ruskin comes the Rev. Whitwell Elwin, whose first five volumes of a new definitive edition of the works of Pope appeared in 1871–2. The remaining five volumes, edited by W. J. Courthope, appeared at intervals up to 1889. Until the appearance of the Twickenham edition the Elwin–Courthope edition was standard. In his introduction Elwin revealed for the first time the full story of Pope's contrivances in bringing about the publication in 1737 of his correspondence with various celebrities, notably Wycherley and Addison, and of his correspondence with Swift in 1741. He also mentioned literary borrowing as a major feature in the poetry of Pope, relating how Bowyer began collecting Pope's borrowings in 1740 and how this annoyed Pope, who bought him off and made him his printer. Elwin notes also the harvest of borrowings collected by Gilbert Wakefield, a later editor of Pope in 1794.

> The sensitiveness which was disturbed at the gleanings of Bowyer would have shuddered at the abundant harvest of Wakefield.

Elwin quotes De Quincey's favourable comments on Pope's character, but can never keep out of his own comments the tone of severe
moral censure. While he does not write as a neutral, he is strictly objective. He writes as a scholar. For every accusation he gives chapter and
verse – to the point of tedium, as he admits. Modern scholars are, one is
inclined to think, relieved not to have to take Elwin's censure into
account, to be able to write it off as an expression of moral rectitude by
a Victorian parson. The Twickenham edition does not include Pope's
letters, which are, however, dealt with definitively in Sherburn's monumental five-volume edition of 1956. Sherburn confirms with scrupulous
detail Elwin's account of Pope's labyrinthine activities in publishing and
editing his correspondence. Elwin censures Pope for reprinting letters
he had written to Caryll, a private friend of no public importance, as if
they had been addressed to the dead Addison. He also denounces Pope's
deception of Bolingbroke, the 'guide, philosopher and friend', in
secretly printing an edition of his political writings against Bolingbroke's
wishes. But the weight of his censure is reserved for Pope's management
of the correspondence with Swift in 1741, achieved by even more
devious means than the earlier volume. Swift had strong and obstinate
views about the publication of private letters, and expressed himself as
being out of sympathy with his friend's desire for 'epistolary fame'.
Having wholly failed to get Swift's agreement to print their correspondence, Pope devised a scheme for issuing it as if by Swift's own
injunction. To this end he had it printed in London and shipped to
Dublin, where it appeared as if by Swift's authority. Swift was by now
seventy-four, and his mental powers were hopelessly impaired. In these
circumstances Pope allowed himself to feel justified in going against
his friend's wishes and protected from any danger of interference or
discovery.

Of all the deceptions which the poet practised to get his correspondence
under the eye of the world, his dealings towards Swift are the worst.
He had failed to gain his consent to putting forth the letters while any
judgment yet remained to him; but no sooner had he sunk into dotage
than, trusting to his inability to detect the cheat, Pope beguiled him
into sanctioning the publication by sending him the volume ready
printed, with a flattering exhortation, the echo of what he had written
on a former occasion, 'importing that it was criminal to suppress such
an amiable picture of the Dean and his private character'. (Pope to
Nugent, Aug. 14 1740.) The moment Swift fell into the pit his friend
had dug for him, his friend denounced him for the act. 'I think,' he
wrote to Mr. Nugent, 'I can make no reflections upon this strange

incident but what are truly melancholy, and humble the pride of human nature – that the greatest of geniuses, though prudence may have been the companion of wit (which is very rare) for their whole lives past, may have nothing left them at last but their vanity. No decay of body is half so miserable.' . . . Infamous language when the deed he reprobated was his own, and Swift the innocent dupe; and when having traded successfully in the mental afflictions of his friend, he proceeded to hold up his victim as the criminal. But the simulated indignation is less revolting than the simulated fondness. 'When the heart is full of tenderness,' he said to the Dean, in the letter of March 22, 1741, 'it must be full of concern at the absolute impotency of all words to come up to it. I value and enjoy more the memory of the pleasure and endearing obligation I have formerly received from you than the perfect possession of any other. Think it not possible that my affection can cease but with my last breath. If I could think yours was exhausted I should grieve, but not reproach you. If I felt myself even hurt by you I should be confident you knew not the blow you gave, but had your hand guided by another.' The hand which guided him was the same hand that was at that moment aiming a blow at his reputation. Taking advantage of his cruel malady and prostrate understanding, Pope was then endeavouring to fasten upon him the stigma of his own personal treachery, and this pretended magnanimity in forgiving a deed which he had contrived and instigated was in itself a calumny and a fraud.

Elwin's moral condemnation is not subtle. To him, as to a prosecuting counsel, there is only black and white. Relativity in matters of conduct has small place in the Victorian scale of values. The delicate assessment of Pope's sincerity is left to later apologists. As a moralist Elwin stands in the line of Bowles. The interest of his attitude is that, in his quarrel with the Byron–Ruskin line of defence, it adumbrates the quarrel between art and morality, ethics and aesthetics, which was rippling the surface of English society from Shelley's time onwards, and broke into a storm in the debate on the Oscar Wilde scandal at the end of the century. That debate is sometimes treated as if it were closed, a mere matter of social history. But the issues are not so simple as they are sometimes taken to be, and we shall hear more of them. To Elwin, however, writing in 1870, they were simple enough:

. . . I do not pretend to think that genius is an extenuation of rascality.

It was left to later critics, developing the implications of Ruskin's aesthetic, to maintain that art – superlative art – is above ordinary morality.

Leslie Stephen made a determined effort to understand the contradictions in Pope's character. The subject of an essay he printed in *Hours in a Library, 1874–1879*, is 'Pope as a Moralist'. He recognizes that Pope is by now the most quoted author after Shakespeare, but says that his 'copybook maxims' are stale. 'We cannot give him credit for being really moved by sad platitudes'. Stephen follows Elwin in finding Pope a 'consummate liar'. 'His mendacity amounts to a monomania.' He comments on Pope's deviousness:

> Almost every publication of his life was attended with some sort of mystification passing into downright falsehood and, at times, injurious to the character of his dearest friends.

Summing up his findings, Stephen says: 'Pope's practical morality was defective'. However, side by side with his defects of character he has a genuine love of goodness, benevolence, and honesty, as well as 'the excessive sensibility of genius'. Stephen is aware of Pope's inconsistencies and calls him a 'mixed character'.

When he comes to consider the moral writings of this mixed character, Stephen is not very happy. He quotes Ruskin's challenging eulogy, and refers to the doctrine that a reader can only think and speak like great men by learning what they were. Stephen has learnt what Pope was, and it worries him. He falls back on something of an equivocation: 'Morality and art are not independent, though not identical.' At first it seems as if Stephen is coming down heavily on the side of the moralists. It is worth quoting him at length because *Hours in a Library* has long been out of print.

> Pope is one of those strangely mixed characters which can only be fully delineated by a masterly hand, and Mr Courthope in the life which concludes the definitive edition of the works has at last performed the task with admirable skill and without too much shrouding his hero's weaknesses. Meanwhile our pleasure in reading him is much counterbalanced by the suspicion that those pointed aphorisms which he turns out in so admirably polished a form may come only from the lips outwards. Pope, it must be remembered, is essentially a parasitical writer. He was a systematic appropriator – I do not say plagiarist, for the practice seems to be generally commendable – of other men's thoughts. His brilliant gems have often been found in some obscure writer, and have become valuable by the patient care with which he has polished and mounted them. We doubt their perfect sincerity because, when he is speaking in his own person, we can often prove him to be at best under a curious delusion. Take, for example, the 'Epistle to Dr Arbuthnot', which is his most perfect work. Some of the boasts in it are apparently quite justified by the facts. But what are we to say to a passage such as this? –

I was not born for courts or great affairs;
I pay my debts, believe, and say my prayers;
Can sleep without a poem in my head,
Nor know if Dennis be alive or dead.

Admitting his independence, and not inquiring too closely into his prayers, can we forget that the gentleman who could sleep without a poem in his head called up a servant four times in one night of 'the dreadful winter of Forty' to supply him with paper, lest he should lose a thought? Or what is the value of a professed indifference to Dennis from the man distinguished beyond all other writers for the bitterness of his resentment against all small critics; who disfigured his best poems by his petty vengeance for old attacks; and who could not refrain from sneering at poor Dennis, even in the Prologue which he condescended to write for the benefit of his dying antagonist? . . .

Thus, we are always pursued, in reading Pope, by disagreeable misgivings. We don't know what comes from the heart, and what from the lips: when the real man is speaking, and when we are only listening to old commonplaces skilfully vamped. There is always, if we please, a bad interpretation to be placed upon his finest sentiments. His indignation against the vicious is confused with his hatred of personal enemies; he protests most loudly that he is honest when he is 'equivocating most genteelly;' his independence may be called selfishness or avarice; his toleration simply indifference; and even his affection for his friends a decorous fiction, which will never lead him to the slightest sacrifice of his own vanity or comfort. A critic of the highest order is provided with an Ithuriel spear, which discriminates the sham sentiments from the true. As a banker's clerk can tell a bad coin by its ring on the counter, without need of a testing apparatus, the true critic can instinctively estimate the amount of bullion in Pope's epigrammatic tinsel.

The argument by which in succeeding pages of his essay Stephen persuades himself of what may be regarded as the aesthetic view of Pope (art is superior to morality) may be summed up thus: Pope was a supreme literary artist; as such he hated dullness (regarded by Stephen as all forms of folly and stupidity); he loved piety and universal benevolence, caring tenderly for his old parents. In the expression of both piety and the hatred of dullness he perfected his art. Perfection of expression – when all allowances are made for Pope's many faults and for his 'mixed' character' – can only be achieved as the distillation of a basically moral nature. We shall see how far Stephen was qualified to judge of the morality expressed in Pope's couplets and of the literary artistry which could only proceed from sound morality.

Pope's constant aim as a literary artist was the perfection of the epigram. Such an epigram must be 'the quintessence of a whole volume of reflection'. This implies 'not only labour, but an unwearied vividness of thought and feeling. The poet must put his soul into the work as well as his artistic power'. Stephen does not, it may be noted in passing, make any allowance for what he has previously called the 'parasitic' nature of Pope's writing; he does not ask himself the question whether the vivid thought and feeling epitomized in the epigram is Pope's or another's.

> Thus, if we may take Pope's most vigorous expressions as an indication of his strongest convictions, and check their conclusions by his personal history and by the general tendency of his writings, we might succeed in putting together something like a satisfactory statement of the moral system which he expressed forcibly because he believed in it sincerely.

Stephen, however, declines to check Pope's expressed convictions against his personal history, and this is just what his argument requires. There is much to be said for his desire to equate energy of expression with sincerity of feeling : what he does not do is to demonstrate that his most energetic writing is concerned with piety and benevolence. The *Dunciad* has more 'energy and continuity' of expression than Pope's other satires, and must therefore be taken as the sincerest expression of his discoveries about human nature. Stephen believes that Pope was the embodiment of literary intelligence and sincerely hated folly. He does not seem to regard the *Dunciad* as purely negative and destructive in its effect.

> It is in some degree creditable to Pope that his satire was on the whole justified, so far as it could be justified, by the correctness of his judgement. The only great man whom he has seriously assaulted is Bentley . . .

The implications of the words 'great' and 'seriously' do not trouble Stephen, who clearly has made very little study of the writings of many of the 'Dunces'. Is it necessary, in Stephen's eyes, to be 'great' in order to escape unjust attack? Is it to Pope's credit that he did not 'seriously' go for Defoe? But all is well : it is the privilege of the supremely intelligent to pillory anything less than itself – clearly an inclusive privilege.

> Pope is the incarnation of the literary spirit. He is the most complete representative in our language of the intellectual instincts which find their natural expression in pure literature . . . The complete antithesis to that spirit is the evil principle which Pope attacks as dullness. This false goddess is the literary Ahriman; and Pope's natural antipathies, exaggerated by his personal passions and weaknesses to extravagant proportions, express themselves fully in his great mock-epic. . . . Seen from this point of view, there is an honourable completeness in Pope's career.

It is only necessary here to comment that, had Stephen studied the writings of some of the 'Dunces' as sympathetically as he has studied Pope, he could scarcely have regarded them all, without exception, as propagating an 'evil principle'. He might also have inquired why certain bad writers and painters were left out of the *Dunciad*.

Not only was Pope superior to his victims in intelligence, he was more successful. Stephen praises him for 'raising [himself] permanently above the need of writing for money' by translating Homer. It is difficult to see why Stephen regards it as a bad thing to have to write for money. True, he says Defoe would have been a better man if he had not always been in debt. But then we might not have had *Robinson Crusoe* and *Moll Flanders*. Clearly the point could be argued indefinitely. There are worse reasons for publication than money. At all events, Pope acquired the most exalted position a poet had hitherto achieved by his own efforts: '. . . what was the morality which Pope dispensed from this exalted position? . . . Is this guardian of virtue quite immaculate, and the morality which he preaches quite of the most elevated kind?' Basing his account partly on the *Essay on Man*, partly on the satires in general, Stephen describes Pope's morality as mainly that of good sense and moderation. It is exactly the morality of the *Spectator*. Its chief appeal is that readers are prepared for it and are not lifted into uncomfortable areas of ethical and metaphysical speculation. Pope's work is studded with graceful compliments to his friends, and 'This vein of genuine feeling sufficiently redeems Pope's writings from the charge of a commonplace worldliness'. The compliments quoted by Stephen are those addressed to Sir Samuel Garth, celebrated elder poet and physician-in-ordinary to George I; to Dr John Arbuthnot, wit and physician-in-ordinary to Queen Anne; to Viscount Bolingbroke, Secretary of State under Queen Anne and leading supporter of the Jacobite cause; to the Earl of Peterborough, admiral, general, and diplomat; to William Pitt, later Earl of Chatham; to Viscount Cobham, soldier and statesman; and to the Prime Minister, Sir Robert Walpole, who employed many of the hack writers Pope attacked. Stephen does not consider whether the sincerity of Pope's compliments to these men might have been enhanced if he had shown as much appreciation of virtue in men of less exalted station.

He examines the *Essay on Man* in some detail; although he does not discover in it the same energy and continuity as had characterized the *Dunciad*, he finds it full of genuine expressions of piety and universal benevolence. Stephen cannot believe that this view of Pope's morality allows of an unsympathetic view of Pope's character in the last analysis.

Yet I must decline to believe that men can gather grapes off thorns, or figs off thistles, or noble expressions of moral truth from a corrupt heart thinly varnished by a coating of affectation. Turn it how we may, the thing is impossible. Pope was more than a mere literary artist, though he was an artist of unparalleled excellence in his own department. He was a man in whom there was the seed of many good thoughts, though choked in their development by the growth of innumerable weeds.

This seems a very robust assertion for one who lived in the age of Chadband. Stephen concludes with a panegyric on an uncharacteristic minor poem, *The Universal Prayer*, which he invites his readers to admire.

. . . they will admit that the little cripple of Twickenham, distorted as were his instincts after he had been stretched on the rack of this rough world, and grievous as were his offences against the laws of decency and morality, had yet in him a noble strain of eloquence significant of deep religious sentiment.

Whatever the quality of the religious sentiment, no one, I suspect, but Stephen has ever admired *The Universal Prayer* as poetry. One stanza may be quoted as being of special interest :

> Let not this weak, unknowing hand
> Presume Thy Bolts to throw,
> And deal Damnation round the land,
> On each I judge thy Foe.

It may be wondered whether Pope's victims in the *Dunciad* considered he had done his best to live up to the spirit of this sentiment.

Leslie Stephen, then, admits serious faults in Pope's character, but comes out strongly in his favour as a moralist. He considers that Pope's genius as a literary artist, a coiner of unforgettable epigrams – a genius he never calls in question and never examines in a truly critical spirit – is sufficient warrant of Pope's sincerity as a moralist. In other words, literary skill is a guarantee of sincerity, and superior morality derives from artistic integrity. We shall hear more of this view.

5 The Victorians II

Matthew Arnold's famous essay on *The Study of Poetry* was published in 1880 as the general introduction to Ward's *English Poets,* and again as the first of the *Essays in Criticism: Second Series* in 1888. His pronouncements on the poetry of Dryden and Pope have acquired considerable currency – more perhaps than they deserve – and have been regarded as a stumbling-block to the twentieth-century rehabilitation of Pope as a poet. Arnold describes in general terms, but with a fair grasp of the situation, the revolution in English literature achieved by Dryden and his followers. He puts his finger on an important truth when he says that they were insensitive to the virtues of English poetry before Waller and the Restoration. They wrote of our earlier English poetry with a certain patronizing superiority, allowing Chaucer, for instance, 'the rude sweetness of a Scotch tune', though in general his verse 'is not harmonious to us'. Dryden venerated Chaucer solely as a delineator of character, a medieval social historian. Dryden's function was to create modern English prose – easy, lucid, and supple. Arnold's praise of this prose is eloquent and generous, 'but it was impossible that a fit prose should establish itself amongst us without some touch of frost to the imaginative life of the soul'. Arnold then goes on to deny solemnly the claims of Dryden and Pope to have created classics of our poetry. He quotes with enthusiastic approval the opening of *The Hind and the Panther* and some lines from one of Pope's imitations of Horace, and calls them classics of our prose, 'admirable for the purposes of the inaugurator . . . [and] the high priest of an age of prose and reason'. He denies Dryden and Pope the highest poetic qualities of 'high seriousness' and an adequate poetic criticism of life.

Few would now accept Arnold's grounds, in so many words, for denying Pope's greatness, but his diagnosis of the virtues and limitations of the 'age of prose and reason' can still command respect, so long as there is anyone left who would regard prose as different from poetry and assign to it a different function. James Sutherland in his *Preface to Eighteenth-Century Poetry* makes the point that the eighteenth-century reader wanted the same lucidity and perspicuity in poetry as he found in, say, the prose of *The Spectator.* In other words, it was the prose values that counted.

It seems to me far from correct to say, as F. R. Leavis, writing of Pope as satirist in *Revaluation*, mysteriously says: 'We may have entirely disposed of Matthew Arnold'. Even if Arnold himself had not the qualities which escape such disposal, what he said was not new,[1] it was more an epitome of views previously held. If Arnold had not written on Pope, we should still have to reckon with the case he so ably presented. J. S. Cunningham, in his study of *The Rape of the Lock*, 1961, deprecates Arnold's distinction between the poetry of imagination and that of ratiocination, but it was not Arnold who first made it. As we have seen, it appeared over a century earlier in the work of Warton, whom elsewhere Cunningham quotes with approval. Yet the idea that Arnold is the villain of the piece dies hard. One of Pope's latest editors, John Heath-Stubbs, writing in 1964, says:

> Matthew Arnold's really rather offhand judgement . . . set a new and unfortunate tone for Pope criticism in the later nineteenth century, from which the twentieth was slow to emancipate itself.

That Arnold's judgement was not offhand, but grave and deliberate, and that its tone was not new, the reader has already seen. But this view of Arnold's decisive rôle in the formulation of what may be called the Victorian fallacy in Pope criticism is repeated like an incantation.

Among twentieth-century critics of Arnold, Geoffrey Tillotson is the most formidable. In an article contributed to *Essays presented to D. Nichol Smith*, 1945, he describes Arnold as only a part-time critic, who can therefore be excused for inadequate reading, and for being ill-informed about the Elizabethan age and the eighteenth century. It might be objected that ignorance of the Elizabethans would be a help rather than a hindrance to the enjoyment of Pope, and that his being a part-time critic at least allowed him time to be, among other things, a part-time poet, which might be some qualification for a general appreciation of poetic values. Has the fact that, say, T. S. Eliot was also a part-time poet and a part-time publisher diminished his authority as a critic? Still, the natural superiority of the professional over the amateur must be taken into account.

Tillotson attacks Arnold for his generalizations, for his expressions of personal liking and disliking of authors and centuries. It is as if the modern professional critic feels that it is unfair for the amateur to use his personal taste and his prestige as sometime Professor of Poetry at

---

[1] More original were Arnold's views, stated much earlier than *The Study of Poetry*, on Pope as a translator of Homer, which are largely overlooked by modern critics. An account of them is given elsewhere.

Oxford to turn the nineteenth century against Pope. Had the high priest of sweetness and light an unfair advantage over the high priest of prose and reason? But under the appearance of professional objectivity, is Tillotson's view of Pope any less personal than Arnold's? Referring to Arnold's quotation from Dryden's *The Hind and the Panther*, he says: 'To reinstate the couplet where it belongs, we need only remember that prose is not concerned with music.' Is this not what Heath-Stubbs would call 'really rather offhand'? For surely Tillotson cannot mean merely that poetry is musical prose. He claims for Pope, not only music, but what he calls 'natural magic' in sensuous description and the use of imagery. To illustrate this he chooses some lines from the 'Grand Tour' passage in the *Dunciad* – those describing the Seine, the Tiber, Venice, and the French monasteries. This excellent passage is discussed elsewhere; it is enough to say here that Arnold would certainly not have denied its merit, but that he would have dissented from Tillotson, as would many others – even perhaps full-time critics – when he comments that Pope's display of 'natural magic' is 'as authentic as anything in Shakespeare or Keats'. To put Pope's mellifluous, literary reconstruction of scenes he had never viewed on a level with, say, *A Midsummer Night's Dream* or the ode *To Autumn* is surely to make as personal a judgement, as arbitrarily stated, as any of Arnold's. It is none the less interesting for that, and it helps in determining Tillotson's status as a critic.

The real difference between Tillotson and Arnold is of course personal: the two men liked different things. Coming down firmly at this point, on the side of bio-criticism, Tillotson discounts Arnold's theoretical objections to Pope and says he (Arnold) does not like couplets because he does not like 'art objects'. Arnold only responds adequately to architecture, and then only when it is large:

> If you do not care for art except when it reaches the scale of cathedrals and town halls, it is unlikely that you will care very much for the heroic couplet . . .

The trouble is that the old neo-Gothic philistine did not like music, paintings, pottery, and china. Tillotson does, and this qualifies him to respond to the heroic couplet. To him a heroic couplet is an art object, like a sonata, a painting, or a Dresden shepherdess. Indeed one suspects that Tillotson likes Pope not for what he was, but because he reminds him of Mozart, Watteau, Dresden china and, perhaps, Georgian domestic architecture.

Arnold's prestige had no doubt had its effect before the end of the century. John Dennis, whose popular handbook, *The Age of Pope*, appeared in 1894, expresses the view which was by this time becoming more or less standard. It had hardly been possible to write before this of an 'age of Pope'. Like most standard views about complex matters, Dennis's is full of unresolved contradictions, by which, however, he is not unduly troubled. He regards the *Essay on Man* as ambitious popular philosophy, but

> Read the poem for its poetical merits and you will forget its defects.

Dennis calls the concluding lines of the *Essay*, addressed to Boling-broke, 'as beautiful as they are false'. A begged question or two does not trouble the writer of the popular handbook. He sits comfortably on the fence between aesthetes and moralists, censuring Pope's injustice in the *Dunciad*:

> To place a great scholar like Bentley, an eloquent and earnest preacher like Whitefield, and a man of genius like Defoe among the dunces was to stultify himself.

A modern reader might think it was more than this. On the other hand Dennis echoes Thackeray and Ruskin in admiring the conclusion to the *Dunciad*, which 'may be almost said to redeem the faults of the poem and they prove incontestably, if such proof be needed, Pope's claim to a place among the poets'.

Dennis's willingness to admire Pope 'as a poet' is, however, qualified by moralistic scruples. Endorsing Leslie Stephen's view of *The Rape of the Lock* in his *English Men of Letters* volume (1880), he says that Pope's praise of women 'is too often a libel upon them'. Puritanism, as well as feminism, is a trait in the late Victorian ethos: but Dennis was not the first to comment on Pope's bawdry, which indeed had been noted by his contemporaries!

> He was not a man to rise above his age, and it would be charitable to ascribe a portion of his grossness to it.

Dennis also comments, as we should expect, on Pope's duplicity. Summing up, he describes Pope as 'the representative poet of his century', and gives him 'first place in the second order of poets'. It will be remembered that Warton had done the same more than a century before. He quotes Scott's phrase about Pope – 'a true Deacon of the craft' – and calls it generous. Scott may have known what Dennis perhaps did not, that 'deacon' is defined as 'minister of the third order'. The late nineteenth-century received view of Pope is perhaps be-summed up by George Saintsbury, whose *Short History of English Literature* appeared in 1898. It contains, as we should expect in such a work, nothing new, but it indicates Pope's standing at the end of the century, a standing somewhat higher than is allowed by modern enthusiasts. As Professor of Rhetoric and English Literature at Edinburgh University, Saintsbury enjoyed considerable authority, and his is the kind of critical view which percolates in course of time downwards from the academic chair into the minds of the reading public generally. He writes with more than his customary coolness of Pope's character, but his appreciation of the poetry is judicious and even enthusiastic. He condemns Pope's 'extreme untruthfulness', and gives a mainly unsympathetic account of Pope as a man. 'But his character,' Saintsbury concludes, *'save for its close connection with his work*, matters very little; his literature matters very much'. The italics are mine, and serve to point out the begged question we have just had occasion to note in another popular critic. It shows also how far the century had moved from Arnold's moralistic position. It does not occur to Saintsbury to attempt a reconciliation between his contradictory views of the man and the poet, for on the whole he admires the poetry. He calls Pope

> . . . within certain narrow but impregnable limits one of the greatest masters of poetic form that the world has ever seen, and a considerable though sometimes over-rated, satirist.

He endorses the Ruskin–Thackeray view of the conclusion to the *Dunciad*, by now more or less stereotyped, adding his personal comment that it is 'Swift done into poetry'. Saintsbury has little to say about the question of originality in Pope, but perhaps it is the implications of that phrase, 'done into poetry', which cause him to deny Pope a place among the greatest. In Saintsbury's view Pope had little humour, but much wit; 'exquisite though limited perfection of phraseology'; and 'the neatest, smartest, sharpest rhyme' to each of his couplets. It is indeed the mastery of the couplet which, as we should expect, evokes Saintsbury's most unreserved approbation. To him poetry was three parts prosody.

> Pope's extraordinary mastery of a certain refinement of the Drydenian couplet which, losing not a little strength and colour, and something of that portion of the poetic vague which Dryden retained, added an incomparable lightness and polish, seems to have been attained very early.

The early poems, however, were 'mere pastiches'; it is the *Dunciad*, the *Essay on Man* and the later satires that are Pope's best work – 'mosaics', but none the worse for that.

Once again we have the critic who distinguishes between the exquisite but limited technique of 'the pen that never stumbles' and the hand that holds the pen, the man of doubtful personal morals. There is no attempt to harmonize this disharmony, no suggestion that there may be a difficulty in accepting flawless poetry as the work of a flawed character. Undoubtedly the aesthetic revolution of the 'nineties has had its influence: any difficulty Saintsbury may have had in harmonizing the poet and the man is eliminated by his willingness to accept poetry purely as prosodic technique. Art for art's sake. The ambivalence of the late nineteenth-century view illustrates Pope's importance, as the Bowles–Byron controversy had illustrated it in the early part of the century. You cannot be consistent about him unless you have a reasonably clear notion, right or wrong, of what poetry is. Saintsbury had no such notion.

Perhaps the last word, so far as the nineteenth century is concerned, should be with a poet – one who was also a prosodist. Tennyson published nothing on Pope, and his opinion could have had little influence in his time. In his *Memoir*, 1897, Tennyson's son, Hallam, records that his father compared Pope unfavourably with Dryden.

'What a difference,' he would add, 'between Pope's little poisonous barbs and Dryden's strong invective! And how much more real poetic force there is in Dryden!'

Tennyson admired the *Elegy to the Memory of an Unfortunate Lady*, but did not find much human feeling in Pope, except in *Eloïsa to Abelard*. He considered his couplets monotonous, although he much admired certain couplets and single lines. He believed that Pope had, here and there, a real insight into nature, and that his satirical 'lancet touches' were 'very fine'. The Laureate was justly proud of his own ear, and especially his skill in dealing with the obtrusive English 's'. Although he responded to Pope's 'musical finesse', he remarked on his difficulty over the letter 's'. Quoting the first line of *The Rape of the Lock*,

What dire Offence from am'rouse Causes springs,

Tennyson commented:

'Amrus causiz springs,' horrible! I would sooner die than write such a line!!

A modern poet, Robert Graves, as fastidious a prosodist as Tennyson, also observes Pope's lack of control over the 's' sound (*The Crowning Privilege*, 1955). This has never, so far as I know, been adduced as evidence that 'the little nightingale', when a child, literally lisped in numbers.

6 Pope in the Twentieth Century I

The first important landmark in Pope studies in the twentieth century is the full-length biography by Miss E. M. Symons ('George Paston'), two volumes, 1909. This has been unjustly overlooked, probably because its author is in places decidedly critical of Pope's character. She is on the whole fair, and her book, *Mr. Pope: His Life and Times*, is still (up to the time of writing) the fullest and most informative biographical study. It has long been out of print and is rarely mentioned in the bibliographies. In his own biographical study, *The Early Career of Alexander Pope*, 1934, George Sherburn gives it grudging recognition in a passing reference, but damns it in the all too familiar formula of professional scholars, 'marred by factual inaccuracies'. How many these inaccuracies are, and how serious in a book of over seven hundred pages, we are not told. The eclipse of Miss Symons' biography is undoubtedly due to the changing temper of Pope criticism in the present century.

Another cause of neglect is that E. M. Symons was an amateur, almost the last amateur to write at length on Pope. It should here be said that I use the words 'amateur', 'professional', and 'academic' – words often charged with critical overtones – in as nearly neutral a sense as possible. When I say, for instance, that in the 1930s Pope was taken over by academic criticism, I mean simply that almost all the important writing on him has been done by full-time professional scholars working in universities. I do not mean that no earlier writers held academic positions; what I do mean, however, is that before the 1930s this field of criticism still had room for non-academic writers. I believe, too, that the take-over of Pope by the universities, to the exclusion of amateurs, has had certain important results, not all good. Few poets have written on Pope, and then only sporadically. Moreover the galloping specialization of academic literary studies is tending to make it more difficult for a generally well-read and widely experienced writer to get a serious hearing. This specialization is unfortunate if it means that those who compose the most important and well-informed monographs on literary subjects, Pope or any other, are able to devote less and less time and energy to the reading of works outside their chosen speciality. The man who has read only, or mainly Pope and his contemporaries is not necessarily the best judge of Pope. Without disparaging the valuable work of academic criticism, especially in the field of textual and historical scholarship, I believe that precision and detail have been achieved at some cost to breadth of outlook.

Before the academic take-over of Pope began in the 1930s, a few isolated voices were heard which indicate the trend of early twentieth-century thinking. In 1919 J. W. Mackail, then sixty years old, delivered the Leslie Stephen lecture on Pope. He had had one foot in the academic world and a career not unlike Matthew Arnold's. He had little to say that was new, and his lecture is beset by those inconsistencies which are inseparable from amateur Pope criticism. But he claims to speak with authority, and he takes it for granted that his audience is prepared to accept general statements about the nature and value of poetry. He speaks as one who considers it important to weigh the poetry of Pope against other poetry. His lecture is a curious mass of contradictions and owes some of its interest to this fact: it illustrates the difficulty of adopting a consistent attitude towards Pope. Mackail goes to some pains to discuss Pope's character, in which he finds little to applaud.

> He fell under the domination of Swift; he fell later, and as disastrously, under the domination of Bolingbroke; he knew it, and stung back by treating both with inexcusable perfidy. . . . His cynicism with regard to women is really sentimentality gone tainted; some would say, gone putrid. . . . His love was febrile and sickly; his hatred was a clear consuming flame.

But this has nothing to do with Pope's poetry, which 'as poetry is not a biographical or historical document'. Poetry has nothing to do with morals; 'Milton was not a shining example of the domestic virtues. Coleridge had no morals at all'. It is when we read statements like this last that we remember that Mackail was the son of a Scots minister. Mackail dismisses Stephen as a critic of poetry, since to him poetry was valuable only for its prose content. Stephen, moreover, 'was without that touch of the poet in him which is necessary for the vital appreciation of poetry'. The 'touch of the poet' in Mackail authorizes him to detect in Pope's *Pastorals* the unmistakable sound of 'a new poetical voice'. He quotes the 'Where'er you walk' quatrain with admiration, and comments: 'These lines, so fine in phrasing, so elastic in rhythm, have become inseparable from the exquisite music to which Handel wedded them' in *Semele*. That Pope was here re-working a traditional conceit of pastoral poetry, with verbal echoes, possibly at second hand, from Waller does not trouble Mackail, for whom poetry is not a matter of content or morality, but of phrasing and rhythm. He refers to the

conclusion of Book IV of the *Dunciad*, 'before which all criticism has
bowed down in admiration'.

Nevertheless, as a good Calvinist Mackail is not quite easy about
adopting the aesthetic attitude. Pope had inborn genius, but squandered
it on unworthy objects. He cannot, as many of his predecessors could
not, see Pope steadily and see him whole, and make sense of what he
saw. He wishes him otherwise, remade in the image of a poet as conceived by a Victorian-born Scottish classical scholar. Aesthetic and
moral criteria having to some extent failed him, Mackail, in his final
judgement, falls back on literary history and an Arnoldian formula
rounded off with an appeal to generalized literary emotion. Pope's
poetry was not, he tells us, 'quite in the central line of evolution', but he
does not tell us just what that line was. In any case, 'nous avons changé
tout cela', a modern critic might claim. Mackail concludes:

> Pope is a limited classic, a classic with a difference. But with that dif-
> ference, within that limit, his poetry is, as only classics are, imperishable.
> No lapse of time, no change of fashion, can abate 'that brilliant genius
> and immense fame'.

In 1925 a refreshing note was introduced into Pope criticism by
Lytton Strachey's once famous and now perhaps underrated essay. This
note may have been the first blast – or squeak – of the trumpet against
Matthew Arnold. Everyone knows that Strachey is more highly regarded for brilliance than for depth, but there is something to be said
for his answer to Arnold's charge against Pope, that he lacked an
adequate criticism of life: 'His poetic criticism of life was, simply and
solely, the heroic couplet.' It is not quite certain that Strachey is not
here deflating Pope as well as Arnold. His judgement may be no more
than a *bon mot*, but it is an antidote to the excessive 'high seriousness'
of the heavier critics. Strachey admired French literature almost to
excess, and he admired Pope's couplets for their antithetical neatness
and their surface gloss.

In 1930 Edith Sitwell produced her book, *Alexander Pope*, a
romantic novel offering itself as a critical biography. It is discounted by
academic critics as a serious embarrassment to the cause of Pope's
rehabilitation. But it is worth consideration for a number of reasons: it is
a pioneer effort in that rehabilitation; it is almost the last serious non-
academic study; much that it contains, when the rubbish has been forgotten, has been adopted by later critics, though in more cautious and
decorous terms. Her admiration for the 'texture' of Pope's verse, for
instance, is the substance of much of Tillotson's analysis and it may be

noted that he also endorses her view of Pope's character. He calls it a 'reasonable attitude' reached by 'the exercise of a vivid intuitive sympathy'. To this combination of reason and intuition he might have added a pretty selective treatment of the facts. Moreover, Edith Sitwell writes as a poet, sincerely and wholly committed to her subject, expressing her *Schwärmerei* for Pope with warmth and passion. Her approach is bio-critical, though she scarcely succeeds in integrating her admiration for the poems with her love of the man. She was excited to profound sympathy by the more appealing elements in Pope's nature and circumstances – his protestations of benevolence, his lonely bachelorhood, and above all his desperate physical handicaps. She reveals an unswerving devotion to his 'genius', a whole-hearted conviction of his 'greatness'. She hardly pretends to see him whole; where she admits his faults, she regards them as venial, explicable by the standards of his time and his pitiable personal circumstances. To her, Pope was a lonely genius, defending himself against the misunderstandings and the cruelties of scribblers, deprived by ill fortune of normal human relationships yet craving them with all his soul, a supreme literary artist traduced by a hostile world.

This picture of Pope, which is still current in some quarters, does not stand up to an examination of the facts, half of which Edith Sitwell is obliged to ignore. But we can at least respect it as a labour of love, even if to some extent a labour of self-love, for it contains a strong element of self-projection. It might be called autobio-criticism. There is an interesting passage in a review by Philip Toynbee of Edith Sitwell's autobiography (*Observer*, 4 April 1965), all the more striking because the reviewer was not writing about Pope:

> There is, I believe, a kind of hatred which not only distorts its object but also reveals elements in that object which love could never have perceived. There is also a kind of love which dares to see its object whole and which is strong enough to be open-eyed about faults and weaknesses. Some of Dame Edith's portraits are full of love; but unfortunately it seems to be nearly always the kind of love which is based on *gratitude* and which repays some debt, of admiration or affection, by seeing its object in angelic colours.

What Toynbee says of Edith Sitwell might be applied with equal force to Pope, though, in my opinion, neither was sufficiently self-forgetting ever to see a love-object whole. Neither had the requisite daring, because each was too self-absorbed. This was their misfortune and it explains the compelling attraction of Pope for Edith Sitwell.

Love is blind, but seldom worthless. Love of Pope persuades Edith

Sitwell that hostility to Pope was a Victorian heresy, with Matthew Arnold as the villain. It was not poets, but schoolmasters, school inspectors, and dons who had disparaged Pope out of jealousy and spite against a creative artist. This was fiction in 1830, and not less so in 1930. Nevertheless, the thirty years before Edith Sitwell's book do, on the whole, represent the low-water mark in the estimation of Pope, and it must be fairly admitted that, hysterical as much of it is, her praise of Pope sets a new tone. It might be deplored, but it could not be ignored. She could scarcely have complained that during the thirty years after her book there was any under-estimation or neglect of Pope in the educational world.

To Edith Sitwell Pope was 'a good and exceedingly lovable man'. His letters to his friends are 'among the most touching letters that any great man has written'. His friendship with Swift was 'a monument of what friendship should be'. This is undoubtedly what Pope intended his readers to think, and Edith Sitwell is a willing dupe. True, she admits that in publishing his correspondence he redirected a letter he had written to Caryll, 'for some inscrutable reasons', as if it had been addressed to Addison. The reason is simple: to Pope's readers Addison was a more impressive correspondent than Caryll, a private Catholic friend. But Pope could not recover his letters from Addison, who by this time was dead. He made use of many of his letters to Caryll in this way, but he did not expect to be found out. In referring to Pope's friendship and subsequent quarrel with Lady Mary Wortley Montagu, Edith Sitwell's hatred – one might almost say jealousy – of Lady Mary knows no bounds. She is much more abusive about the pioneer bluestocking than ever Pope was. On the other hand, Edith Sitwell has a mild protest to make about the illiberal treatment of Broome and Fenton over their reward for help with the *Odyssey*. 'These gentlemen were, comparatively speaking, unoffending.' If Edith Sitwell had troubled to read Johnson on Fenton, or had had access to the correspondence of Broome and Fenton, she could hardly have written 'comparatively speaking'. She does not think Pope's treatment of the bookseller Curll in the incident of the emetic reprehensible, but she condemns his subsequent exploitation of it in print. She admits Pope's tortuousness and his 'constitutional inhibition against speaking the truth', but she cannot condemn them. 'I have so often found both these faults in myself, that I do not dare to blame them.' Nor would any of us blame Edith Sitwell unless she had, like Pope, made frequent protestations about her spotless moral character.

To Edith Sitwell Pope is not merely a lovable and misunderstood

man, but also a 'great and – at his best – flawless poet'. Without pausing
to question whether any poet worthy of a full-length monograph is not
'*at his best* flawless', we may ask what it is that Edith Sitwell admires in
his work. For you cannot write at length on Pope, or any poet, without
revealing your personal definition – or lack of a definition – of poetry,
even if only by implication. It is clear, from *Alexander Pope* and from
the introduction to her anthology, *The Pleasures of Poetry*, 1930, that
to her poetry is 'texture'. This is also abundantly evident from her own
poetic practice, at least until the time of World War II. She had spent
many years in fiddling about with 'verbal music' and with building up
a reputation as an avant-garde poet, and this strengthens her sense of
affinity with Pope. Brushing aside the views of those who believe,
allegedly, that poetic beauty is 'dependent upon subject alone', she
advances the view that poetry is more or less a matter of superlative
expression: Pope is a great poet because he achieves triumphantly what
Edith Sitwell was trying to achieve. She admires the 'murky and
Tartarean' texture of the *Dunciad* – 'just as beautiful in its own way,
and just as strange, as *The Ancient Mariner*'. As for verbal music, it is
to be found everywhere. Edith Sitwell singles out for quotation two
lines from the *Ode on St. Cecilia's Day*:

> Thy stone, O *Sysiphus*, stands still;
> *Ixion* rests upon his wheel.

Untroubled by the presence of eleven 's' sounds in sixteen syllables, and
a faulty rhyme, Edith Sitwell calls these lines 'superb'. Is love deaf as
well as blind? In Pope's *Odyssey* the 'lines and the heroes walk with the
pomp and majesty of waves', but

> . . . we do not find the astonishing variations in texture that we find in
> *The Dunciad*, nor the incredibly subtle variations of *The Rape of the
> Lock*. The poem is more uniform, but had it been otherwise, the technique
> would have been unsuited to the matter.

This is interesting. Texture is the most important attribute of Pope's
poetry. In the *Odyssey*, magnificent as it is, the texture varies little.
Half of it was written by Broome and Fenton, and not much of their
contribution, so far as we know, was substantially altered by Pope.
Pope's greatest achievement, therefore, is not hard to imitate. Is this
the inference we are meant to draw?

Before leaving Edith Sitwell it would be worth while to exhibit her
at her most ingenious and imaginative. She quotes a couplet from the
Dunciad, IV:

> Thick and more thick the black blockade extends,
> A hundred head of Aristotle's friends.

and comments:

> The first line of this couplet is very interesting from a technical point of view, with the deliberately muddy arrangements of the 'ck's', which give exactly the impression of mud clinging to our feet and delaying our progress. The mere dullness of the 'i' sound in 'thick', the slight lengthening sound (delaying the line still further) of 'black' and the heel-over dark impenetrability of the 'block' in 'blockade' seems the very essence, in sound, of stupidity itself. 'Black blockade' conveys, in its sound, the impression of an enormous wooden figure at the head of a procession, heeling over, and righting itself by an effort.

This is a fine example of the 'texture' school of Pope criticism. Meanwhile:

> ' "Impenetrability! That's what I say!"
> "Would you tell me, please," said Alice, "what that means?"
> "Now you talk like a reasonable child," said Humpty Dumpty, looking very much pleased. "I meant by 'impenetrability' that we've had enough of that subject...".'

The academic take-over of Pope already referred to began, significantly, with the work of the American scholar, George Sherburn, whose *The Early Career of Alexander Pope* came out in 1934. It is an account of Pope's life and writings up to the period when, in his late thirties, he was preparing to bring out the *Dunciad*. The choice of the word 'Career' make an important bio-critical point. The excellence and usefulness of this book established Sherburn as the leading authority on Pope. It is not clear why he did not complete his study of Pope's career.[1] It may be that he felt a growing distaste for the man and his work. At all events he appears to have devoted much of his later energy to more purely scholarly and bibliographical studies, culminating in his monumental and definitive edition of Pope's correspondence, published in 1956. All students of Pope are permanently in his debt.

Sherburn exemplifies humane and balanced scholarship at its best. He writes of his subject *con amore* but has too much integrity not to reveal doubts about Pope's character and conduct. The very thoroughness of his editing of the correspondence shows up Pope's defects, and while the editor attempts sometimes to condone them, he does not hide them. He

---

[1] In this connection it may be noted that Vol. I of Peter Quennell's substantial *Alexander Pope: The Education of Genius 1688–1748* appeared in 1968 and that Vol. II has not been published up to the time of writing (March 1974).

combines a certain naïveté with a degree of scholarly scepticism. In *The Early Career* he finds himself obliged frequently to use expressions such as 'if the poet is to be believed'. In discussing Pope's relations with such men as Theobald, Broome, and Fenton, Sherburn takes Pope's side somewhat uncritically. On the other hand, he can rarely praise Pope without reservation.

> It is certainly a tenable position that an author's personality should have no influence with a critic of his writing; but few will deny that Pope's supposed personality daily prejudices readers against his work.
>
> (Preface to *The Early Career*.)

It is clear that Edith Sitwell's contribution had made little impact on the American scholar. 'I do not expect,' he writes, 'to revolutionize the conceptions that have been current concerning Pope's character'.

Our gratitude is due to Sherburn as a literary and bibliographical scholar; we do not look to him for criticism. No work of literary scholarship, however, is wholly without critical overtones. One brief contribution Sherburn makes to the critical debate must be noted. Commenting on the accusation made against Bowles that he applied Wordsworthian standards to the poetry of Pope, he says

> To judge Pope by romantic criteria is of course to condemn him by the laws of a country in which he was no citizen.

This is a point frequently made by academic admirers of Pope, who do not see that, by introducing the word 'romantic' to designate the kind of poet that Wordsworth and his contemporaries were and that the Augustans were not, they demarcate poetry in a way which poets do not accept. Both Pope and Wordsworth, Shakespeare before them and Tennyson after them regarded themselves simply as poets, working under the same laws, if laws there are, as other poets. Edith Sitwell, writing as a poet, has no compunction in comparing the *Dunciad* with *The Ancient Mariner* and awarding Pope, even under the laws of Coleridge's country, high rank. Literary historians may call Shakespeare a dramatic poet, Pope a classicist or a satirist, Wordsworth a Romantic and Tennyson a Victorian; to invent an exclusive category for every major poet or his 'school' is in the end to make critical anarchy by denying the reality of 'poetry'. It is as if there were no poetry, only poems. A major purpose of criticism must be to insist on the laws under which all poets work, not to deduce from their work mutually incompatible sets of laws. To a poet all poets are citizens of one country.

7 The Twentieth Century II

Between the publication of Edith Sitwell's book in 1930 and the appearance of the first volume of the definitive Twickenham edition of the poems on the eve of World War II no major monograph appeared except Tillotson's *On the Poetry of Pope* in 1938. This title is significant, illustrating as it does the trend away from biography manifested in the 1930s. A number of interesting briefer studies of Pope appeared during the decade, indicating the direction of academic thinking. These vary in length from casual, but seminal, remarks to essays. T. S. Eliot (who, as a critic, began his career in the rôle of a kind of extramural professor) had, in the preface to his 1928 selection from the poems of Pound, dropped a hint:

> . . . indeed it might be said in our time that the man who cannot enjoy
> Pope as poetry probably understands no poetry . . .

This is one of the *ex cathedra* pronouncements which, in those days, were taken very seriously in Cambridge. True, a few years later Eliot characteristically withdrew from any appearance of over-enthusiasm for the age of Pope which his earlier hint might have given. In *The Use of Poetry and the Use of Criticism*, 1932, he wrote that the

> History of every branch of intellectual activity provides the same record
> of the diminution of England from the time of Queen Anne. It is not
> so much the intellect, but something superior to intellect, which went
> for a long time into eclipse; and this luminary, by whatever name we
> may call it, has not yet wholly issued from its secular obnubilation. The
> age of Dryden was still a great age, though beginning to suffer a death of
> the spirit, as the coarsening of its verse-rhythms shows; by the time of
> Addison theology, devotion and poetry fell fast into a formalistic slumber.

Meanwhile I. A. Richards was communicating to his Cambridge students his enthusiasm for the *Elegy to the Memory of an Unfortunate Lady*, and William Empson in his *Seven Types of Ambiguity*, 1930, expressed delight in the lines on 'Timon's villa'. Both of these enthusiasms were elaborated by F. R. Leavis, whose essays on Pope and the Augustan age appeared in his *Revaluation*, 1936. Writing from a consciously post-Arnold standpoint, Leavis finds in the *Elegy* (whose 'rare fineness . . . has not had the recognition it deserves') evidence of affinities between Pope and the Metaphysicals. He claims to find this affinity in the style of Pope's performance, and is not concerned with the possibility of a total absence of temperamental affinity, nor with the fact of literary history that Pope, refining on Dryden, had done his best to eliminate from his poetry the most characteristic qualities of the Metaphysicals. A brief examination of what Pope did to Donne in attempting to regularize the style of his satires is enough to convince us of the justice of Eliot's judgement and of Pope's incapacity to respond to the subtlety of the Metaphysicals' rhythms.

Leavis is also opposed to bio-criticism:

> It is, in some ways, a pity that we know so much about Pope's life. If nothing had been known but the works, would 'envy', 'venom', 'malice', 'spite' and the rest have played so large a part in the commentary?

But we have Pope to thank for most of our knowledge of his life. By 'works' Leavis means 'poems', but Pope took just as much trouble to give us his letters, and the whole conduct of his life was such as to encourage the proliferation of gossip, malicious or otherwise. Leavis's wish to isolate the poems from their biographical context is symptomatic of the whole trend of academic criticism, which seeks to minimize the crucial importance of that word 'Career' in the title of Sherburn's book. Leavis denies the relevance of the moral-aesthetic debate over Pope. Commenting on a quotation about Pope from an American critic, he says: 'An "understanding of the basic moral values" is not a claim one need be concerned to make . . . for a poet, . . .' I have re-read Leavis and considered very carefully my comments and this commentator's. On the whole I think I have given a very fair account of Leavis's views and represented them fully enough for the reader to form his own judgement. Naturally there is always room for differences of opinion. But it is certainly a claim Pope made for himself, and if we take 'understanding' as meaning 'apprehension' rather than something more articulate, it is a claim which some critics, and certainly many poets, have been prepared to make. The question of whether it *ought* to be made is one that Leavis might be expected to be concerned with. Elsewhere he often writes as if the moral-aesthetic dichotomy vitally concerns him; he is never wholly at ease among the pure aestheticians. He gives sometimes the impression of believing that morality somehow matters in art but not in conduct.

Turning to the poems, Leavis praises 'the intense destructive capacity of the Sporus portrait', and is 'inclined to think' *Dunciad*, IV 'the most striking manifestation of [Pope's] genius'. It should be noted that both passages are destructive; yet elsewhere Leavis insists on the essentially positive and creative character of Pope's achievement. Summing up his findings, Leavis concludes:

> In the Augustan poet, then, the development associated with Waller's name fulfils itself and exposes its full significance. Yet, as the fourth book of the *Dunciad* along with a great deal else of Pope shows, the Augustan poet, using an idiom and forms that insist so on the authoritative reality of the social surface, is not necessarily confined to that surface . . . Pope's greatness, we remind ourselves, is of such a kind as to enable him to transcend his age: his profound poetry has in it an essential element of the Metaphysical (and no other poet of Pope's century so communicates with the seventeenth). The representative Augustan poems are rather *The Rape of the Lock,* the *Essay on Man* and the *Epistle to Arbuthnot,* and these too it took a Pope to write: they stand far above anything by any contemporary of his. In Pope, alone, in his time, the tradition he represents may be said to bring into poetry the full vitality of the age.

Well-expressed and cogently argued as are these conclusions, it is impossible to follow them to the point of enthusiasm felt by Leavis. Questions which have to be considered elsewhere are these: What development in poetry, other than a sterile one, is associated with Waller? How far does Pope get below even the limited area of the surface of Augustan society with which he was familiar? Can the poetry of the Augustans, even Pope, be said to express the full vitality of an age which also contains Defoe, Hogarth, Vanbrugh, Cibber, and Swift? In *The Common Pursuit,* 1952, Leavis states with still more emphasis his position on the Augustan age. Writing of the *Dunciad,* he insists on the distinction between its materials and its poetry, which is what 'matters'.

> For eighteenth-century readers it must have been hard not to start away continually from the poetry to thinking about the particular historical victim and the grounds of Pope's animus against him . . .

Not only was it hard; the distinction did not exist for them. It is an invention of academic criticism. For the poet Owen the 'pity' of the war was its poetry. To the eighteenth-century reader the poetry of the *Dunciad* was its malice, though Leavis cannot recognize this, as his comments seem to indicate that he could in the case of the 'Sporus' passage. Contrasting Pope and Swift as poets, Leavis maintains that Pope is always engaged in 'positive creation', while Swift is aridly negative. It is necessary to Leavis's view of Pope as the greatest poet of his age that Swift should be written down and, I believe, fundamentally misrepresented. Leavis sees Pope as 'a great and ardent representative of Augustan civilization'. What he cannot see, since he prefers to discount the biographical facts, is that Pope was basically satisfied with Augustan civilization as he knew it. He was thus a satirist without a mission. Had he not written, 'Whatever is, is right'? His fulminations against money and corruptions are the mere rhetoric of the *persona* he had assumed. He loved money, and if some of his friends were not corrupt, it was because they were out of office. The view that Pope stood for an ideal 'Augustan' order (he never, so far as I know, used the word) is, however, a part of contemporary Pope criticism and will have to be considered elsewhere. As for Swift, even if we ignore such 'positive' creations as *Mrs Frances Harris's Petition* and other unpretentious pieces, we shall find in the verse evidence of a far more profound, because more immediately felt, realization of what was corrupt beneath the Augustan surface. We shall find, too, a continuous concern for linguistic vitality – a concern which acquits Swift, more than any of his contemporaries, of the charge levelled by Eliot of rhythmic degeneration. This has to do with the responsiveness of Swift's ear to the common tongue with which he had so much sympathy.

It is no part of my purpose to examine Swift as a poet, still less to upgrade him at the expense of Pope or anyone else, but our view of his poetry would have to take into account our view of the nature of poetry itself and of the relation between a poet, his times and his writings. How far was it possible to be at once a poet and a member of Augustan society? Swift destroyed himself in trying to find the answer, but his poems fulfil themselves by facing, not evading, the issues, terrible as he found them. Leavis makes much of Pope's positive creativity and admires the *Dunciad* as an expression of his concern for 'order' and an 'ideal Augustan civilization'. I do not believe this view of Pope's poetic purpose can be sustained; it depends on putting too much strain on the term 'Augustan', which, in the whole context of Pope's life and work, means little more than 'as Pope would have it'. The relation of Pope to his age is a matter for more detailed study. It is, however, we are told, the poetry that matters, not the thought. Quoting the opening of *Dunciad*, IV, Leavis invites his readers to 'consider how triumphantly it enlists Milton into an Augustan sublime'. This is a matter of taste. Are we to infer that to the Augustans sublimity means no more than an accomplished pastiche of *Paradise Lost*? Referring to the famous close of *Dunciad*, IV, Leavis finds himself in company with Thackeray and Ruskin. He has done much to discredit vague terms of literary appreciation, and it is disappointing to find him, when committing himself

o an expression of personal admiration, falling back on such a phrase
as 'that tremendously imaginative and moving grandeur'.

David Nichol Smith, in *Some Observations on Eighteenth Century
Poetry*, 1937, says that 'the call for the reopening of the case' for a
reassessment of the eighteenth century had come mainly from the
universities, and that the Americans had taken the lead. He is unwilling
to regard Pope as esoteric, though he does not explain why the call has
come from the universities rather than the common reader. Dryden's
aim, he says, was to reform poetry by making it more natural than that
of the Metaphysicals and more able to appeal to a wide audience.

> The poet does not write for a coterie, a privileged few who know his
> special point of view and are prepared to wrestle with his conundrums;
> the poet writes for the community. . . . The leadership passes to Pope,
> and he is a loyal successor who, despite his strongly marked individuality,
> never falters in his admiration. He has the same ideals . . . the differences
> between his work and Dryden's do not spring from different aims.

Of Pope's aims in the wider sense nothing is said. How far he may
truly be said to have shared Dryden's aim of making poetry more
natural, more accessible to the 'community', must be judged in the light
of his actual performance. Nichol Smith, after a long eulogy of Pope's
capacity for natural word order and emphasis, holds up for admiration
the following couplet:

> But grant, in Public, Men sometimes are shown,
> A Woman's seen in Private life alone.

By any standards this is abominable English, to be admired only by a
very sophisticated or a very insensitive reader, or by one for whom Pope
never puts a foot wrong. True, Nichol Smith praises this couplet for
compression, declamatory ease and pace. But if these are achieved at the
cost of natural diction and clarity of meaning, what becomes of the claim
for Pope's mastery of the natural style and his appeal to the common
reader?

Nichol Smith discusses Pope's diction as it were *in vacuo*. This is, of
course, a legitimate and to some extent necessary critical practice, but it
has its drawbacks, notably the implication that poetic value may reside
in diction irrespective of what is said. The corollary, as we have seen,
is that poetry is 'texture' – a common assumption among Pope's
admirers. Fundamental questions may be treated with something
approaching frivolity. Quoting the passage from the *Epistle to Augustus*
beginning

> Of little use the man you may suppose,
> Who says in verse what others say in prose

Nichol Smith calls this Pope's 'light-hearted rejoinder to the question
which I suppose we have all heard – what is the use of poetry and
poets?' Here Pope merely enumerates some of the practical uses of verse
as distinct from prose – the education of children and foreigners and the
teaching of oratorical facility. Nichol Smith adds that the passage contains Pope's 'ultimate verdict on Addison as a writer, and never has
Addison received higher praise'. It also contains high praise of Swift.
But the tributes to Addison and Swift are concerned with these writers,
not as poets, but as the authors of *The Spectator* and such prose tracts as
The Drapier's Letters. There is an element of intellectual trickery in
this which would seem to call for some comment other than the praise
of its diction. Nichol Smith also quotes the 'Where'er you walk' quatrain
and comments, 'I suspect that not everyone who is familiar with the
music is aware that the words are by Pope'. I suspect that Nichol Smith
either was unaware, or did not care, how much Pope was here indebted
to earlier poets. He quotes a couplet from Johnson which is in every way
as good as Pope:

> There mark what Ills the Scholar's Life assail,
> Toil, Envy, Want, the Patron, and the Jail.

He quotes also a sustained passage from *The Vanity of Human Wishes*,
which also is as good as Pope in versification, but superior in warmth
of feeling and genuine pathos. He does not draw the inference that it
was perhaps not very difficult for an eighteenth-century writer to compose effective heroic couplets; and if it is objected that it was easy for
Johnson to do so after Pope, the answer would be that it was equally
easy for Pope to do so after Dryden. Diction, rhythm, texture – these
cannot alone afford criteria for poetic evaluation.

In an interesting study of *The Inspiration of Pope's Poetry* in a
volume of essays presented to David Nichol Smith, 1945, John Butt
indicates clearly some of the directions criticism was now taking. Butt's
distinguished academic career culminated in the Professorship of English at Edinburgh University, by which time, as general editor of the
Twickenham edition, he became the leading British Pope scholar. His
essay on *The Inspiration of Pope's Poetry* makes it quite clear that he
regards Pope as caviare to the general and ideally suited for the
academic take-over in which he himself played so important a part.
He says that the 'unsophisticated' reader finds it hard to appreciate

Pope. He makes the point that the poetry is topical and cannot be fully understood without extra-poetic knowledge. The literary historian is to be the high priest mediating between the common reader and the poetic godhead.

> To say merely that Pope's ethical and topical poetry transcends its occasions is asking too much of a reader's faith. Yet this is the result of Pope's treatment of his materials.

Butt admires the *Dunciad* where 'Pope's enemies and the traditional enemies of good taste and sense are flayed in his most grave and imaginative poetry', and where he is working simultaneously at several 'levels', – that of personal revenge, that of conferring upon his revenge universal significance, and that of 'satisfying his imagination with poetry which is beautiful in itself, apart from any satiric significance'. This simplified account of the motivation of the *Dunciad* has gained a fair measure of assent in academic quarters. Others too, notably Edith Sitwell, found the *Dunciad* 'beautiful'. The status of Pope as arbiter of taste and watchdog of civilized values is certainly a matter for the historical study which Butt so persuasively demands.

In another important respect the 'common reader' needs the help of the scholar. On these grounds alone, Butt seems to be saying, we need a monumental critical edition of the poems. He is writing of what he calls Pope's 'literary inspiration' and what has elsewhere been variously called his allusions, borrowings, echoes, plagiarism. Pope came to regard his early descriptive poetry as fanciful and later thought of himself as 'moralizing his song'.

> After 1717 Pope preferred to subdue his powers of imagination . . . He liked to think that he had not wandered long in Fancy's maze.

To some this might sound like a good prescription for poetic suicide, but

> . . . neither Milton nor Pope wished to limit themselves to the comparatively mean resources of nature. Truth of description, like all other aspects of truth, Pope reserved to strengthen his moral purpose.

The fact is, of course, as is abundantly clear to any student of the first volume of the Twickenham edition, that even in his 'fanciful' period Pope had never got very close to nature. This does not trouble Butt. 'Literary inspiration,' he says, 'is not essentially different from inspiration derived from life.' How does the Professor know this? It is a belief commonly held by non-creative critics and, as one of the major heresies to be propagated since the academic take-over, it calls for special consideration. Butt writes as if to look at nature through the spectacles of books is the same as to look at it without spectacles. Certainly the habit of 'literary inspiration' practised by Pope and others is of immense assistance to the case for exhaustive editorial scholarship and exegesis.

It is not easy to do justice to Geoffrey Tillotson's small, compact book *On the Poetry of Pope*, first published in 1938, and reissued in slightly revised form in 1950. It is, perhaps, the best general appreciation, and should be read as a whole. If any single book could persuade a sensitive reader of the merits of Pope, it is this. It is good because it reflects throughout its author's sincere personal pleasure in his subject, and shows no trace of sophisticated exhibitionism. Tillotson genuinely loves the poetry of Pope, and is genuinely anxious to convert others to his view. In taking issue with him, both over his main contention, and on many points of detail, I have to admit that some of my differences are those of personal taste, of individual sensibility. Tillotson writes in the Bowles–Byron tradition, and in his book we are continually coming up against matters of basic poetic principle where disagreements are larger than, and antecedent to, any consideration of Pope alone. It is clear, for instance, that Tillotson delights in Latin poetry, and admires Pope because he is 'half a Roman poet. His profoundest kinship is with Virgil. After Virgil came Ovid and Horace.' Tillotson defends the Latinism of Pope's diction in the earlier poems, and claims that it makes for compression and elegance. He takes immense pleasure in the 'texture' of the poems, but recognizes that texture is not all. Under the surface he detects in Pope something of a suppressed romantic, whose lyricism is present more by implication than directly. His lyrical impulses, Tillotson writes, moved him not to elation but to 'something nearer melancholy'.

> In this he was like his favourite Virgil in whom the tears of things ache and burn behind the solid epic. And it is this quality which constitutes part of his profound kinship with Mozart and Keats.

This is to relate a personal aesthetic experience, but not to add anything to the understanding of Pope, since no illustrations are given in support of the comparison. To introduce the respected name of Virgil and the favoured names of Mozart and Keats is to create a sympathetic atmosphere for the reading of the poet you are recommending, but it has no objective critical force. True, Tillotson elsewhere elaborates on the Mozart comparison, but he says no more, perhaps, than that Mozart and Pope are both classical artists. It is easy enough to associate among one's aesthetic experiences those which give us the keenest pleasure – Shakespeare and Beethoven, Debussy and Botticelli, Bach and Giotto, Haydn and Wren, Spenser and Vivaldi. The possibilities are endless, but of limited use, except in telling us about the mind of the critic.

In invoking Keats, Tillotson seems anxious to present Pope as a much more romantic poet than has generally been allowed. It is in fact to his credit that he attempts to give Pope a high place by poetic standards which do not exclude romantic poetry: he has no qualms about judging Pope by the laws of a country of which he is no citizen. Whether or not he makes good his claims is to be judged by the degree to which his quotations bear them out. Tillotson believes, for instance, that, despite his aim of 'correctness', he had about him much 'wildness, sensitiveness, happy valiancy'. Tillotson's quotations simply do not bear this out. The reader begins to suspect that to Tillotson 'wildness' is something tamer than to most people. He finds Pope's *Iliad* 'fiery'. He is, indeed, at great pains to represent Pope as at the same time controlled and fiery. He speaks of the *Iliad* as if it were a sort of slow-combustion contrivance, like an Aga cooker.

> We know from a hundred independent sources that Pope had the true fire in him, but he did not set it before the reader's eyes as a bare flame. He set it instead to turn '. . . every wheel of that unweary'd Mill
> That turned ten thousand verses . . .'

This is an ingenious plea, but it could be equally well applied to anyone who tries hard and continuously to write good poems, but achieves only frigid, clever verse. 'Where is the fire?' you ask. 'You can't see it,' comes the answer; 'it is used up in writing the verses.'

Tillotson acknowledges the imitative quality of Pope's poetry, its constant element of translation and adaptation. 'Among English poets Pope is one of the most greedy of other poets' phrases.' He speaks of some of the material in Pope's longer poems being 'given its poetry'. The impression his comments leave is indeed that he regards poetry as a means by which prose is processed into verse. He argues that Pope's poetry provides the same sort of emotional satisfaction as La Rochefoucauld in prose.

> Before such material became poetry, it required to be radically changed. One can see what this transformation amounted to if one compares the passage on Addison's character in Pope's prose letter to Craggs . . . with the character as it appears in the verse *Epistle to Arbuthnot*. . . . The transformation here is radical.

There is, as a matter of fact, no evidence that the verse character of Atticus did not precede the prose letter to Craggs in date of composition; in any case, what was being given its poetry in the form everyone knows was not a prose thought, but an assortment of hints and phrases from earlier poets.

Not only is Pope's poetry smouldering with unrevealed fire, it is also charged with latent pity. Pope, we are told,

> . . . attains those moods in which pity is found trembling like a frightened dove or in which it moves over the mind like a slow dumb wave, a bulge of deep water.

To illustrate this, Tillotson cites, among other passages, the lines on Gay in the *Epistle to Arbuthnot*:

> May Dunce by Dunce be whistled off my hands!
> Blest be the Great! for those they take away,
> And those they left me – For they left me *Gay*,
> Left me to see neglected Genius bloom,
> Neglected die! and tell it on his Tomb;
> Of all thy blameless life the sole Return
> My Verse, and Queensb'ry weeping o'er thy Urn!
> Oh let me live my own! and die so too!
> ('To live and die is all I have to do:')

To me there is no pity in this, only an affected pathos, an egocentric incapacity to realize the death of Gay except in terms of self-congratulation for having composed Gay's epitaph, with perhaps a subsidiary touch of pride in being associated with so illustrious a person as Gay's patron, the Duke (or Duchess) of Queensberry. Gay was not a neglected genius. *The Beggar's Opera* had been a phenomenal success, but he had squandered the fortune it brought him and was in some difficulty when the sequel, *Polly*, was refused a licence by the Court.

Not only was Pope a suppressed romantic, he was also a nature poet. Quoting a number of couplets from the *Dunciad*, Tillotson remarks on Pope's capacity for suggestion. 'There is no other poet who habitually catches so much in a small glass.' Whether such couplets as this are to be admired is a matter of taste:

> As to soft gales top-heavy pines bow low
> Their heads, and lift them as they cease to blow.

It is doubtful if there are pines so top-heavy and so pliant as to bow low 'to soft gales'. Elsewhere Tillotson calls this couplet 'a simile perfect for its beauty', and points out that it is adapted from a simile by the

Latin poet Statius, who was writing of cypresses, not pines. Cypresses, of course, are remarkable for their pliancy; pines might well snap. This is not nature poetry, but literary adaptation. Of all the descriptions quoted from the *Dunciad* the only one which may have been partially observed from nature is:

> The sick'ning stars fade off th'ethereal plain.

This, however, is more likely to be an echo from *Hamlet* with a Miltonic overtone.

> . . . and the moist star,
> Upon whose influence Neptune's empire stands,
> Was sick almost to doomsday with eclipse.
> *(Hamlet,* I, i, 123–5.)

If Pope is to be called a nature poet, the term must be extended to include reworking of literary models and possibly the study of landscape painting. Tillotson cites as proof of Pope's aesthetic sensibility his remark in a letter to Caryll that 'small black and white landscape drawings can give no idea of "beautiful country", since they deprive it "of the light and lustre of nature" '. He had evidently never seen the miniature etchings of Rembrandt. Tillotson defends Pope against the criticism that he left nature out of his later poems on the ground that he felt obliged to devote himself more and more to the study of men in society, 'since this was the eighteenth century'. A major poet is not directed in his choice of subject-matter by the demands of his age. If Pope had really wanted to go on writing nature poetry, there was nothing whatever to stop him except that he might have lost the interest of the polite world of London society. After all, Thomson's *Seasons* had begun to appear before the publication of the *Dunciad*.

When he comes to discuss Pope's character, Tillotson admits that 'as a man Pope does not come up at all points to the ideal which readers elect for great authors', but hopes that scholarship may in time clear him of many of the charges made against him.. He cites his two predecessors, Sherburn and Edith Sitwell, in support of this optimistic view. As we have seen, the latter simply ignored many of the facts; as for Sherburn, his edition of the correspondence was not destined to help much. No one, of course, now believes the more outrageous accusations made against Pope during his lifetime; but much remains, or has subsequently come to light, which Pope's admirers could wish to have explained away. The *Dunciad*, Tillotson argues, 'strictly speaking, was not personal in origin. It was part of the programme of the Scriblerus

Club . . .' This is equivocation. The Scriblerus Club in its original form had ceased to be a going concern when Pope began to write the *Dunciad*; whatever may have been the origin of the poem, Pope used it to attack his enemies, to some extent against the wishes and advice of his friends, Swift and Arbuthnot.

> Whatever people may think of his private character – and of this there have been and are very few who are qualified to have an opinion – that character as it is revealed positively in the poetry is almost wholly admirable . . . The tone of this poetry and this prose [i.e. the letters] must convince the reader that he is in the presence of one whose sense of virtue is as alert as the trembling, vivid eye one notes in his portraits..

This is all highly debatable. The extent to which Pope's poems and letters were tuned to a conscious intention of presenting their author as the man of virtue seems not to be fully realized by Tillotson. For him, as for so many other readers of Pope, the expression of virtuous ideas and motives is synonymous with the posession of them. 'Pope's letters seem more concerned with friendship than with any other subject.' Precisely: but friendship is as friendship does, and there is such a thing as protesting too much. When Tillotson calls Pope 'a great critical intelligence, the most vigilant and subtle discriminator of intention and conduct in the whole gamut of our literature', the reader cannot help asking himself how far critical bravado can go.

Tillotson is much happier when he deals with the niceties of texture and diction than when he discusses the larger questions. 'The problem for the critic of Pope's poetry,' he frankly admits, 'is that of relating the mechanics of the verse to its quality for the emotions.' This problem does indeed hang like a cloud over Tillotson's book, as over so much other Pope criticism, and it is to Tillotson's credit that, unlike some others, he faces the problem and makes a determined effort to solve it. His best pages, however, are those in which he describes the origins of Augustan poetic diction and the influences which went to mould Pope's style. That this style could in any way be regarded as a distortion or a debasement of the English language never occurs to him because, like Pope, he seems insensitive to the qualities of any English poetry before Waller. He really enjoys Latinate diction and syntax, which he believes to be elegant and civilized, like Mozart, porcelain china, and landscape gardening. Here lies the danger to a critic of identifying himself too closely with his subject. Tillotson can appreciate Pope in a context which includes Keats and even Shakespeare, but he cannot stand back from him far enough to put him in perspective with the run of English poetry from Chaucer, through the Tudor poets, Jonson and the Meta-physicals to Blake and Coleridge.

Eloquent in the praise of Pope's technical ingenuity, Tillotson de-precates the practice of regarding Pope's genius as expressing itself fully 'in the supersensitive surface of his technique'.

> But the truth is that this triumph in technique is the counterpart, and no more than that, of a triumph of content . . . the same measure in the satires, burned out of its lacquered placidity and then frozen again into metal, is the medium for a vision of men and things which is as elaborate as intense. So malleable are its twenty syllables that the couplet never stereotypes the vision . . . One does not know where more praise is owing, for the vision or the verse.

This is impressive; but what does it mean? Wherein lies this 'triumph of content'? What is this 'vision of men and things'? We are not told.

Tillotson is, as has been said, most at his ease in discussing what he calls the 'mechanics' of Pope's verse: alliteration, onomatopoeia, syntax, literary echoes, variations in couplet structure. He gives us many fascinating pages in illustrating his pleasure in such things, and almost persuades us that the appreciation of poetry is an aesthetic game for the well-read. It is when he comes to deal with the larger significance of the mechanics that he is least convincing. Writing of *The Rape of the Lock* (though the application is general), he says:

> This presence of brain-work in such quantity and quality cannot be said to rob the poem of any of its emotional value even for a reader whose nineteenth-century sympathies incline him to think that poetry is a divine afflatus dependent upon the brain only so far as to divide it from madness. There are elements in Pope's poetry which adequately provide for this kind of reader. But for other readers all these accurate mechanics of the brain are themselves found to contribute to the emotional value of the poem.

It is not 'nineteenth-century sympathies' which cause a reader to de-mand evidences of divine possession in the greatest poetry. The same demand would occur to an enthusiast for Marlowe or Shakespeare. Nor do readers of Donne or Marvell need to be told that 'brainwork' is not incompatible with the best poetry. To imply, as Tillotson does, that reservations about the greatness of Pope are a nineteenth-century aberra-tion is simply to repeat the Victorian fallacy by which modern critics are obsessed. Where the modern reader, who doesn't object to the presence of brainwork in poetry, feels sceptical is in the claim that the brainwork contributes to the emotional value of the poem. There is, after all, a mass of brainwork in that favourite Victorian, Browning, and its presence did not inhibit the appreciation of his poetry in its time. For all his eloquence, Tillotson does not persuade. He nowhere tells us what the emotional value of Pope's poetry is, apart from its power to remind him of Virgil, Mozart, and Keats. It seems as if the real emotional value lies in the satisfaction afforded to the reader in working out the mechanics and analysing the brainwork, just as the pleasure of fox-hunting is said to derive from the chase, not the kill. Does not Tillotson admit as much?

> One's emotions rage like tigers round the intellectual circle and rage all the more powerfully for the complexity of Pope's methods.

There is not much evidence of tiger-like rage in Tillotson's pages of cool technical analysis, and one is left with the impression that he is trying to turn Pope into the poet he would like him to be. He concludes:

> Pope's verse is, of course, almost faultless. Its faultlessness indeed has sometimes been made a reproach . . . Perfection at the pitch attained by Pope is itself mysterious. The 'heights' were within Pope's reach and he reached them.

What 'heights' were reached by Pope's 'almost faultless' verse, his technical 'perfection', must be discussed more fully, but even if the claim were allowed, the only 'height' Pope is shown to have reached would be that of textural complexity; this, for Tillotson as for other critics, seems to be value enough. Pope's criticism of life was 'simply and solely, the heroic couplet'. Had not Lytton Strachey said it before?

8 The Twentieth Century III

The appearance in 1941 of *The Poetical Career of Alexander Pope* by the American scholar, Robert Kilburn Root is important for several reasons. It marks the decisive adoption of Pope by the American universities – the inauguration, one might almost say, of a major American academic industry in Pope criticism. Most of the important studies in the next quarter of a century were to be American. The Twickenham edition, proceeding at intervals during this period, is a joint Anglo-American undertaking. Root's book adopts the idea of 'poetical career' from Sherburn, the founding father, and is in its general lines typical of contemporary attitudes to Pope. These attitudes represent not so much something new as a new selection from among former attitudes. All the old contradictions and inconsistencies are to be found, as well as the old doubts and uncertainties about basic poetic principles. The preface contains a fair statement of what was at that time the generally accepted view :

> Of all our English poets none has suffered more in his reputation from shiftings of literary taste than has Alexander Pope. To his delighted contemporaries he was the 'Prince of English Poets', his throne on the topmost peak of the English Parnassus. In the nineteenth century critics could dispute as to whether he was really a poet at all. Since the beginning of the present century there have been many indications that the tide of taste has turned the other way. People are now disposed to like rather than to distrust the eighteenth century. Though no one, I imagine, would restore Pope to the supreme eminence which was his two hundred years ago, there are few lovers of our older literature who do not recognize him as a very considerable poet.

We have seen how nearly every statement in this calls for modification or reservation in the light of the facts of literary history. Not all Pope's contemporaries regarded him as a 'prince'; the dispute about his status was not a nineteenth-century one; people have always liked the eighteenth century, though not necessarily its poetry; the 'tide of taste' is observable less among general readers than in the universities. General readers in the Victorian age, as Stephen noted, could quote Pope with less frequency only than Shakespeare. My grandmother, an average reader educated in the third quarter of the nineteenth century, could remember long passages of the *Essay on Man* well into the present century. Outside academic circles it might be maintained that the tide of taste has, if anything, turned against Pope.

Root gives a good account of the special qualities of Augustan poetry. 'For Milton,' he writes, 'poetry is a sacramental mystery; for Pope it is an exacting social art.' The development of this art was based on the belief that pre-Restoration English poetry was uncouth, rustic, provincial, barbaric. 'Pope found an extravagance and turbulence of spirit' in Shakespeare and Milton. Poetry must be corrected in line with French models, according to principles laid down by the French critics, notably Boileau. Pope's aphorism about 'true wit' as the polished expression of 'what oft was thought' is a rewording of Boileau's 'Un bon mot n'est bon mot qu'en ce qu'il dit une chose que chacun pensoit, et qu'il la dit d'une manière, vive, fine, et nouvelle'. The ideal is politeness, smoothness, urbanity, as distinct from fire, imagination and inspired madness. Root is enthusiastic in his praise of *The Rape of the Lock* as a demonstration of these aims:

> Trifle though it is, the poem is constructed with the nice craftsmanship of a watchmaker. In the whole of its conduct, in its conception and in its expression it is the perfect illustration of that balance of wit and judgment which was the goal of neo-classic art . . . On any principle of criticism it is a great masterpiece of poetic art, one of the permanent achievements of English poetry.

Note the sleight of hand by which 'poetic art' is used interchangeably with 'poetry', as if there is a difference but we are not supposed to notice it.

The *Dunciad* is 'not only great satire, but *in its kind* great poetry'. The italics are mine. How can a work be 'in its kind great poetry', if that kind is different from other great poems? Root elaborates this:

> The *Dunciad* is great poetry not only in the music of its verse, but in its power to evoke images which carry immediate conviction, if not to the imagination in the higher meanings of that word, at least to the poetic fancy of the reader, images which with nicest accuracy embody the poet's thought . . . From the nature of its substance, it cannot often touch our sensibility or move our sympathy. It offers instead that keen joy of recognition which comes as we watch the flashing play of a disciplined mind, which is also indubitably the mind of a poet.

This is almost an echo of Tillotson. The *Dunciad*, Root seems to be saying, is not really a great poem in itself, but acts like one because it exhibits a poet's mind in action. It is difficult to deduce the nature of poetry as conceived by Root, but he seems to regard it as something *applied* to prose thought and content, rather than something co-extensive with the poem as a whole. In this he is very near Tillotson when he talks of a passage being 'given its poetry'. Root writes of the lines on the spider in the *Essay on Man* as being 'packed with poetry'. Uncertain as to whether his readers will accept Pope as a great poet, for he is not happy about their obstinately 'romantic' habit of mind, Root claims confidently that at least he was a great satirist; he admits that satire is not poetry of the highest order, but it has a place on Parnassus, even if only on the lower slopes. It is interesting to note how many critics, uncertain of the final implications of their analysis, resort to metaphor, especially high-sounding metaphor, to blur the edges of definition. Root believes that the motive of Pope's satire is a sincere concern for truth and virtue. He sees no reason to doubt the sincerity of Pope's frequent utterances to this effect. He is not concerned to define sincerity, nor does he see the need to postulate the Horatian *persona* of later criticism. For him it is enough to quote from the *Epilogue to the Satires, Dialogue II*:

> When Truth or Virtue an Affront endures,
> Th' Affront is mine, my friend, and should be yours.

Root does not find it necessary to test the sincerity of such an assertion by the known facts of Pope's life. He admits Pope's deviousness, but his personal character 'is, I believe, in spite of some obvious defects, both lovable and noble'. There is no reason to think this a mere echo of Edith Sitwell. It may be remarked that Pope's character seems to be even more a matter of disagreement than his poems. This is one reason why the debate about them is still open and may never be closed. After so recent an assertion by an American scholar it would be surprising, were the subject almost any other writer, to read the beginning of an anonymous and well-informed review in the *Times Literary Supplement* for 29 December, 1961:

> Alexander Pope is the most unlikeable of all the great English poets whose personalities can reasonably be considered an abiding interest in their work.

Not only does Root love Pope as a man; he reveres him as a poet, obstinately regarding him as 'great' and 'major', despite all the arguments he has adduced in the course of his book to limit these claims. Much that he says could be used directly to support the arguments of earlier critics that Pope was no more than an accomplished versifier and the high priest of an age of prose and reason. But if Byron may be said to have inaugurated a 'Pope can do no wrong' line of criticism, and Edith Sitwell to have strengthened it, though with reservations, R. K. Root must be admitted to be a loyal follower. After recording Pope's death he writes:

> He was cured at last of that 'long disease' his life; but English literature had lost one of its major poets. Between the death of Dryden in 1700 and the emergence of Wordsworth and Coleridge in 1798, he is the only English poet for whom we can confidently predict a continuing memory of poetic fame.

The meaning of the last six words is extremely obscure, perhaps deliberately so; but if it means that Pope will live when Swift, Gray, Collins, Smart, Cowper, Crabbe, and Blake (not to mention the Scotsmen Thomson and Burns) are forgotten, we can only marvel at the effects of enthusiasm on judgement.

To realize how far the 'rehabilitation' in academic quarters has proceeded, it is worth while to take an unchronological look at an American study of *The Major Satires of Alexander Pope* by Robert W. Rogers, which appeared in 1955. By this time it is possible to virtually ignore previous hostile criticism and assume Pope's greatness and even his goodness. In his preface Rogers, while admitting that Pope is 'one of the more controversial English poets', and that his premises may be challenged, confidently asserts his belief that 'Pope was a great poet and that satire can be a form of great poetry'. As for Pope the man:

> I have also assumed that Pope's moral character cannot be explained by easy generalizations and formulae. He had a large capacity for growth and development; and basically he was sincere and honest. He may occasionally have acted from mean motives, but personal animus alone will not do much to explain why he wrote as he did. He may sometimes have been guilty of distortion and misrepresentation, but he was not an inveterate liar. I have accepted throughout this book the hypothesis that his own remarks, treated with little more than ordinary caution and imagination, are the most reliable index to his aims and desires.

Few assert, or have asserted, that Pope's character can be explained by easy generalizations and formulae, nor has 'personal animus alone' ever been seriously adduced as the motive of Pope's writings. Leaving aside the Aunt Sally suggestions, however, and the question as to *which* of Pope's remarks are to be taken as an index to his aims and desires, it may be observed that it was scarcely possible before the post-war years to base a study of Pope on such assumptions. The grounds for making

them, in the case of Rogers, are not stated; they must be presumed to
be part of the general climate of Pope criticism in the universities. We
have seen how the climate has gradually changed, especially in America.
No doubt the influence of Sherburn and Root was considerable, and
Austin Warren's ambitious study of Augustan poetry, *Rage for Order*,
1948, played its part.

Warren's argument is very sophisticated, attempting as it does to
postulate a situation for poets after Milton in which the hitherto
accepted canons of poetry do not operate and special circumstances
give their work a new and different appeal.

> The idea of the Great Poem, of the Great Genius, of the (often corre-
> lated) Great Style intimated many Augustan poets, 'froze the genial
> current' of their souls. Only, it seems, if they could say to themselves,
> 'This is of course not poetry, or not *really great* poetry,' could they have
> a fair chance of writing it.

Warren goes on to speak of the difficulty of reconciling neo-classical
ideals with the idea of Great Poetry. One method is burlesque.

> The mock epic is not mockery of the epic but elegantly affectionate
> homage, offered by a writer who finds it irrelevant to his age. As its
> signal advantage, burlesque (with its allied forms, satire and irony)
> allows a self-conscious writer to attend to objects, causes, and persons
> in which he is deeply interested, yet of which, in part, or with some part
> of him, he disapproves.

The reader may feel that, with its capitalized or italicized pseudo-
quotations, the discussion of poetry has reached a new level of indirect-
ness. Is Warren suggesting that the Augustan age is one in which great
poetry cannot be written, or does he mean rather that 'great poetry' is
a relative term whose meaning can change with changing times? Why
is epic 'irrelevant' to the age of Anne, and is it the only form of great
poetry?

Warren goes on to instance a number of writings by Pope which are
in one way or another burlesque, imitation, pastiche. *Eloïsa to Abelard*
is at the same time an imitation of Ovid and a tragic soliloquy *à la*
Racine. The *Pastorals* are verbal music; Warren makes a comparison
between their composition and the writing of a string quartet. *The
Rape of the Lock* is praised for its zeugmas ('stain her honour or her
new brocade'), a form of pun which constitutes 'one of Pope's most
poetical resources'. It is not certain that Warren knows exactly what he
means by 'poetical', nor is it certain that Pope would have so regarded
the zeugma. That he regarded it as witty and effective is implied by his

repeated use of this device in *The Rape*. The poem is admired as a mock-epic which plays with the fires of sex and religion; it succeeded where other post-Miltonic epics failed, because it was written in an unheroic age. Pope's later mock-epic, the *Dunciad*, appeals to Warren as a statement of Pope's sense of the precariousness of civilized values; it transcends the personalities of its victims and is justified by its expression of the 'rage for order' as experienced by Pope. We shall hear more of this view of the *Dunciad*. The work of Warren is symptomatic of the concern shown by modern critics with the purpose and content of Augustan satire and of the difficulty they experience in accommodating it to any accepted general notions of the nature of poetry.

Warren's *Rage for Order* is part of the general reappraisal of eighteenth-century poetry by which Pope is, *a fortiori*, considerably upgraded in the poetical hierarchy. This reappraisal produced an excellent *Preface to Eighteenth Century Poetry*, 1948, by James R. Sutherland, a British professor, whose Twickenham edition of the *Dunciad* had first appeared in 1943. Sutherland begins by detailing the course of what I would call the counter-revolution in poetry inaugurated by Dryden and consolidated by Pope. It was a revolution against extravagance, enthusiasm, imagination. It reflected the ideas of Shaftesbury, Locke, and especially Hobbes, who did more than any other to establish the ascendancy of reason; he was inclined to equate imagination with madness and condemn it as childish. Children, it will be recalled, were not respected for themselves at this time. Dryden himself was opposed to anything irrational, anything that savoured of enthusiasm in religion or anything else; hence he sneered at inspiration in poetry. One of his gibes at the unfortunate Elkanah Settle was that he believed he 'has a light within him, and writes by inspiration'. Almost a century later, it will be remembered, Johnson, who should by that time have known better, was sneering at Gray for a similar 'fantastic foppery'. The poet wrote not by supernatural inspiration nor by the light within himself; he wrote by the light of public favour and at the dictates of the *beau monde*. Sutherland points out that the public for poetry was limited to the professional classes and their social superiors; it was an expensive luxury. The poetry-reading classes, who got their standards from the rationalist philosophers filtered through the pages of periodicals such as *The Spectator*, mistrusted the expression of personal feeling and demanded stereotyped ideas in recognizable poetic forms.

> The eighteenth-century poet's consciousness of this public inhibited the expression of emotion, unless it was of a recognized and acceptable kind.

Poetry, in short, was a social art bound by rules and conventions. That it could be anything else was scarcely conceivable. Sutherland aptly quotes Pope's enemy Dennis: 'In short, poetry is either an art, or whimsy and fanaticism. If it is an art, it follows that it must propose an end to itself, and afterwards lay down . . . rules.' There is of course the 'Persian fable' which Pope told Spence and Judith Cowper he had considered writing, 'in which I should have given a full loose to description and imagination. It would have been a very wild thing, if I had executed it.' To Tillotson this indicates the suppressed romantic in Pope; but the significant thing about Pope's Persian fable is that it was never executed.

'Either an art, or whimsy and fanaticism' – this was the crux of the matter and it is still at the centre of the Pope controversy. Pope would certainly have agreed with Dennis, whose critical standards were more or less indistinguishable from his own. It may be mentioned in passing that when Sutherland, like others, praises the *Dunciad* for its genuine concern 'to maintain the threatened standards of polite literature', he seems to forget that many of Pope's victims were animated by exactly the same concern. In attacking Dennis he pilloried an ally.

Sutherland has some illuminating pages on the nature of eighteenth-century poetic diction as the means by which a poet 'clothed' his thoughts and distanced them from the meanness and vulgarity associated with plain prose. Readers who are inclined to think that the eighteenth century got its prose values right and its poetic values wrong will find support here; they may also wonder whether we have, in Leavis's phrase, 'entirely disposed of Matthew Arnold'. Sutherland quotes a revealing remark by Saint-Evremond, which appeared in an English translation of 1728, the year of the *Dunciad*: 'Poetry requires a peculiar genius, that agrees not overmuch with good sense. It is sometimes the language of gods, sometimes of buffoons; rarely that of a gentleman.' Perhaps the Frenchman was more logical and more realistic than English writers in recognizing that the neo-classical counter-revolution had debased poetic values. Sutherland is aware of this. He is less happy about the merits of mock-heroic than is Warren :

> In some ways the reputation of this genre is a disquieting sign; it seems to point to a public which can respond contentedly to what has the sound of poetry without the substance, a public that likes to have its knowledge flattered by being invited to recall what (of Homer, Virgil, Milton) it already knows.

Sutherland writes eloquently of Wordsworth and of the differences between Romantic and neo-classical poetry. 'All through the eighteenth century,' he insists, 'poetry was regarded as an art: the art of making poems. Coleridge and Shelley, you might almost say, wrote poetry: Dryden and Pope wrote poems.' This is a revealing distinction. And what kind of an art, what kind of poems were they? Like Tillotson, Sutherland sees the representative eighteenth-century poem as an artefact.

> Why so many people come with an open and receptive mind to eight-teenth-century furniture, architecture, or music, and yet approach the poetry of that period with a closed and even hostile mind is something of a mystery. A Chippendale chair is a period piece and is willingly accepted as such; but when the reader of poetry comes upon some equally perfect period piece in the work of John Gay he is, as often as not, far less ready to respond to the fashion of an earlier age. The average reader of poetry, it may be, is not content with a purely aesthe-tic pleasure; he looks for some reflection, or at least adumbration, of his own habitual thoughts and feelings in the poem he happens to be reading . . . much of it [eighteenth-century poetry] – at its most remote, and even because of that remoteness – is capable of yielding a genuine aesthetic pleasure, the sort of pleasure that he may be accustomed to receiving from a Chelsea shepherdess or a conversation-piece by Zoffany.

Gay, not Pope, is the occasion of these remarks, but the application is general. The reader is being asked to approve of poems as if they were elegant furnishing pieces. There is of course no quarrel with a critic who values *vers de société* for what it is, but higher claims than this are made for Pope. Perhaps, too, higher expectations are aroused in the mind of the average reader when he opens a book of poems than when he inspects a Chippendale chair; after all, you cannot sit on a poem, so you expect it to offer different satisfactions from even the most elegant and craftsmanlike chair. The reader may demand more of a poem than that it should be a 'period piece'. Besides, it is possible that a period which is good for the domestic arts may be bad for poetry. At all events, neo-classical poetry is the only English poetry which the reader is seriously invited to admire because it has the same virtues as *objets d'art*. No critic asks us to like or dislike Victorian verse because it re-minds him of pot-plants and bamboo furniture. Can it be that the average reader, as distinct from the don, looks to poetry for something other than 'aesthetic pleasure'?

Indeed, it is difficult to escape the impression that Sutherland himself prefers post-eighteenth-century poetry as yielding him higher satisfactions, but that he is prepared to fall over backwards to avoid judging the eighteenth century by Romantic criteria. For all his wide reading, his sympathetic tolerance and the eloquence with which he invests his special pleading, he betrays, by his critical honesty, something like a fundamental lack of enthusiasm for eighteenth-century ideals in poetry. It is significant that he excludes Swift from his account. His book, it seems to me, offers the most effective support given in the present century for Arnold's view of the age of Dryden and Pope. This support is all the more effective for not being intended.

9 The Twentieth Century IV

One aspect of the Pope debate that has always been implicitly present begins to come into sharper focus with the post-war years. This is what I have called the bio-critical approach. The opponents of this approach take up the simple standpoint that it is the poems that matter; the historical man is irrelevant. Supporters of bio-criticism believe that the historical Pope is important; they are not altogether happy about his character, but they believe his defects have been exaggerated or that they are counterbalanced by other factors. Despite the valuable biographical work done in America, the recent tendency of the most advanced and sophisticated American criticism is away from biography and towards concentration on the text and nothing but the text, or the text and its context in literary, as distinct from personal history. Another tendency of modern American criticism is towards finding in Pope a necessary influence on twentieth-century literature. Both of these tendencies are illustrated in an Anglo-American collection of essays presented to George Sherburn under the title, *Pope and his Contemporaries*, 1949. In an interesting article on Pope's imagery Maynard Mack says: '. . . Pope writes a poetry with striking prose affinities.' He seems to be claiming for Pope the mastery of a kind of poetry much nearer to prose than was either that of the Romantics or the Metaphysicals. There is nothing particularly new in this: Arnold had, after all, noticed something of the kind. Mack's analysis, however, has further implications. He concludes:

> But the task of criticism for the future, when we are likely to be paying more and more attention to Pope as our own poetry moves in the direction suggested by Mr Auden and Mr. Eliot in his *Quartets*, is not with Pope as a pre-Romantic or a post-Metaphysical, but as an Augustan poet whose peculiar accomplishment, however we may choose to rate it on the ultimate scale of values, was the successful fusion of some of the most antithetical features of verse and prose.

This is a modest enough claim, suggesting as it does that we are (or were in 1949) on the edge of a new Augustan age. Whether or not this is an exciting prospect, Mack is too discreet to say. It would depend on how far the work of Eliot and Auden was regarded as a reliable guide to the future, and on how important are other manifestations of contemporary poetry than those which may be called neo-Augustan. A rather more disturbing implication, faint though it is, is that poetry is to some extent a by-product of critical theory. It should be noted, too, that academic criticism seems willing to isolate and analyse in even greater detail yet another poetic category – 'Augustan' – to be placed side by side with the others. Criticism, we can't help feeling, is piling up for itself a big task of deciding between its various categories 'on the ultimate scale of values'. Or will another Pope arise to say of literary criticism, as was said of philosophy in the famous conclusion to the *Dunciad*, IV, that it:

> Shrinks to her second cause, and is no more.

For all the 'mountains of casuistry' that are likely to be manfactured before the debate is concluded, it will be difficult to sustain the idea that it is a peculiarity of 'Augustan' poetry to achieve 'the successful fusion of some of the most antithetical features of verse and prose'. It is the greatness of English poetry in many periods to have done this.

An even more extreme statement of the alleged relevance of Augustan poetry to our own age is made in another essay in the same volume – *Pope and Our Contemporaries*, by Joseph Wood Krutch. His conclusion is so persuasively phrased and so resonant with overtones that it must be given in full, to avoid misrepresentation.

> To the charge that Pope is deficient in 'sensibility' and that he sticks too closely to the normal, waking, daylight world to appeal very strongly to a generation proudly neurotic, dissociated and doubtful, I should be inclined to reply neither with denial nor with apology, but with the forthright assertion that we need, at this moment at least, his qualities rather more than a turning of the face against them. Even sensibility, however good it may be, is good only in so far as it can be disciplined and used, and it seems obvious enough that modern literature has culti-vated it to a point where it now has more sensibility than it knows what to do with. No doubt Augustan poetry finally died because it lacked fresh feelings and fresh thoughts. Perhaps romanticism revives poetry by supplying both. But to call now for still more of mere naked sensibility is to put oneself in the position of the enthusiast – described by the elder Samuel Butler and recalled by Samuel Johnson – who would go crying 'Fire! Fire!' in Noah's flood. It is generally agreed that the ideal of the eighteenth century was best summed up in 'Let us cultivate our garden'. One might, I suppose, say that the ideal of romanticism (and I mean in science as well as in art) could be summed up in some such exhortation as 'Let us explore our wilderness'. More than a century has been devoted to the attempt to do just that. Could a redeemable section of the long-neglected garden be found again?

It is by no means certain that the metaphor of the contrasted garden and wildnerness is a helpful description of modern literary tendencies, nor does Krutch tell us who is now supposed to be calling for 'still more of mere naked sensibility'. What is more probable, however, is that it is the poets, not the critics, who will decide whether the direction (if there is to be a direction) for poetry will be towards anti-Romanticism. There is, perhaps, some substance in Saul Bellow's complaint at the 1966 P.E.N. Congress in New York that the professors had appointed themselves directors of contemporary literature. Professor Bellow has allowed me to quote from an article as yet unpublished as follows : 'The universities have done great damage to poetry and fiction. Professors of literature, members of the academic intelligentsia, are not interested in poetry but only in what can be said about it. The classics are their raw materials. From these they make discourse. Discourse is valuable. How many accounts of *Moby Dick* have I not read which do the novel *right* – translating it into theology, philosophy, social history and other intellectual staples. For the professors are, of course, intellectuals and wish only to be intellectuals. In their intellectual role they are far too greatly excited and agitated to submit to the enchantments of art. In his last book of essays, for instance, Professor Trilling goes so far as to say that the modern Authentic Individual cannot be held spellbound by a story. Not even Homer, I suppose, could hold him, or *Crime and Punishment*. Our case is such that even these are no longer interesting. What, then, *is* interesting? Why the life of an Authentic Individual – i.e. an intellectual.' So far as America is concerned, we are likely to hear more of this kind of criticism from creative writers.[1]

Returning to the subject of the bio-critical approach, we find support for it, somewhat surprisingly, in an essay in the same collection from

---

[1] In this context it is worth recalling a passage from the poet Randall Jarrell's essay, *The Age of Criticism*, from his book, *Poetry and the Age*, 1955: 'A novelist, a friend of mine, one year went to a Writers' Conference; all the other teachers were critics, and each teacher had to give a formal public lecture. My friend went to the critics' lectures, but the critics didn't go to his; he wasn't surprised; as he said, "You could tell they knew I wasn't really literary like them." Recently I went to a meeting at which a number of critics discussed what Wordsworth had said about writing poetry. It was interesting to me to see how consciously or unconsciously patronizing they were to – poor Wordsworth, I almost wrote. They could see what he had meant, confused as he was, layman that he was; and because he had been, they supposed they must admit, a great poet, it did give what he had to say a wonderful documentary interest, like Nelson's remarks at Trafalgar. But the critics could not help being conscious of the difference between themselves and Wordsworth and my friend: *they* knew how poems and novels are put together, and Wordsworth and my friend didn't, but had just put them together.'

Geoffrey Tillotson on Pope's *Epistle to Harley*. 'When a poem is declared to be occasional,' he roundly asserts, 'we can only call ourselves readers of it if we recover as much of its occasion as we can.' For all its caution this is in some respects an incautious assertion. Tillotson is in fact referring specifically to Keats's sonnet *On first looking into Chapman's Homer*, whose title certainly 'declares' the poem to be occasional. But it would be a bold critic who would attempt to divide poems into the occasional and the non-occasional simply on the ground of such a declaration. Personally I would prefer to defend the assertion that all true poems are occasional.

Tillotson begins his essay:

> To be a poet is, to begin with, a matter of being; from time to time being becomes doing, and the poet writes down a poem.

This is well said, as far as it goes. He develops this into a limited commitment in favour of a bio-critical approach to the poetry of several poets, especially Keats:

> . . . ultimately we cannot divide the man either from his poems or from his career. Some part of our minds is aware of Keats the man even when we are reading the 'Ode to Melancholy'.

'We cannot divide the man either from his poems or from his career.' This is exactly what some modern writers on Pope would like to do, and it is the crux of the matter. In an interesting and highly sophisticated essay on *The Muse of Satire*, published in *The Yale Review*, Vol. XLI, 1951, Maynard Mack attempts to remove Pope's work from the familiar context of its author's actual character and career, and transplant it to a dual environment consisting on the one hand of satire as a literary *genre* with a long pedigree and on the other the satirist's *persona*. Biographical and even aesthetic considerations must be supplemented by the analysis of a poem in terms of 'rhetoric', the medieval program for a work of literature as an artefact.

> Inquiries into biographical and historical origins, or into effects on audiences and readers, can and should be supplemented, we are beginning to insist, by a third kind of inquiry treating the work with some strictness as a rhetorical construction: as a 'thing made', which, though it reaches backward to an author and forward to an audience, has its artistic identity in between – in the realm of artifice and artefact.

True, Mack says 'supplemented', not 'supplanted'. But new doctrines, introduced with becoming decorum, are apt to get out of hand; everyone knows the import of remarks such as 'we are beginning to insist'.

Even in this single essay we can see how far such 'insistence' can go. In deprecating bio-critical attacks on Pope's satires Mack says that:

> we overlook what is most essential if we overlook the distinction between the historical Alexander Pope and the dramatic Alexander Pope who speaks them.

Even in Pope's most personal satires Mack insists on the distinction between man and satirist. The 'Muse of Satire', whom Pope continually invokes, gives him, in Mack's view, a perpetual alibi under cover of which he can disclaim responsibility for his utterances. Mack elaborates this special pleading by suggesting that behind any good satire is a 'fiction' – which seems to mean that a satire must not be taken at its face value but as fulfilling conditions laid down by the nature of the genre. This would have been a cheering thought to Lord Hervey, Lady Mary Wortley Montagu, Theobald, Curll, and Concanen.

Not only has satire its 'fiction', it must have its 'ethos'.

> For the satirist especially the establishment of an authoritative *ethos* is imperative. If he is to be effective in 'that delightful teaching', he must be accepted by his audience as a fundamentally virtuous and tolerant man, who challenges the doings of other men not whenever he happens to feel vindictive, but whenever they deserve it. On this account, the satirist's *apologia* for his satire is one of the stock subjects of both the classical writers and Pope : the audience must be assured that its censor is a man of good will, who has been, as it were, *forced* into action.

Mack then analyses the *Epistle to Arbuthnot* in terms of the commonplaces of classical satire and its 'ethos'. Mack here seems, to the average reader, to be documenting most effectively Pope's built-in insincerity. If the satirist's friends 'happen to be out of power, or drawn in part from a vanished Golden Age, so much the better for *ethos*: our satirist is guaranteed to be no time-server.' One cannot help wondering how Pope would have developed as a satirist if Swift and Bolingbroke had 'happened to be' in power. Mack attacks those who find Pope insincere or vain, on the ground that the *Arbuthnot* is a piece of self-portrayal in the image of the classical satirist and his necessary 'ethos'. He points out that the publication of Pope's letters, as well as the notes to the *Dunciad*, 'significantly accompanied his turning satirist. Pope felt the necessity of supporting the *ethos* a satirical poet must have'. In other words, all the fuss made in the nineteenth century about Pope's faking of his letters was beside the point: Pope was simply creating for himself a dramatic *persona*, so that the world might accept him as a neo-classical satirist. A satirist is obliged to be a hypocrite. Is that what Mack means? If so, what is to be made of the verse-satirist, Swift, whose real effectiveness as a scourge of Anglo-Irish political jobbery and self-interest is enhanced by the personal integrity which glows in every line? Why didn't Swift feel the necessity to deal in 'fictions', to fabricate an 'ethos', to assume a 'dramatic' self? I am tempted to say that, on Mack's showing, with Swift satire was life, as with Keats poetry was life, and that with Pope both were a neo-classical game – an 'artifice', to use the current word. Again, on Mack's theory what are we to make of Defoe's brilliant and effective satires, *The True-born Englishman* and *Hymn to the Pillory*? Defoe felt no need for a *persona*, for 'fictions' and a fabricated 'ethos'. He merely spoke from his own mind, heart, experience. If this disqualifies him from the ranks of neo-classic satirists following the rules of the *genre*, does it diminish his stature as a writer of English satire?

It is doubtful if Pope would have recognized himself in Mack's description. Mack distinguishes three elements in the dramatic *persona* of the satirist: the plain-living, high-thinking man of friendships; the naïve, simple man unable to comprehend the wickedness of the world; the public defender, a hero who puts himself on a pedestal of righteous indignation. The three voices may be summed up as those of the *vir bonus*, the naïf, and the hero. The hero speaks, for instance, in the denunciation of Sporus, the enemy of mankind, Satan himself whispering into the ear of Eve. Mack admits that here Pope speaks from personal animus. It is impossible to avoid the inference that Pope the man occasionally breaks through the mask of public defender. It is as if the voice of the heroic *persona* is momentarily adulterated by a tone of sincere hatred. As for the voice of the naïf, that is heard in the 'I lisped in numbers' passage, which is based on Ovid and Boileau. It is not so much that Pope invents a *persona* for him; he synthesizes one from the texts of foreign satirists. Perhaps Mack's elaborate special pleading in favour of the satirist as hypocrite is attractive because of the fundamental modesty of the claims made for Pope. Clearly Mack believes that satire is different from poetry, and that the 'Muse' of satire makes very limited personal demands on her devotees.

The most questionable assertion in Mack's thesis is that 'the establishment of an authoritative *ethos* is imperative' for the satirist. I do not know enough about the private lives of Horace and Juvenal, nor the conventions of Latin satire to know whether an authoritative *ethos* was considered imperative in Rome; to regard it as imperative for an English satirist is clearly wrong, and any English writer who composes

satires according to classical conventions invites the charge that he is
content to offer mere pastiche. That any convention of Latin poetry
should be regarded as having authority in English poetry is a suggestion
which critics ought to resist.

A useful summary of the general critical situation in the post-war
period, so far as Britain is concerned, is offered by Bonamy Dobrée in
Volume VII of the *Oxford History of English Literature,* 1959. Dobrée
is an enthusiast for Pope; already in 1951 he had published a small
monograph, *Alexander Pope.* Unlike the Americans, Dobrée carries
his enthusiasm almost to the point of naïveté. Admittedly he is writing
for the general reader as distinct from the specialist. Even so, there is a
note of almost blind admiration which has been rare since the appearance of Edith Sitwell's book.

> He exists, he is a quality; he continually gives us an addition to life, a
> delight which releases in us springs of understanding.

This is the voice of spontaneous personal enthusiasm not so often heard
in academic criticism. That Dobrée should reveal in detail the sources
of this delight and understanding to every reader is hardly to be expected; but at least he convinces us that he really enjoys Pope for his
own sake, not because he reminds him of music and old china. He gives
us a hint of what he admires in Pope – and it has been admired before
by critics from Walsh onwards – when he speaks of the 'superb mellifluous poetry', which 'gave a sheen and a dazzle to the utmost sordor,
making even the *cloaca* honorable and vituperation lovely'. 'Superb
mellifluous poetry' – one begins to guess that for Dobrée the poetic *is*
the mellifluous.

But love is blind, and Dobrée is almost rapturously blind both to
some of the facts of the situation and to some of the faults of his hero.
His passionate advocacy puts him on the defensive, and it is a curious
fact that nearly all favourable Pope criticism since the days of Bowles
and Byron has had and still has a defensive note. It is curious also that
so much defensive propaganda and critical rhapsody should appear in
what is called a 'History' of literature. To Dobrée Pope can scarcely do
wrong. He quotes Byron in agreement : 'It is Pope's misfortune that
quotations from his work have become commonplaces.' This is naïve.
They were always commonplaces and they were meant to be quoted.
Dobreé believes that 'the ceaseless flow of vituperation to which he was
subject' was 'nearly all unjustified'. It was Pope himself who, as a young
man, wrote that 'the life of a wit is a warfare upon earth'. Pope encouraged many of the attacks; he relished, if he did not always enjoy them;

they were fuel for his satiric purpose. Pope knew very well the publicity value of constant vituperation and the sympathetic attention it evokes; he knew that the only real disqualification for success in the life of a wit is to be ignored. The picture of an innocent lover of peace and retirement stung to frenzy and desperation by the unmotivated attacks of mere malice and ignorance is as false as it is sentimental. The 'unjustified' attacks are listed by Dobrée as being on 'his character, his honesty, his ingratitude, his greed, his physique, and his capacity to translate Homer'. Leaving aside his physique, which aroused sympathy as well as derision, there were certainly grounds for attacking Pope on each of these scores, and in the 'warfare upon earth' Pope gave as much as he got, and better. His wit at its best was a rapier; that of his enemies often a broadsword or a cudgel. What the sentimental admirers of Pope do not see is that one who claims for himself a high moral character is expected to rise above the sordid quarrels of his time. We are constantly told that Pope transcended his age. In some respects he did not. He played the Grub Street game and played it with greater skill than his opponents. It brought him fame and profit. No one who has read the notes to the *Dunciad* or the *Dunciad* itself can doubt this. It is one thing for a bluestocking or a don in the twentieth century to savour the mellifluous dazzle of the honourable *cloaca* in the *Dunciad* II; it was quite another thing for Pope's living contemporaries who were immersed in the filth. Not all Pope's attacks, however, were with the rapier; some were as crude as those to which he was subjected. Even here, in Dobrée's eyes however, Pope can do no wrong. Writing of the attack on Dennis in the *Essay on Criticism*, he says that Dennis's anger was excusable, his revenge inexcusable. Certainly Dennis's pamplet against Pope, written with the rage of a humourless, irascible and not very successful author more than twice Pope's age, contained cruel and unpardonable passages. But in his attack on Dennis in *The Narrative of Dr. Robert Norris* Pope was equally cruel, as well as coarse. The sensitive young man was enjoying his 'warfare upon earth'. Dobrée calls this 'inspired buffoonery' and 'glorious high spirits'. Dobrée is not wholly consistent in his views on Pope's attitude to his enemies. In his earlier monograph the picture of Pope as a spider does not quite suggest the innocent victim of unjustified onslaughts.

> In one of his early squibs, *The Club of Little Men*, when making brave fun of his littleness, he describes himself as 'a lively little Creature, with long Arms and Legs: A Spider is no ill Emblem of him': from this centre he could feel everything that was going on either at great country houses or in Grub-Street, sensitive to it all:

> The Spider's touch, how exquisitely fine;
> Feels at each thread, and lives along the line.

But also the creature dashes out to get its nutriment, or its prey. And Pope, of course, was always busily harvesting material for his poetry, or brooding over the ills done him and his art, making the ills themselves matter for his poetry.

Indeed, it is possible that Dobrée became even more enthusiastic about Pope between the appearance of the monograph in 1951 and writing the section on Pope in the *Oxford History of English Literature,* Volume VII, 1959. For in the monograph he admits – cheerfully enough, it is true – some of Pope's failings : lying, sycophancy, avarice, and vanity.

Dobrée calls the opening to the *Essay on Man,* Epistle II ('Know then thyself . . .') 'as glorious a piece of "philosophic" poetry as ever was penned'. Such a judgement raises so many issues that no brief comment is appropriate. All that can be said here is that if glorious philosophical poetry is written by amalgamating into nine couplets ideas and phraseology derived from Pascal, St. Paul, Charron, Cowley, Addison, Bezaleel Morrice and others, Dobrée's rapture can easily be understood. Even as an editor of Shakespeare Pope is praised. 'His preface is impeccable,' Dobrée's readers are told. Turning to Pope's preface to his edition of Shakespeare, what do we find? After some enthusiastic general comments based on Dryden, Pope tells us that with Shakespeare's excellences, he has 'almost as great defects'. These defects, Pope says, were due to his having had to appeal to 'the meaner sort of people'; to his having no knowledge of Aristotle's rules; to his having been an actor, mixing with actors, 'the worst of company'. Impeccability, that's what I say.

When he gets closer to the text of Pope's poems, Dobrée discovers two Popes – the textural perfectionist and the satiric moralist. He is stronger in his advocacy of the former. General epithets of approval in which his pages abound are : 'magnificent', 'splendid', 'brilliant', 'triumphant', 'glorious'. In his estimation the laurels are pretty evenly divided between the *Epistle to Arbuthnot* and the *Dunciad, IV.* The former is 'more than any other single piece, the poem which established Pope as having added something essential, something rarely individual, to the canon of English poetry'; the latter is 'the most weightily serious, the most genuinely and deeply felt of all the poems of his maturity'; Dobrée accepts the generally received belief that in the final lines Pope expressed a profound emotional concern for what he took to be the imminent collapse of European civilization. These judgments are widely accepted in current Pope criticism.

As a scholar Dobrée is well aware of Pope's borrowings. Discussing the *Elegy to the Memory of an Unfortunate Lady*, he notes the echo from Jonson in the opening line (which not everyone has noticed), and then quotes the passage beginning

> Most souls, 'tis true, but peep out once an age,
> Dull sullen pris'ners in the body's cage;

and calls it 'a passage which might have come from a later Metaphysical'. It comes, in fact, from Dryden, with perhaps some help from Waller and others. But it scarcely matters where it comes from, since to Dobrée, as to a growing number of contemporary critics, all borrowing is good. Borrowing and imitation are described by Dobrée as Pope's 'dedicated task of integrating English poetry into one splendid whole'. As to why anybody should want to do anything so grotesque, Dobrée, alas, is silent. But perhaps he means simply that Pope was doing it for fun. The *Dunciad*, he tells us, gives us 'delight':

> It is not a poetic delight in the full sense of the term, but it is an aesthetic delight in the sense that any game beautifully played conveys that quality.

If only Dobrée had developed this distinction between poetic and aesthetic pleasure. It must be admitted that the term 'aesthetic' comes in handy when you are trying to convey the idea that something is slightly different from what it is generally supposed to be, but not necessarily worse. We learn of Pope as the exponent of an 'aesthetic morality'.

> For all his inconsistencies there is a guiding integrity in Pope, the integrity of the artist given to something bigger than himself, a fine aesthetic morality establishing a standard from which he never swerved.

If we could be convinced that this really means anything precise, it would indeed afford a resolution of the art *versus* morals controversy which has troubled the critical waters ever since the time of Bowles and Byron. But Dobrée seems to have hit on the phrase 'a fine aesthetic morality' more by a happy chance than as the result of a process of reasoning. Is not his conclusion, after all, a variation on the old 'art for art's sake' doctrine and its corollary that art is above morality? For the most part Dobrée does not offer anything new, but sums up twentieth-century attitudes to Pope as represented in the writing of Edith Sitwell and Tillotson. To these he adds a reference to the idea of the satiric *persona*. 'And after all, it was part of the "rhetoric" of satire for the author to make himself out to be the Stoical *vir bonus* : Pope could assume a *persona* when he wished.' Dobrée has evidently read Mack and realized what a useful escape the notion of 'the rhetoric of satire' offers when awkward questions are raised about Pope's sincerity. The question of whether this makes Pope a rhetorician more than a poet does not occur to Dobrée. Nevertheless, he is an eloquent propagandist for Pope, and the confusions into which his advocacy leads him are not of his making. They are inherent in the two hundred and fifty years old controversy.

10 The Twentieth Century V

I described Edith Sitwell's *Alexander Pope* as almost the last critical study by an amateur. If I call G. Wilson Knight's book, *Laureate of Peace*, 1954, the last, it is not through ignorance of his professional standing; it is because, for all practical purposes, he temporarily vacates his chair, throwing scholarly caution to the winds. His book is, I believe, not widely admired by academics, who perhaps feel that his rhapsodic, almost frenzied transports of admiration do the cause of Pope little good. But there is something for which they might be grateful. Wilson Knight shows no concern whatever with the biographical side of the Pope debate, almost as if the mere facts of Pope's mundane existence were beneath consideration when poetry of such sublimity is under discussion. Indeed, it is one of the attractions of *Laureate of Peace* that its author seems scarcely to be aware that anyone has ever doubted Pope's greatness. The only doubt is as to whether he has been thought great enough. Then again, the book has a certain irresistible energy in its determination to seat Pope finally and immovably among the very highest peaks of Parnassus. Such overwhelming assurance must be the secret envy of more timid critics who perhaps think what he thinks but dare not say it.

> Pope's work, though profiting by the general tidying up that stands so firmly to Dryden's credit, has that pulsing heart for lack of which Dryden's remains a little cold; it is a single, organic, whole, as surely as Dante's or Shakespeare's; and it shows a wondrous harmony.

It is evident that Wilson Knight is ready to pull out all the stops in his jubilant acclaim of one whom he regards as embodying the prophetic voice of Augustan London speaking to England and the world. He writes of 'the whole rich, pulsing, solid achievement in all its human wisdom and excelling power of Pope's created world'.

It is when he comes to scale down this Metro-Goldwyn view of Pope to take account of the actual poems that he is less impressive. Of *Eloïsa to Abelard* he says: 'This is certainly Pope's greatest human poem, and probably the greatest short love poem in our language.' The 'greatness' of the poem seems to lie in the now almost too familiar quality of 'texture'. 'Watch now,' he says of a descriptive passage, 'the darkly rich vowel-colourings.' We are also invited to admire the opening three lines:

> In these deep solitudes and awful cells,
> Where heav'nly-pensive contemplation dwells,
> And ever-musing melancholy reigns;

in which Wilson Knight is not at all troubled by the obvious blemish of the false distinction between 'dwells' and 'reigns'. He persists in calling the poem 'Websterian': it is a favourite critical, or pseudo-critical, device of his to secure overtones of admiration by introducing the names of other widely esteemed writers, whether appropriate or not. *Windsor Forest,* for instance, reminds him of Shakespeare. Of *The Rape of the Lock* we are told: 'Shakespeare gives us drama and Milton epic, and Pope builds from both in *The Rape of the Lock.*' Referring to a passage in Canto V of this poem, Wilson Knight says that it is 'done with a glorious sense of the trivial sublimated to heroic stature'. Is this the language of the critic or of the advertising copy-writer?

With critical intrepidity Wilson Knight discusses at length *The Temple of Fame,* an early Chaucerian imitation which most readers have found too stiff, artificial, and contrived to give much pleasure. He notes, as any reader must, the comparison between the description of the building of the Temple and that of Pandemonium in *Paradise Lost*; Pandemonium is of course a council chamber for fallen angels, and its inappropriateness as a model for the Temple of Fame does not worry Wilson Knight. The poem reminds him of *Kubla Khan,* one of the masterpieces of Romantic poetry at its most imaginative. But the comparison is in favour of *The Temple of Fame,* even with one of Keats's finest poems thrown into the opposite scale for good measure.

> Eternal insight is not enough. *Kubla Khan* had that, and so has Keats' *Grecian Urn,* but do either make any contact with morality?

This is not quite so bizarre as it sounds; but we shall return to the question of morality. For the moment it should be noted that Wilson Knight is interested in the poem chiefly for its thoughts and sentiments that is to say, as versified prose. The same applies to his comments on the *Essay on Criticism,* of which he gives an admirable prose summary, a summary so good and so detailed as to make it unnecessary for anyone to read the poem unless he enjoys literary criticism in heroic couplets. When he comes to the *Essay on Man,* Wilson Knight's judgement is almost paralysed by the effort to express his admiration. After invoking the names of Goethe, Blake, and Nietzsche, he goes on:

We are watching something very rare: a poetic genius of the first order deliberately setting himself in maturity to create a compact and coherent system from his own creative centre.

'A poetic genius of the first order' – this is almost as far as anyone has ever gone: Wilson Knight's is a respected name, and this is the kind of phrase that is remembered. What is the quality of the genius evinced in the *Essay on Man*? Wilson Knight is in no doubt.

With what imperturbable and untroubled ease, comparable to that of Shakespeare's 'cloud-capp'd towers', the couplets roll out their mighty images.

One of several couplets selected for commendation is

> ... Heav'n;
> Who sees with equal eye, as God of all,
> A hero perish, or a sparrow fall.

Even if, in this synthesis of echoes from Spenser, St Matthew's Gospel, and Shakespeare there is no objection to the false antithesis in the last line (why not 'A sparrow perish, or a hero fall'?), that anyone can compare this to one of the finest passages in *The Tempest* suggests a total atrophy of critical discrimination. *The Dunciad* also is extravagantly praised because it is 'Dantesque'. Its coprophily is admitted and defended, as are Pope's sneers at his victims' poverty. Wilson Knight commends the couplet on the bookseller Lintot –

> As when a dab-chick waddles thro' the copse,
> On feet and wings, and flies, and wades, and hops;

– without apparently noticing that it is a deliberate parody of Milton, to whom, therefore, and not to Pope the credit for its graphic realism should go.

We begin to realize the motives for this unique critical extravaganza when we recall that Byron is one of Wilson Knight's heroes, and that Byron also revered Pope. Most even of Pope's most fervent advocates consider that Byron went too far. Not so Wilson Knight, to whom half-measures are unknown. Byron praised Pope above all for the 'morality' of his writings – not the equivocal 'aesthetic morality' of recent criticism, but whole-hearted, honest to God ethical morality. Commenting on the alleged failure of *Kubla Khan* and the *Grecian Urn* to 'make any contact with morality'. Wilson Knight goes on:

Life to Pope, as to Byron, takes precedence over art, even though that very procedure becomes again art's subject.

(The picture of Coleridge and Keats, of all men, as anaemic aesthetes preferring art to life is a poignant one, but let it pass.) Wilson Knight elaborates:

> His [Pope's] final purpose is to set 'the Passions on the side of Truth'; to deliver morality from her 'false guardians'; to establish, as Byron saw, a virtue which is not cant; and to charge with a newly enlightened significance the traditional values of patriotism and fame.

Wilson Knight is not one of those who feel the need to postulate a dramatic *persona* and a satiric *ethos* in order to escape the dilemma produced by the contradiction between Pope's character and his professions. Pope can do no wrong. No breath of adverse criticism is allowed to cloud the roseate window through which he is viewed. He is 'a poetic genius of the first order', and that is all that matters. Wilson Knight accepts everything he says at its literal face-value. The truth is that he is really interested in ideas, not poetry. He reads Pope for his didacticism, the ethical system set forth in his poems. The fact that Pope's moral doctrines are, as everyone admits, at best second-hand, frequently third- or fourth-hand, does not bother Wilson Knight in the least. If his other intellectual heroes – Shakespeare, Goethe, Nietzsche and the rest – were as unoriginal, the imaginative literature of Europe would indeed be a sorry affair. Others have attempted, with more or less success, to reveal Pope as a poet: Wilson Knight is content to regard him as a preacher, a moralist, a thinker. He is interested in morality in the strictly homiletic sense. He makes much of a supposed affinity between Pope and Shakespeare on the ground that Shakespeare also was a moralist. Wilson Knight claims to be able to understand Shakespeare's moral purpose. No one would deny that Shakespeare was interested in moral problems, as he was interested in all manifestations of human life; but few would maintain, and no one has satisfactorily demonstrated, that his plays have a moral purpose. They are as far removed as it is possible to imagine from the didacticism of the *Imitations of Horace* and the 'comfortable metaphysics' (in Byron's phrase) of the *Essay on Man*. Where does Shakespeare ever lecture his age on avarice and corruption, as Pope does in the *Epilogue to the Satires*?

Apart from some textural comment of the familiar kind, Wilson Knight pays little close attention to the text of Pope's poems, since he is interested mainly in their prose content. In order to commend him as a poet, and establish him solidly in his own poetic Pantheon, he relies on the associative effects of almost indiscriminate name-dropping: Dante, Shakespeare, Goethe, Byron, Keats, Nietzsche, and even Jesus

Christ – in such company almost any writer can be invested with a reverential halo, an aura of sanctity. I am reminded of Nicolas Bentley's clerihew :

> Cecil B. de Mille,
> Rather against his will,
> Was persuaded to leave Moses
> Out of 'The Wars of the Roses'.

Wilson Knight's infatuation with Pope is interesting because it shows the lengths to which subjective self-delusion can go, and it proves that anyone can find the Pope he wants to find, if he is sufficiently determined. But it is embarrassing because he is a teacher and a critic who has earned respect.

I do not know whether 'finding the Pope he wants to find' can be justly applied to *Pope's Dunciad: A Study of its Meaning*, 1955, by the American scholar, Aubrey Williams. But I think parts of it would have surprised Pope. When the Rev. William Warburton published his defence of the *Essay on Man*, whose orthodoxy had been seriously impugned, Pope wrote to him gratefully:

> You have made my System as clear as I ought to have done and could not. It is indeed the Same System as mine, but illustrated with a Ray of your own . . . I am sure I like it better than I did before, and so will every man else. I know I meant just what you explain, but I did not explain my own meaning so well as you: You understand me as well as I do myself, but you express me better than I could express myself.

Pope would have had equal cause to be grateful to Williams. His study is important, if only because it is, so far as I know, the first full-length monograph in recent times on a single work by Pope. He treats the poem, within the tradition of mock epic, as a wholly serious defence of the culture and cultural values which, derived originally from the east, pervaded European civilization from the Middle Ages onwards. Pope saw this culture threatened, according to Williams, by the growth of bad writing, and the purpose of his poem was to extinguish this writing and its writers by the power of ridicule. Moreover, this bad writing was deliberately encouraged by political patronage drawing its strength from the commercial Whig oligarchy flourishing in the City of London. The 'progress of dulness' is thus seen as beginning in the City and moving towards Westminster and the Court at St James's, the traditional champion of true culture. Williams' thesis will have to be taken into account in discussing the *Dunciad* in a later chapter. Meanwhile, a few general observations are not out of place here.

If his book is to be the type of Pope criticism in the future, certain lines of development are to be expected. It is assumed that Pope is an important, even a great poet, a representative Augustan personality linking English culture in the early eighteenth century with a European tradition much larger than anything English literature can be said to have stood for hitherto. The question of 'sincerity' or a dramatic *persona* for the author scarcely arises. Pope is taken to have intended to say what the critic discovers him to have said, whether directly or by implication, and this is taken to be of major importance. The matter of a personal or biographical relation between the poet and the import of what he is discovered to have meant is taken no account of, presumably as being an irrelevance. After all, as Williams' sub-title indicates, his book is a study of the *meaning* of the *Dunciad*: that is, the meaning for the modern critic and his readers, not necessarily for Pope and his. Williams discovers its meaning, not in what others have regarded as its 'poetry', nor even wholly in its prose content, but in his own special view of it. Whether the poem stands up to Williams' interpretation, whether this is relevant to it as a poem, whether its author aptly fits the rôle assigned to him by the critic – these questions must be left till later.

Robert W. Rogers' study of *The Major Satires of Alexander Pope*, published by the University of Illinois Press in 1955, has already been referred to in passing. Rogers is at heart an adherent of the 'Pope can do no wrong' school, though he is, as one would expect of an academic, more cautious and sophisticated than Byron, Edith Sitwell, or Wilson Knight. Indeed, he admits some of the faults attributed to Pope, notably his deviousness, though he seems not to regard this as a fault. He reveals Pope as an adroit manipulator of his own reputation, especially as regards publicity for the *Essay on Man*. Rogers describes carefully what he calls the 'manoeuvres' accompanying this event – the anonymity of the first edition, the hints thrown out in influential quarters that here was the work of a new young poet, a possible rival to himself – and quotes Johnson:

> Those friends of Pope, that were trusted with the secret [of Pope's authorship] went about lavishing honours on the new-born poet, and hinting that Pope was never so much in danger from any former rival. To those authors whom he had personally offended, to those whose opinion the world considered as decisive, and whom he suspected of envy or malevolence, he sent his Essay as a present before publication that they might defeat their own enmity by praises, which they could not afterwards decently retract.

This is all very amusing, and Rogers does not consider it necessary to reconcile it with his belief in Pope's 'basic sincerity and honesty'. Moreover, 'manoeuvres' of this kind accompanied Pope's dealings with the public throughout his life; their motive was to gain not only reputation but also sales, the two being directly connected. It is not considered necessary by critics like Rogers to enquire whether such procedures in any way qualify the claims of Pope as a denouncer of venality and the lust for gold.

Rogers works through Pope's principal satires, giving a conscientious account of their conception and execution and of their prose content. It is difficult to discover much in the way of a manifestation of personal enthusiasm for Pope as a poet. It is as if he assumes that his careful analysis will be taken as sufficient evidence of his enjoyment of the satires. He admits, for instance, that the *Essay on Man* is a hotch-potch of received ideas derived in part, though not wholly, from Bolingbroke, and he summarizes these ideas at some length, as if the ideas constituted the poetry. 'The *Essay on Man*,' we are told, 'must be judged as an example of rhetoric designed to assure men that the universe is perfectly planned . . .' In other words, we are asked to believe that popular metaphysics derived from Shaftesbury, Locke, Addison and others is more persuasive when turned into heroic couplets by a non-metaphysician, and that it is the function of poetry to provide this kind of satisfaction. Rogers admits that some of the bloom of the *Essay on Man* has worn off with the passage of time, but it remains 'magnificent' and 'moving'.

> The *Essay on Man* and the *Ethic Epistles* are magnificent undertakings. Changes in sensibility that the poet could not have anticipated have partially obscured the merits of the poems; but they do not prevent readers from appreciating the grandeur of the conception of the subtlety with which moral corruption, its 'mean compromises, sullen vanities, and secret brutalities', is detected and interpreted . . . [Pope] had shown that moving poetry could be created out of the most highly prized speculative materials of his day.

It might be remarked in passing that the merits of any poem may be obscured by changes in sensibility, though if it is a great poem its merits will be recognized in time. No poet can possibly anticipate such changes, but it would be interesting to know what modifications in the *Essay on Man* such foreknowledge on Pope's part would have produced. What we look for in vain is more guidance as to where Rogers finds the 'moving poetry', and how it moves him. When he comes to particularize the grounds of his admiration, he is inclined to take refuge in the vaguely magniloquent. Of the two concluding Horatian dialogues (*Epilogue to the Satires*) he says: 'The passages occurring at the climax of each dialogue are apocalyptic in their splendor and suggestiveness.' He calls the satires as a whole 'a distinguished protest against depravity' and accepts at its face value Pope's statement of his motivation as 'The strong Antipathy of Good to Bad'. He affirms with reasonable reservations the honesty of Pope's intentions and the nobility of his purpose:

> He assumed that social good depended upon the morals of individuals in a society; and Pope's business is therefore private morality. By examining the moral state of persons, he hoped to enlarge prevailing conceptions of pleasure and happiness, and to improve thereby the moral tone of the times. His end was essentially noble. It remains noble, even if at times expressed in savage invective, and even if at times distant from his own actual achievement in conduct.

The claim that Pope's end was noble would need to be based on evidence outside Pope's written professions. I believe there is little evidence that Pope really cared for the moral tone of society, and that his reasons for proclaiming his concern were complex and can only be analysed against a bio-critical background larger than Rogers allows himself. Nevertheless his forthright and unambiguous statement of his faith in Pope's satiric mission is creditable, and cannot be merely brushed aside. The hesitation I feel in accepting it is partly expressed in an admirable passage which occurs earlier in Rogers's own study:

> Perhaps the most distinctive method by which Pope makes clear the virtues he seeks to recommend is through the development of a well-rounded picture of the personality and character of the satirist . . . the attributes ascribed to the satirist always help to define Pope's idea of what is worthy. In the *Epistle to Dr Arbuthnot* there is a carefully evolved portrait of Pope as a man of letters – modest, unassuming, hostile to vice and friendly to virtue. One important purpose of this self-portrait is to develop a picture of an ideal and successful man of letters. The implied character of the satirist is similarly important to the positive argument of the *Epilogue to the Satires*, in which Pope appears as the outspoken citizen incensed by corruption in high places. He is no flatterer or time-server; he is incomparably patriotic, honest, uncompromising, and fearless. In every way he is an admirable citizen, representative of that civic virtue which the times so badly needed.

This is the now familiar notion of the *persona*. Of the several elements used by Pope to build up this self-portrait, the most substantial is a series of adaptations, especially in the *Epistle to Arbuthnot*, of the autobiographical parts of the satires of Boileau.[1] A problem which exponents of the *persona* theory do not face is that of the relation between the Boileau-figure and the historical Alexander Pope. The question which Rogers does not ask is, if Pope's intentions are honest and his purpose noble, if his character (apart from minor deficiencies) qualifies him to set up as a reformer of the morals of his time, why is it necessary for him to express his intentions and clothe his personality in the ideas and phrases of others? What becomes of Rogers's claim that Pope's professions are to be taken at their face value?

Such questions as this, as well as others which have been asked by readers of Pope for more than two centuries, would perhaps seem naïve in the context of the latest American academic criticism, and consequently not worth asking or answering. The most ambitious and sophisticated study of recent years is Reuben Brower's *Alexander Pope: the Poetry of Allusion*, 1959. This is a book which neither admirers nor detractors of Pope can ignore. It makes a strenuous, conscientious, and sincere attempt to establish Pope's elevation to the heights of the poetic hierarchy on secure critical, even scientific foundations. Brower follows the lines laid down by previous academic critics and strikes out along paths of his own. It is an important book because undoubtedly much more will be heard of his claims for Pope and of his views on poetry. That they are, in my judgement, almost wholly pernicious does not destroy my respect for Brower's scholarship and his sincerity: he clearly admires and enjoys Pope's poems, and the quality of his responses calls for comment. Nor, if I am right, does my view diminish the importance of Brower's book. Rather it enhances it, since it calls in question the value and rightness of the general trend of recent academic criticism of poetry, at least so far as America is concerned.

There is much that may be – must be – said of the book: this is sufficient warrant of its interest and importance. That a reader may find cause for disagreement on almost every page, even violent disagreement, at least it makes it necessary that he keeps his own judgements and assumptions continuously under review. The difficulty I feel is in keeping my own commentary on it within reasonable bounds, for the book continually raises fundamental questions, though without enquiring

[1] See *Boileau and the French Classical Critics in England 1660–1830*, Paris, 1925, by the literary historian A. F. B. Clark, who documents in great detail Pope's debt to Boileau, summing it up by saying, 'He clothed himself in Boileau's personality.'

into them. For instance, commenting on the distinction drawn by Horace between satire and poetry, Brower says:

> In one of the early satires [Sat. I. IV. 39–62] Horace further muddied the waters of criticism by raising the ugly and unnecessary question as to whether his poems were poetry.

Here is the passage from Horace in Christopher Smart's translation:

> In the first place, I would except myself out of the number of those I would allow to be poets: for one must not call it sufficient to tag a verse: nor if any person, like me, writes in a style bordering on conversation, must you esteem him to be a poet. To him who has genius, who has a soul of a diviner cast, and a greatness of expression, give the honour of this appellation.

Whether or not Brower is right in calling this insincere and merely mock-modest (and this is very doubtful), it is significant that he should regard it as muddying the critical waters for a poet to raise this fundamental question – 'ugly and unnecessary' he calls it – about his own work. After all, Horace, of whom the English neo-classic movement took a rather selective and specialized view, was well aware of the difference between poetry and familiar satire. He deprecated the use of the word 'poetry' to describe his satires and said that a poet must have not merely art but also genius (*ingenium*), and imagination, and could not move a reader unless he himself was first moved. Admirers of the poetry of 'art' are apt to forget that it was Horace who said '*Poeta nascitur non fit*'. Brower's account of Pope has the assurance of one who believes that the cause is won, and that the defensive tone which has characterized so much Pope criticism in recent times is now wholly out of place.

> When planning this book twenty years ago, I thought of dedicating it 'To the Readers of Pope'. The irony, perhaps not timely then, is certainly out of date now. Thanks to a revolution in taste and to the efforts of critics and scholars, Pope has more readers at present, it seems safe to say, than at any time since the eighteenth century.

Has there been a revolution in taste outside the ranks of critics and scholars? Has there been a real revolution in taste even among their pupils? Certainly it is safe to say so, for there is no means of proving or disproving it. What I am waiting for is a revolution in favour of Pope among poets. But what we have here is perhaps a symptom of the academic take-over noticed earlier. There is throughout the book so much mere paraphrase, however, that a reader is tempted to suspect that Brower's audience is not as familiar with Pope as he could wish.

But his enthusiasm is genuine, even if the detailed attention he focuses on Pope raises a doubt as to how wide is his understanding and how keen his enjoyment of the whole range of English poetry. He does indeed admire Pope because he reminds him of Yeats, Milton, and others held in high estimation. But there is no doubt that the main source of his admiration for Pope is that he writes against, not with, the authentic stream of the English tradition. Here, I believe, is the first of Brower's major heresies – heresies which to anyone who cares about English poetry, as distinct from the work and reputation of certain major poets currently much discussed in academic quarters, must be regarded as pernicious.

The emphasis on this line of thought is something new in Pope criticism – a line adumbrated in Aubrey Williams's study of the *Dunciad*. Throughout his book Brower reveals a personal preference for classical – in effect Latin – poetry over English. Everything in Pope that derives from the Latin poets directly or – as is more usual – through translation is praised; so pronounced is Brower's admiration for the classics that it is enough for him to record Pope's indebtedness – say to Theocritus and Virgil in the *Pastorals* – to imply approval of Pope's poems. Brower records the influence of Dryden in 'Latinizing' English poetry. He presents Dryden as reaffirming the rôle of the poet as spokesman in public affairs – a function of which Brower clearly approves. He compares the effect of the changeover from the private man to the public spokesman at the Restoration on Dryden and on Marvell, greatly to the latter's disadvantage. 'The spectacle is rather painful: the earlier Marvell could not address this world [of the Restoration] without sacrificing many of his virtues as a poet. Dryden could . . .' The comment that leaps to the mind is that if he did, the poet of the Nun Appleton poems had much, much more to sacrifice. Perhaps, too, Marvell's political satires are now underrated. At all events we know what Dryden thought of the situation in which the poet found himself as spokesman on public affairs. It is worth while to remind ourselves of the great words of his dedication to the *Examen Poeticum* written towards the end of his life.

'Tis a vanity common to all Writers, to over-value their own productions; and 'tis better for me to own this failing in my self, than the World to do it for me. For what other reason have I spent my Life in so unprofitable a Study? Why am I grown Old, in seeking so barren a Reward as Fame? The same Parts and Application, which have made me a Poet, might have rais'd me to any Honours of the Gown, which are often given to Men of as little Learning and less Honesty than my self. No Government has ever been, or ever can be, wherein Time-servers and Blockheads will not be uppermost. The Persons are only chang'd, but the same juglings in State, the same Hypocrisie in Religion, the same Self-Interest, and Mis-management, will remain for ever. Blood and Mony will be lavish'd in all Ages, only for the Preferment of new Faces, with old Consciences. There is too often a Jaundise in the Eyes of Great Men; they see not those whom they raise in the same Colours with other Men. All whom they affect look Golden to them; when the Gilding is only in their own distemper'd Sight. These Considerations have given me a kind of Contempt for those who have risen by unworthy ways. I am not asham'd to be Little, when I see them so Infamously Great. Neither, do I know, why the Name of Poet should be Dishonourable to me, if I am truly one, as I hope I am; for I will never do any thing, that shall dishonour it. The Notions of Morality are known to all men; None can pretend Ignorance of those Ideas which are In-born in Mankind: and if I see one thing and practise the contrary, I must be Disingenuous, not to acknowledge a clear Truth, and Base, to Act against the light of my own Conscience.

To what extent Dryden and Marvell respectively were destroyed as poets by the situation so trenchantly summarized is a matter of opinion. In my opinion the English tradition expired – or went underground – with Marvell. It is left to the critics to acclaim Dryden's success in finding a new direction – what I have called the neo-classic counter-revolution. 'Dryden,' according to Brower, 'marks the reaffirmation of "Europe" in English poetry and culture after an experiment in insularity . . .' Typography has no resources to express my amazement at such an assertion. Brower proceeds: 'By following Dryden and surpassing him, Pope became after Chaucer, Shakespeare and Milton the most European of English poets.' The basic reason for Brower's high estimtion of Pope thus becomes clear: 'Pope is thus perhaps the last major English poet to feel at home with the whole European and English tradition in poetry.'

Let us call this 'the European heresy'. Brower is thoroughly committed to it; it is worth some reflection, as we shall certainly hear more of it. To him, as to others, Europe ends at Calais. One would suppose that Britain was not part of Europe and had severed her connection with it at the death of Chaucer in 1400. The notion that there was something insular, something provincial about all English culture from the Reformation onwards is one we have met before. But despite the growth of nationalism in the fifteenth and sixteenth centuries English poetry never lost contact with its roots on the other side of the channel. That ties were loosened after the Reformation was indeed a necessary condition of the free growth of the truly national poetry which found its greatest expression (at least until the later eighteenth century) in the poets of the Elizabethan age. But to regard Tudor and Stuart England as outside Europe, and to speak of 'an experiment in insularity', is a travesty of literary history. How can any sensitive reader of English poetry write off as an insular deviation all poetry (except that of Shakespeare and Milton) between Chaucer and Dryden? Leaving aside the implied Europeanism of Shakespeare and Milton (does the critic perhaps mean that any English poet conventionally called 'major' is 'European'?) we are to suppose perhaps that Skelton (whose fusion of native English with medieval Latin elements is notable), Wyatt (whose naturalization of Petrarch was highly influential), Ralegh, Sidney, Greville, Campion, and Herrick (both accomplished classicists), Davies, Donne, Drummond (who, according to some literary historians, first perfected the heroic couplet), Herbert, Carew, Suckling, Crashaw, Vaughan, as well as Marvell and all the dramatists from Marlowe and Chapman (both classicists) to Webster – dramatists saturated in the spirit of Italian and Spanish literature – we are to suppose that these poets are to be relegated by modern criticism to the rubbish-heap where neo-classic doctrine consigned them. (I omit Spenser, as there is some indication that Brower regards him as European.) And to say that Pope was 'at home' with the tradition they represent is ridiculous.

A reasonable case could be made out for saying that there was something insular and provincial about English cultural achievements in architecture and the graphic arts, and perhaps in music, in the period in question; but no such case could possibly be made out against English poetry, if only because the evolution of poetry is bound up with that of a nation's language, a national possession. By the time of Shakespeare and the King James Bible, if not before, England had achieved a poetry second to none in Continental Europe or anywhere else. This is partly because the English language is the most poetic instrument ever evolved in the minds of men. It may be added that it is in the seventeenth century, before the 'Europeanizing' influence of Dryden was felt, that American poetry has its roots.

The second of Brower's major heresies consists in his advocacy of imitation and allusion, combined with a distaste for originality. This is, indeed, the principal theme of his book:

> While there is a value in recognizing the conventions Pope used and some pleasure in hearing echoes of earlier poets in his verse, it is more important to see how he used the poetry of the past for his own expressive purposes. For Dryden and for Pope allusion, especially in ironic contexts, is a resource equivalent to symbolic metaphor and elaborate imagery in

other poets. Through allusion, often in combination with subdued meta-phors and exquisite images, Pope gets his purchase on larger meanings and evokes the finer resonances by which poetry (in Johnson's phrase) 'penetrates the recesses of the mind'.

No doubt there is a certain scholarly satisfaction to be had from identify-ing Pope's innumerable literary borrowings; but the task of sorting out the concealed echoes which demonstrate Pope's basic deficiency in primary experience from the calculated parodic quotations from, or references to, the classics (to Homer and Virgil in *The Rape of the Lock*) or to Milton (in the *Dunciad*) is a difficult one. The whole question will need to be considered in the context of general notions of poetic theory and practice. Phrases such as 'gets his purchase on larger mean-ings and evokes the finer resonances' are high-sounding and seem to need more justification than Brower offers. What are these 'larger meanings'? What are these 'finer resonances' except literary echoes from a well-stored but unoriginal mind? Brower does not value originality.

> Feeling no nineteenth-century compulsion to be merely original, he took
> pleasure in imitating the poets he read and admired, one and all.

This is a really astonishing view. It is difficult to comment adequately on the idea that there is anything 'mere' about the process by which poetry renews itself and revitalizes our aesthetic experience instead of copying and refining on existing poetry. If there is anything 'mere', surely it is imitation. It is also impossible to accept the notion of origin-ality in poetry as a nineteenth-century aberration. Keats, we know, owed something to Milton; Tennyson was glad to learn from Keats; the Pre-Raphaelites learned from Keats and Coleridge and the ballad revival. Arnold intelligently imitated Homer, Browning adapted the manner of Byron. Indeed, Hopkins alone was strikingly original, and his originality exiled him from the nineteenth to the twentieth century. Originality, however, was never 'mere', even in Pope's own day; ex-pressly or implicitly it has at all times been regarded by poets as in some degree a necessary condition of full self-realization and poetic growth. No doubt Pope took pleasure in imitating what he admired; nor was he at all averse to borrowing from forgotten poets whom he professed not to admire. The question is, how are we to rate poems conceived and composed on this basis?

But Pope, it seems, was able to have it both ways. 'From Dryden,' Brower tells us, 'he learned how to imitate without loss of originality.' The reader must give Brower full marks for critical dexterity. Referring elsewhere to this topic, he tells us that ' "original" is always a relative term when used of Pope; his latest successes like his earliest were all more or less "imitations".' 'Original', it may be observed, is always a relative term except perhaps when used of the scribblings of psychopaths. Brower goes on to defend 'imitation' in the sense in which it was understood by the Renaissance, but his examples are, significantly, taken from architecture. The poems of Pope are to be judged by the canons of architecture.

The cumulative impression of Brower's book is that he is giving a detailed account of the processes of a thoroughly second-rate talent. We are repeatedly told of the dependence of Pope on the writings of others, of the inescapable influence of their work on the minutest particulars of his. 'For Pope, almost invariably, a mode of expression includes a mode of imitation or allusion.' This is well put. Again: 'For Pope at the start of his career, as at the end, the imitation of life is also the imitation of literature.' This is a dexterous play upon two allied but distinct meanings of 'imitation', for with Pope the imitation of literature involves the incorporation of fragments of actual literature into his own work; in the Aristotelian phrase, the imitation of life implies an imaginative transubstantiation into verbal-dramatic form of non-verbal matter having no precedent formal permanence. To Pope, then literature is the imitation of an imitation. Throughout the book he is praised for his allusions to Milton, himself one of the most allusive of English poets. Milton makes continual reference to Homer, the Latin classics, Shakespeare, and many others. Pope alludes to Milton. Where is the process of poetic in-breeding to end? Perhaps an ideal future postulated by academic criticism would give us yet more subtly resonant poetry incorporating Pope himself as well as all that has been written in the two centuries since his death. What a paradise for the textural editors of tomorrow, and what a bleak prospect for the unspecialized reader! Or are we to suppose that there is no place for the unspecialized reader in the future of literature?

The adoption by Brower of what I have called his two major heresies makes it possible for him, of course, to take a very favourable view indeed of Pope's poetic achievement. If Latin poetry is superior to English, and if the Continental 'European' tradition is greater than the 'insular' tradition of England, then clearly Pope ranks very high. If the kind of originality which consists in the wholesale imitation of other poets is an estimable quality, the appeal of Pope is immense. As we should expect, in Brower's eyes Pope can scarcely put a foot wrong. He admires the *Pastorals* for their evocation of Theocritus and Virgil and for the musical quality of their language. He selects, as others have done, the 'Where'er you walk' quatrain for special commendation. No mention is made of Pope's debt to Waller. Instead, he is praised for his 'choreographic' view of nature and for his 'naïve' dramatic sense, especially in 'trees crowd into a shade'. 'Crowd' is of course a beautiful stroke, and it is lifted straight from Waller. Thus Pope is praised for beauties not his own.

Windsor Forest is admired for its evocation of Homer, the *Georgics*, and Milton's *Paradise Lost*. Anything which reminds Brower of Homer is admired, even the appalling early rendering of the lines from the *Odyssey*, Book VII, on the garden of Alcinous. Here is a sample:

> The balmy spirit of the western gale
> Eternal breathes on fruits untaught to fail:
> Each dropping pear a following pear supplies,
> On apples apples, figs on figs arise.

Among critics Brower almost alone commends such 'gradus epithets' (in Saintsbury's exact phrase) as 'balmy'. He notes the 'subdued gloom' of the description of Windsor as evidenced in such phrases as 'russet plain', 'bluish hills', 'purple dyes' and 'sable waste'. Pope is praised not, of course, for the originality of these phrases but for his painterly skill in selecting and combining them. Brower admits the inaccuracy of many of Pope's images from nature and says that they are derived from art, not observation. But this literal inaccuracy is claimed as a virtue, since as a poet Pope was interested in the idea, not the minute circumstance. Is it not possible to be interested in the idea of an object without falsifying its appearance? The fact that Pope's Windsor Forest, like the scene of his *Pastorals*, might be almost anywhere is presumably to Pope's credit. *Eloïsa* and the *Elegy* are praised, though with reservations, the former because of its reference to the heroic epistles of Ovid. In company with many critics, Brower maintains that Pope's readers would recognize and enjoy the classical allusions throughout his poems. The evidence for this seems to me slender; I think it just as likely that, apart from the more obvious allusions, he may have banked on his reader's having forgotten them. After all, what did he say of the education of the class for which he wrote?

> All Classic learning lost on Classic ground.
> (*Dunciad*, IV, 321)

The implication of Brower's verdict on Pope's *Iliad* is that it was an elaborate act of flattery to please the subscribers. Pope makes the Greek and Trojan lords talk and behave like Augustan lords, because his readers

knew very well – as we can hardly know – how a noble lord behaved, how
he walked and how he talked on great occasions. A chief or a prince in
council could not quarrel like a fishwife as Achilles and Agamemnon
seem to in any literal translation of their speeches.

Surely this is as much as to say that, by yielding to the social pressures
of his time, Pope disqualified himself as a translator of Homer, and to
concede the justice of Bentley's famous comment on Pope's *Iliad*: '. . . it
is a pretty poem, Mr. Pope; but you must not call it Homer.'

Brower devotes to *The Rape of the Lock* as much critical solemnity as
if he were dealing with a major novel by Henry James. He regards the
sylphs as an important device linking the little world of Belinda with
popular country beliefs on the one hand and 'Heathen mythology' on
the other. Pope thus 'makes us feel the presence of forces greater than
Belinda and the Baron and their friends'. I doubt if many readers before
Brower have felt this way about the effect of a device so artificial, literary,
and derivative. There is no evidence that Pope has the least interest in
popular country beliefs. The general impression left by Brower's account
of *The Rape* is that it is one of the least original poems ever written, but
of course this is of no account if a low value is set on originality. By
treating the poem as a novel, however, Brower does lend it considerable
interest and enhances its appeal for readers who are not over-critical
of the verse. Brower tells us that 'Pope's poetry of wit' is 'probably most
perfect in the passage on the ceremony of afternoon coffee and the
cutting of the lock'. It is worth while to pause and take a critical look
at the latter of these passages.

> He takes the Gift with rev'rence, and extends
> The little Engine on his Fingers' Ends,
> This just behind *Belinda*'s Neck he spread,
> As o'er the fragrant Steams she bends her Head:
> Swift to the Lock a thousand Sprights repair,
> A thousand Wings, by turns, blow back the Hair,
> And thrice they twitch'd the Diamond in her Ear,
> Thrice she look'd back, and thrice the Foe drew near.
> Just in that instant, anxious *Ariel* sought
> The close Recesses of the Virgin's Thought;
> As on the Nosegay in her Breast reclin'd,
> He watch'd th'Ideas rising in her Mind,
> Sudden he view'd, in spite of all her Art,
> An Earthly Lover lurking at her Heart.
> Amaz'd, confus'd, he found his Pow'r expir'd,
> Resign'd to Fate, and with a Sigh Retir'd.

> The Peer now spreads the glitt'ring *Forfex* wide,
> T'inclose the Lock; now joins it, to divide.
> Ev'n then, before the fatal Engine clos'd,
> A wretched *Sylph* too fondly interpos'd;
> Fate urg'd the Shears, and cut the *sylph* in twain,
> (But Airy Substance soon unites again)
> The meeting Points the sacred Hair dissever
> From the fair Head, for ever and for ever!

In a passage such as this the manipulation of verbal counters – phrases drawn from literary sources, parody references to commonplaces of epic poetry – is skilful enough; the rhetoric or artifice of the writing is effective so long as Pope is dealing with the invisible and the unreal – so long, that is, as he remains in the sphere of mere verbal manipulation within a preconceived prosodic pattern. But the weakness of the writing on the poetic level appears the moment he is obliged to adjust the rhetorical tone to the actual happening which the passage is supposed to be about. In his early poems at any rate, it is always in the sphere of the actual that Pope fails; he does so because his eye is not on the object but on a book (for instance, Dryden's *Aeneid*); and where his books fail him and he is, so to speak, on his own, he is lost. It is difficult to believe that Pope had never seen anyone use a pair of scissors or used them himself, but this is the impression left on anyone who tries to extend a pair of scissors 'on his Fingers' Ends'. Nor is the couplet in which the Baron actually cuts off the lock any more exact. The two halves of a pair of scissors are already 'joined', but Pope is too interested in making a clever antithesis to be concerned about the inaccuracy of the picture. He is not, in fact, realizing this crucial moment poetically; he is merely making word-play on an action which the reader is left to visualize from his own experience. We think we are seeing the Baron performing the act, but we are not. Again, in the last line but one 'blades' would have been more accurate than 'Points'. These may be hypercritical objections, but we are discussing what is offered as poetry of almost the highest order.

Brower is one of those critics, who, increasingly, invoke the name of Shakespeare to express their feelings about Pope and thereby enhance his prestige.

> Our 'liking' or disliking' do not seem particularly relevant, just as when we are faced with Lear's horrible nightmare of adultery and lechery. The integrity of vision and effect in the portrait of Sporus is in a definable sense Shakespearean . . .

The *Epistle to Arbuthnot,* which contains the portrait of Sporus, was not regarded by Pope or his readers as generalized drama in which vices common to many men are attacked by a *dramatis persona* on the verge of madness in retribution for his own folly. Lord Hervey was a known historical individual, with a known and widely publicized quarrel with Pope. Pope's portrait was a libel and would have earned its subject big damages in a modern court of law. No question of libel on an individual could arise, even in the circumstances of today, over Lear's attack. Hervey's misfortune – probably bisexual tendencies rather than, as Pope hints, impotence – was not imputed, like adultery and lechery in *Lear,* to mankind in general. Moreover, Lear undergoes an agony of personal suffering at the state of mankind, with whom, as the play goes on, he increasingly identifies himself: that is one of the things the play is about. Pope's attitude to Hervey is one of superiority. He cares nothing about Hervey's misfortune and is connected with him only by hatred, not by compassion. The Sporus passage seems to me in a quite definable sense *un*Shakespearian. Brower maintains that Pope's 'great' satiric portraits – for instance, that of Atossa – can be compared with Shakespeare's Thersites or Caliban. But the portrait of Caliban is not a detached diploma piece; it is an element in a dramatic whole containing other contrasting elements – for instance, Ariel and Miranda. Nor is Caliban, so far as we knew, an attack against an individual, real or fictitious; it is not even an attack against a type. Prospero, as another character in the same drama, may condemn him savagely, but Shakespeare the poet does not. He gives him some of the most poetic lines he ever wrote, portraying even the bestial Caliban with some love and humanity and even investing him with a kind of dignity. Pope's satiric characters are drawn for the most part without love or humanity, and are deliberately stripped of all dignity. It must surely be evident to any reader not out to make a special case for Pope that to write of him as in any sense Shakespearian is pure hyperbole.

It need hardly be added that to Brower the biographical connections of Pope's work are an embarrassment which he tries to treat as an irrelevance.

We must not then confuse the history of Pope's portraits with the poetry. Pope's own fury may have set him writing, but as he wrote he transformed his victims – if that is the word – into something quite unreal.

There is no question of confusion. We can appreciate whatever poetry there is in Pope without forgetting its biographical background. It is no good pretending that Sporus was not meant to represent Hervey, once we know he was; Pope deliberately set himself to draw recognizable personal portraits, and he would have been very surprised, perhaps affronted, to learn that they were 'unreal'. A portrait is not necessarily less real for being a caricature.

11 The Twentieth Century VI

No major work on the poetry of Pope has appeared either in England or America since the publication of Reuben Brower's *The Poetry of Allusion*. While it looks as if any new theory and research is likely to come from America, where the academic take-over has proceeded for over thirty years, England has been content to consolidate the now more or less standardized view and to work for the rehabilitation of Pope among university students and the general public as a 'great' major poet. It is becoming increasingly difficult to discover any serious dissent from the standardized view. It is still possible to trace a defiant, propagandist note in references to Pope; but in England, as in America for some time past, it is now not essential for an admirer to adopt the defensive attitude prevalent not long ago. True, an anonymous reviewer in the *Times Literary Supplement* in 1961, as has been noted, had the temerity to call Pope's personality 'unlikeable', but the 'greatness' of his poems is regarded as axiomatic. A reviewer in a later issue of the same journal for 20 August 1964, commenting on an American book about the poems of Allen Tate, goes out of his way to reprove Tate for hostility to Pope in his poem, *The Last Days of Alice*. '. . . a reader may feel,' writes this reviewer, 'in the end that a fine poet should not take such liberties with a great one.' Pope, then, is one who must not be taken liberties with.

Two introductory essays to recent selections of poems by Pope express very fairly the currently accepted view among intelligent writers in what may be called the sub-academic field. John Heath-Stubbs, in his introduction to *Selected Poems of Alexander Pope*, 1964, shows himself a sincere, enthusiastic, and for the most part judicious admirer of both the man and the poems. He is a victim of what I have called the Victorian fallacy, believing that Matthew Arnold 'set a new and unfortunate tone for Pope criticism in the later nineteenth century, from which the twentieth was slow to emancipate itself'. I have already, I hope, done something to dispel the myth of Arnold as the villain of anti-Popery. Heath-Stubbs speaks of the 'far more balanced view of Pope which has grown up over the last quarter of a century or so'. Which is the more balanced – Arnold on the one hand or Edith Sitwell and Wilson Knight on the other – the reader has had an opportunity to judge.

Heath-Stubbs, indeed, singles out for praise what he calls 'the highly individual, but imaginative and stimulating interpretation of Mr. G. Wilson Knight'. We hear, too, once more of the Horatian *persona* which 'enables him effectively to appear as a detached moralist and commentator on his own age'. But even without the *persona* Pope's character, Heath-Stubbs maintains, is on the whole admirable. He writes of his qualities as a 'tender, affectionate and loyal friend, and the generous encourager of young poets of talent'. He writes also of Pope's courage in winning literary pre-eminence in the teeth of continuous attacks by his enemies. All this praise, of course, requires considerable modification if the view of Pope it implies is not to be dismissed as merely sentimental. Heath-Stubbs makes a good deal of Pope's rôle as up-holder of cultural standards in an age which 'saw the beginnings of that expansion of mass sub-literature which in our own day has reached frightening proportions, and which is a real threat to genuine culture'. The defence of literary purity is, Heath-Stubbs believes, the subject of the *Dunciad*. Of this simplified view something will be said later. A few observations may be made in passing: Pope himself profited more than any other single writer from the expansion of publishing in the early years of the eighteenth century; that worse writers should also compete for profit was inevitable; not all Pope's 'dunces' were bad writers by any means; the cultural level of Pope's own publications – especially anonymous ones – was not in all cases high, and he himself employed Grub Street hacks to fight his battle. It was sheer hypocrisy to pretend to be above the battle. The bookseller Curll, who existed on the in-creased demand for books of all kinds, reputable as well as disreputable, was also used by Pope for his own purposes. Commenting on the pro-phecy of the return of Chaos at the end of the *Dunciad* IV, Heath-Stubbs, it seems to me, allows himself to be carried away.

> The vision here presented is dark indeed . . . but as a prophecy we may see it as having been largely fulfilled in our own time. As a poet, then, Pope is, I suggest, more than the mere spokesman of his age.

Yet we can seek comfort in Heath-Stubbs's own words. 'For Pope's reputation today,' he asserts, 'once more stands high – probably higher than it has for two centuries.'

In *An Introduction to Pope* originally published in America and reprinted in *Essays on Literature and Ideas*, 1963, John Wain takes an equally enthusiastic view which is interesting as being an expression of contemporary thinking. Gone is the note of defence, the discussion of Pope's personality, the debate between ethical and aesthetic values

Pope was simply 'the finest English poet of the eighteenth century. Only Burns outreached him, and Burns was not an Englishman'. This is the second time we have come across this word 'fine', and it leaves us wondering about its significance, except as a subjective term of general approval which does not commit its user to anything so positive as 'good' or even 'great'. It would have been helpful if Wain had told us what he means by 'finest', and in what sense Burns is finer than Pope and others less fine. But Wain goes further. Pope, he maintains, 'was a poet in the full sense of the word – imaginative, brooding, responsive to the non-rational side of his nature'. But he found himself in an age which was not poetic 'in the full sense of the word'. It was an age of rationalism and scepticism. Fortunately, however, a solution of this dilemma was to hand; and it must be admitted that on this point Wain is ingenious.

> There was much in his genius that naturally wished to overflow the bounds of eighteenth-century compromise . . . Fortunately there was a way out. . . . The eighteenth century was a great age of parody and burlesque . . . The poet writing a wild and fanciful burlesque was able to use his imagination in a way that would not be permitted in more sedate forms of writing . . . Hence the vogue for burlesque epics. It was one kind of outlet for the poet who longed to write a real, 'straight' epic but was restrained by the decorous poetic climate.

There is much that might be said about this. Just how 'wild' Pope's mock epics were is a matter of opinion; and we have already noted his confessed rejection of the impulse to write a 'wild' Persian tale. We can also see what became of Homer's wildness in the hands of Pope. There were, moreover, other forms of poetry than the 'straight epic' available to poets who were not over-anxious about sacrificing the acclaim of readers who were interested only in what was 'sedate' and 'decorous'. It seems to me that Wain is reviving the notion adumbrated by Tillotson, of Pope as the suppressed romantic confined by the iron shackles of eighteenth-century convention to forms that were alien to the genius of a true poet. If only, one feels, Pope had had the independence of spirit to reject convention and give this romanticism full scope, what poems we might have seen – or if only some of Pope's contemporaries had had the degree of 'genius' ascribed to him. But that Pope's compromise with convention was not the only way out of the dilemma is indicated by the attempts of the Countess of Winchelsea, Young, Thomson, Green, Blair, and Akenside. What must be asked is whether parody and burlesque were the best which the 'finest English poet of the eighteenth century' could accept as the vehicle for his genius. If he set himself up as a prophet with a 'message' for his age, no doubt it was so. Writing of the *Dunciad,* Wain remarks :

> Whether or not he was being just to the particular people he describes is beside the point. The message of *The Dunciad* is that 'dulness' is not just a mistake or a misfortune, but a crime. And if we think of Dulness as including nonsense, falsity, insincerity, and at times plain lying, we shall read the poem with more chance of understanding.

Momentarily one almost imagines that Wain is being ironical; for if falsity, insincerity, and plain lying are substantial ingredients of 'dulness', why is not Pope himself rather than Theobald or Cibber the hero of the *Dunciad*? And if justice to living individuals is beside the point, how serious a crime is mere 'dulness'? How seriously are we to take the message, the moral propaganda of the *Dunciad,* when we weigh the amusement extracted by Pope and his readers from the burlesque of Lewis Theobald against what we know of the man he pillories?

   To have begun a study of a writer by embarking on a long and detailed examination of the opinions of others may seem to some readers perverse. My reasons for having done so are several. The chief, perhaps, is that it was these opinions, expressed at fairly frequent intervals during the past two and a half centuries, which led me to attempt a study of Pope. The diversity and persistence of these views and the lack of agreement among Pope's critics are indications of his importance and of the importance of the questions about which there has been disagreement. It is not as if Pope had been forgotten for a century and then revived; it is not as if he had once been famous and had then fallen into a disrepute from which he had to be rescued; it is simply that there is something about Pope which invites disagreement. Neither his admirers nor his detractors can agree among themselves as to which are his best poems and which are his worst faults. There is no major work by Pope which has not been proclaimed his best by one voice or another; this can hardly be said of any other writer. Shakespeare, for instance, has been the subject of even more controversy and speculation, but there has been fairly general agreement as to which of his plays are the greatest. It is true that certain plays which were at one time neglected have received closer critical attention than formerly, but not to the point of displacing any of the undisputed masterpieces. That Pope himself, both as man and poet, is of compelling interest there is no doubt. But there is a sense in which the discussion is of greater interest than its subject: no writer has ever attracted such *personal* attitudes and reactions. Some writers on Pope have written almost in the spirit of one whose opinions on religion or patriotism are under attack. The discussion of Pope is, as has been said, a discussion of principles and standards; it is a discussion about the aesthetic and moral values of those who have engaged in it.

Another reason, therefore, for documenting the Pope debate so fully is that it is of intense interest in itself. I have attempted to represent all facets of it fairly and to throw some light on views which have been obscured, forgotten or misrepresented. Thus the later eighteenth century has been shown to be a time when Pope was regarded not altogether with that uncritical reverence which is sometimes ascribed to it. Nor was the Victorian period, on the other hand, one in which Pope was universally undervalued. It has been shown, too, that the views of Pope held by writers of the Romantic period were by no means entirely hostile. It is rather that, at all times since the death of Pope, and even before it, his poems and his character have been a battleground for irreconcilable opinions among individuals of differing temperament. How this has come about I shall try to show. It has been for me one of the chief features of interest in this enquiry.

Another reason for the importance of the Pope debate, especially in this century, is the attractions it has offered to professional scholars and critics working in the academic field. The magnificent definitive editions both of the poems and of the correspondence are proof of this. Since critical investigation of one kind or another – textual, biographical, exegetic, prosodic, interpretive – is the field of academic criticism, it is natural that critics should place a high value on what calls for investigation. That high critical value, so to speak, may be taken to constitute high poetic value is a possibility which may perhaps disturb some readers outside the academic field.

The history of the Pope debate may be seen almost as a miniature history of literary criticism, at any rate in England and America, from the Augustan age onwards. We have seen how varying aspects of the debate have engaged the interest of writers at different periods – the question as to whether Pope is to be ranked among poets of the 'first order' or whether he is simply the most accomplished exponent of an inferior kind of poetry; the relation between character and poetic worth, first as more or less avoided by Johnson, then as treated by Romantic critics as of cardinal importance; the 'moral' quality of Pope's poems as asserted by such admirers as Byron and Wilson Knight; the rejection of moral in favour of 'artistic' standards by later writers;

more recently, the assumption, especially by American academics, of Pope's 'greatness' as axiomatic and the increasing sophistication of their methods of analysis and discussion of particular works. All these matters are bound to come up in any reasonably full account of the Pope debate.

If the final stage in the debate is that of what I have called sophistication, this makes it all the more difficult, and perhaps all the more necessary, to return to the simpler questions. For the suspicion is not altogether to be avoided that sophistication, the refinement of terms, the adoption of complex and ambivalent attitudes, may conceal fundamental hesitations and uncertainties on the part of critics. To write a very subtle book about Pope may prove no more than that Pope is a suitable subject for subtle treatment: it does not really prove anything about the value of his poems. There must be a point at which the sophisticated critic has to put his cards on the table and say what he considers valuable in a poem, apart from the possibilities it offers for subtle analysis. This is the point which some critics strive to avoid. It is as if the critic said, 'We shall never agree on what constitutes value in a poem. Let us stop talking about anything so simple, so fundamental, so insoluble. Let us rather concentrate on what we can agree about – namely that such-and-such a passage offers us the refined pleasure of recognizing "larger resonances" through its verbal references to other poems. That at least is a solid pleasure: we need not concern ourselves with the embarrassing question of how valuable the passage is, once we have spotted the references, or whether it is really worth such close analysis.' To this attitude the reply has to be made that, if you admire a poem because it reminds you of other poems, it is the function of poetry to remind you of other poetry. Is this really the case? Pope, in short, is a scholar's poet, the admiration of trained specialist readers. But this is exactly what Pope was formerly claimed not to be. A value that was once attributed to him was the availablity of his poems to the ordinary reader as expressed in the number of quotations familiar to him. The sophisticated critic would presumably be the last to maintain that it is the function of poetry to perpetuate copybook maxims; but that is precisely what the ordinary reader remembers in Pope. The non-specialist, on the other hand, has little use for poems which owe their attraction to their capacity for reminding him of other poems – poems he has probably not read. The conclusion can only be that both kinds of attraction are perfectly valid, but that neither has, in itself, much to do with poetry as such. It is certainly to Pope's credit that he can appeal in different ways to the simple and the clever, the lover of copybook maxims and the connoisseur of 'larger resonances'. But what of the average intelligent reader who is looking neither for 'comfortable metaphysics' (in Byron's phrase) on the one hand nor 'the poetry of allusion' on the other? He may admit that no one can deny the presence of the copybook maxims or the allusions and ask 'But where is the poetry?' That is the main question to be considered.

In evading the simple question 'What is poetry, and what constitutes poetic value?' the sophisticated critic is also enabled to evade another question – a question which has indeed been pretty completely submerged in the later stages of the debate. I mean the question of the relation between the man and the poet. The modern line is to regard the man – the historical Alexander Pope – as an irrelevance. What matters, we are to assume, is the *persona*, the poet as he wants to appear. Whether you accept this view or whether, as I do, you regard man and poet as indissolubly identified is ultimately a matter of taste or personal preference. But nothing is more important than personal preference. Whichever of these attitudes you prefer, all I can do is to try to show you what you prefer; if you 'enjoy Pope as poetry' (in Eliot's phrase), all I can do is to try to show you what you enjoy.

II

THE POEMS

1 The Pastorals

I think a good deal may be said to extenuate the fault of bad Poets. What we call a Genius, is hard to be distinguish'd by a man himself, from a strong inclination: and if his genius be ever so great, he can not at first discover it any other way, than by giving way to that prevalent propensity which renders him the more liable to be mistaken. The only method he has, is to make the experiment by writing, and appealing to the judgment of others: now if he happens to write ill (which is certainly no sin in itself) he is immediately made an object of ridicule. I wish we had the humanity to reflect that even the worst authors might, in their endeavour to please us, deserve something at our hands. We have no cause to quarrel with them but for their obstinacy in persisting to write; and this too may admit of alleviating circumstances.

The author of this humane, tolerant, and sprightly defence of bad writers was Alexander Pope. But at the time of writing it he was only twenty-eight, and was about to put his reputation to the test by publishing his first considerable collection of poems. Another ten years were to pass before he felt sufficiently established to embark on the composition of the *Dunciad*. It would be interesting to know if any of the 'Dunces' remembered its author's eloquent defence of writing ill, 'which is certainly no sin in itself'. Some of Pope's modern critics have forgotten it. The document from which this quotation comes is the revealing, and now not often read Preface to the 1717 collection of Pope's poems. This Preface, with its strange combination of manly pride and earnest humility, of independence and concern for public favour, betrays an obsession with the question of fame. It is difficult to be sure whether the young man is excusing himself or pleading for himself. He seems to be aware of a connection between good verse and a good character.

If I have written well, let it be consider'd that 'tis what no man can do without good sense, a quality that not only renders one capable of being a good writer, but a good man. And if I have made any acquisition in the opinion of any one under the notion of the former, let it be continued to me under no other title than that of the latter.

Here is Pope at twenty-eight already asking to be regarded as a good man, not merely a good writer. Let it not be said that the notion of a connection between morality and genius is a nineteenth-century heresy.

The 1717 Preface shows, at any rate, that however deeply Pope had or had not thought about morality, he had thought a good deal about reputation. 'For (what is the hardest case imaginable) the reputation of a man generally depends upon the first steps he makes in the world, and people will establish their opinion of us, from what we do at that season when we have least judgement to direct us.' This is very shrewd for a young man. He had an old head on young shoulders, having enjoyed conversation and correspondence with much older men – Wycherley and Congreve, Sir William Trumbull and Henry Cromwell. He appears to be claiming the privileges of youth and inexperience; but of course he had good reason to be satisfied with his first steps in the literary world, since the composition of his *Pastorals* had, according to his own account, been accompanied by very favourable auspices. They were written at the age of sixteen and submitted to William Walsh, who, Pope had cause to believe, was the best judge to whom he might send them for an opinion. Walsh was a bad poet, facile, and superficial, and a Whig MP. But what chiefly attracted Pope was that Dryden, whom Pope adored as a poetic father-figure, had called Walsh 'without flattery the best critick of our nation'.

An elegant and formal, rather than vigorous and independent writer, Walsh decried originality and believed that it was useless for a modern poet to try to outdo the 'ancients'. He told Pope that the only way left for a modern writer to excel was through 'correctness'. No one knows precisely what he meant by this, but what he had in mind was evidently prosodic regularity, smoothness of diction, and perhaps a certain coolness or propriety of thought and sentiment, by which the polite reader would be soothed, not shocked. In the main, Pope took 'correct' to mean 'mellifluous'. Walsh was evidently impressed by the performance of the boy of sixteen, and showed his *Pastorals* to influential men in the literary and social world. We have only Pope's authority for the statement that Walsh told Wycherley in 1705 that "Tis no flattery at all to say, that *Virgil* had written nothing so good at his age'. A year later the London publisher Tonson, who had earlier published Dryden's translation of Virgil by subscription, wrote to Pope to say that he had seen part of the *Pastorals* in the hands of Walsh and Congreve. He

invited the boy of eighteen to submit the whole work to him for publication when it should be completed. The boy wisely did not rush into
print, and the *Pastorals* were given to the public in Tonson's *Miscellany*
in 1709.

> So Pope, still a youth, still unknown, entered on the scene, not under
> the protection of a great lord, nor of a statesman, but under the imme-
> diate auspices, and almost at the request, of a publisher[1]

This is not quite true, since Pope already enjoyed the favour not only of
critics and authors but also, according to his account, of a number of
peers, including George Granville, later Lord Lansdowne, an influential
statesman, and a dull writer. Nevertheless, this event marks an important stage in the history of publishing: the system of patronage by titled
men was beginning to give way to the modern commercial system, in
which the final arbiter of taste is the reading public in general. It is
they who decide ultimately whether publishers and authors fail or
prosper. Pope was the first writer to make an independent fortune by
writing for the reading public. This fact is of considerable significance
in following his professional career.

Estimates of Pope's *Pastorals* have varied considerably. In his notes
to the 1736 edition of his works Pope himself gave them a pretty fulsome
puff. He also told Joseph Spence that he regarded them as his most
correct and musical composition, and the analogy with music is repeated
by Austin Warren, who writes of their 'quasi-musical' character and
compares their composition with that of a 'string quartet'. Their extreme artificiality has been alternately attacked and defended. Edith
Sitwell, for instance, defends it on the ground that 'he was writing in
a form which is completely foreign to our language, and which has its
roots in a tradition which is very distant from ours'. Pope was indeed
writing 'in a form foreign to our language'. Rejecting the Spenserian
idiom, he adopted the more modish view of the Pastoral drawn from
the French critics, Rapin and Fontenelle, who based their theories on
the classical models of Theocritus and Virgil. It is for this reason, no
doubt, that the French critic, Louis Cazamian, admired Pope's
Pastorals.

> It has even been possible to say that the *Pastorals* remain in a sense
> the masterpiece of Pope . . . but they also evidence a precocious talent,
> the sincerity of which is here indistinguishable from artifice.[2]

[1] Alexandre Beljame, *Men of Letters and the English Public in the Eighteenth
Century 1660–1744* (trans. E. O. Lorimer) London, 1948.
[2] Legouis and Cazamian, *A History of English Literature*, 1957 edition, London.

Tillotson, too, seems to be fascinated by the sincerity which is 'indistinguishable from artifice', but he is more cautious in his assessment of the poems. In the course of a list of the five major poems extending from the *Pastorals* to the *Essay on Man* by which Pope is not to be judged except under special conditions, he asserts:

> Nor must he be judged by his *Pastorals* and *Windsor Forest*, unless the judge will qualify his sentence by understanding into what context of historical principles these poems fall.

A fair-minded reader is always willing to make this qualification; but it means either that it makes no difference at all to his critical assessment or that almost any poem is worthy of some degree of esteem.

The *Pastorals* were in fact apprentice-work. Most of what Tillotson has to say about them is really a demonstration, with a wealth of detail, that Pope was engaged in an elaborate word-game, primarily as the amusement of an invalid, and then as a means of gaining reputation. As personal experience he could have had no interest in the subject-matter of the *Pastorals*. They express an interest in, and a familiarity with books, not nature. Warton's disappointment with their extreme literary quality has already been noted. That they owed much, if not most, to earlier authors was recognized from the start; but it has hardly been possible to realize the extent and variety of Pope's sources until the appearance of the Twickenham edition. In this matter of 'borrowing', as he calls it, the young Pope had an uneasy conscience. In 1706 he enquired of his mentor, Walsh:

> I wou'd beg your opinion too as to another point: It is how far the liberty of *Borrowing* may extend? . . . I desire you to tell me sincerely, if I have not stretch'd this License too far in these Pastorals?

The critic's answer was reassuring. Walsh wrote:

> As for what you ask of the *Liberty* of *Borrowing*; 'tis very evident the best *Latin* Poets have extended this very far; and none so far as *Virgil*, who is the best of them. As for the *Greek* Poets, if we cannot trace them so plainly, 'tis perhaps because we have none before them; 'tis evident that most of them borrow'd from *Homer*, and *Homer* has been accus'd of burning those that wrote before him, that his Thefts might not be discover'd. The best of the modern Poets in all Languages, are those that have the nearest copied the Ancients. Indeed in all the common subjects of Poetry, the Thoughts are so obvious (at least if they are natural) that whoever writes last, must write things like what have been said before: But they may as well applaud the Ancients for the Arts of

eating and drinking, and accuse the Moderns of having stol'n those Inventions from them; it being evident in all such cases, that whoever live first, must find them out. 'Tis true, indeed, . . . when there is one or two bright Thoughts stol'n, and all the rest is quite different from it, a Poem makes a very foolish figure: But when 'tis all melted down together, and the Gold of the Ancients so mixt with that of the Moderns, that none can distinguish the one from the other, I can never find fault with it. I cannot however but own to you, that there are others of a different opinion, and that I have shewn your Verses to some who have made that objection to them.

This abominable piece of literary criticism is significant. The ancients borrowed – or stole, for the 'borrowings' soon become 'thefts' – and as a modern cannot do better than copy the ancients, he might as well steal too. The art of writing poems is much the same as that of eating and drinking: we have no choice but to copy the ancients in both. It seems, however, that so long as the theft is well disguised, the moderns are to be pillaged like the ancients. Walsh does not make it clear what he means by the 'gold of the moderns': is it what is borrowed from a modern poet or what is supplied by a modern poet to 'melt down' with the gold of the ancients? I am inclined to think he means what has been borrowed from the moderns, since in his *Pastorals* Pope took even more freely from modern poets, such as Dryden, than he took directly from the classics, such as Virgil. Finally, Walsh admits candidly that his view of borrowing is by no means universal: some readers who had seen the manuscript took exception to Pope's 'liberty of borrowing'. This is an illuminating admission, for it makes nonsense of the often repeated assertion that in Pope's day borrowing was common and no one objected to it.

Walsh was a Whig politician, and it is likely that some of those to whom he had shown Pope's verses and who had taken exception to the borrowing were among Addison's politico-literary circle. At all events it was in this circle that Pope's first literary quarrels originated, and it was here that his reputation as a plagiarist was established right at the start of his career. It was a member of this circle who, in a pamphlet, dubbed Pope 'A—P—E', punning on his name.

Once he had Walsh's authority for wholesale borrowing, so long as it was skilfully done, Pope seems to have had no further compunction about it. The *Pastorals,* it is no exaggeration to say, are a mélange of echoes, borrowings, and commonplaces from appropriate contexts in the Latin poets, mainly in translation, and the English poets, dead or living, fused together into a mellifluous compound. Pope's principal

Latin sources are Virgil, Horace, Ovid, and Lucan; among his older English sources are Sidney, Spenser, Waller, Milton, Denham, and Cowley; recently dead poets from whom he borrowed were Oldham, Roscommon, Dryden, and Sedley; living poets whom Pope laid under contribution were Addison, Garth, Walsh, and Fenton. Random examples, not necessarily the most striking, of borrowings are: from the Latin poets –

> VIRGIL (*Eclogue V* in Dryden's translation):
> *Daphnis*, the Guest of Heav'n, with wondring Eyes,
> Views in the Milky Way the starry Skies.
> POPE (*Winter*).
> But see ! where *Daphne* wondring mounts on high,
> Above the Clouds, above the Starry Sky.

(It is usually claimed that Pope's borrowings are improvements: can anyone honestly claim this of the above example?)

> From MILTON (*Il Penseroso*):
> And every Herb that sips the dew.
> POPE (*Summer*):
> Once I was skill'd in ev'ry Herb that grew,
> And ev'ry Plant that drinks the Morning Dew;
> From a living contemporary, ADDISON (*The Campaign*):
> Or where the *Seine* her flow'ry fields divides,
> Or where the *Loire* through winding vineyards glides.
> POPE (*Summer*):
> In those fair Fields where Sacred *Isis* glides,
> Or elsewhere *Cam* his winding Vales divides?

Addison can hardly have regarded his younger rival's version of his lines as an improvement: the Seine and the Loire are accurately characterized, but the contrast between the Isis in its 'fair fields' (an echo perhaps of Milton) and the Cam dividing non-existent vales would be recognized by no one. Addison's couplet is probably based on experience; Pope's is mere word-play. Had Pope been in the least concerned with actuality, he would have done better to locate the Isis among the vales and the Cam amidst fields. It cannot even be said that Pope improved on Addison in the matter of melody: Addison has quite enough 's'-sounds, but Pope doubles the number.

An example of Pope's precocious virtuosity in improving his material and giving it smooth correctness is the famous 'Where'er you walk' quatrain, which, as we have seen, has been admired by more than one critic.

Where-e'er you walk, cool Gales shall fan the Glade,
Trees, where you sit, shall crowd into a Shade,
Where-e'er you tread, the blushing Flow'rs shall rise,
And all things flourish where you turn your Eyes.

(Summer, 73–76)

The origin of this conceit, as the Twickenham editor points out, is probably the legend connected with the birth of Aphrodite, who rose from the sea and appeared on the shores of Cyprus, whereupon grass sprang and flowers bloomed. The conceit was used by Persius and later by Ben Jonson. Two of Pope's contemporaries who used it were Granville and Charles Hopkins, but Pope's immediate inspiration was Waller's *At Pens-hurst,* in which he writes of the trees as follows :

If she sit down, with tops all towards her bow'd,
They round about her into Arbors crowd;
Or if she walk, in even ranks they stand,
Like some well-Marshal'd and obsequious band.

Some may think that Waller is more lively in presenting his trees as well-bred courtiers, and that Pope, in putting formal elegance first at all costs, loses in energy. His 'walk' and 'tread' are little more than interchangeable verbal counters.

'Criticism of the *Pastorals,*' writes the Twickenham editor, 'has ended from the beginning to prize the craftsmanship revealed in their verse and to minimise the worth of their substance . . . At any rate, an examination of the verse itself should be a means of gaining entry to whatever substance these poems possess.' We seem to be promised some revelation about the 'substance' of the *Pastorals,* but it never comes. We are thrown back on the brilliance of the versification, the skill of the craftsmanship. These qualities have surely been exaggerated. Giving Pope full credit for precocity, it must be admitted that his mellifluous smoothness has a soporific quality which tends to deaden the reader's ear to a certain amount of syntactical weakness and vapidity of thought. Take, for instance, these two lines from *Spring*:

Now Hawthorns blossom, now the Daisies spring,
Now Leaves the Trees, and Flow'rs adorn the Ground

Here the word-order of the second line is barbarous. Word-order in English is always of vital importance, because it is an uninflected language, and because so many words do duty as more than one part of speech. Until the verb is established as 'adorn', the word 'leaves' might be taken as a verb. 'Now leaves adorn the trees, and flow'rs the ground' would have been better, but Pope evidently preferred the awkward juxtaposition of 'leaves' and 'trees' to the equally awkward juxtaposition of 'flow'rs' and 'ground'. One feels that one of Pope's admirers should have told him that his line was impossible in any form.

A more extended passage is the lament for Daphne from *Winter*.

> No grateful Dews descend from Ev'ning Skies,
> Nor Morning Odours from the Flow'rs arise.
> No rich Perfumes refresh the fruitful Field,
> Nor fragrant Herbs their native Incense yield.
> The balmy *Zephyrs,* silent since her Death,
> Lament the Ceasing of a sweeter Breath.
> Th'industrious Bees neglect their Golden Store;
> Fair *Daphne's* dead, and Sweetness is no more!
>   No more the mounting Larks, while *Daphne* sings,
> Shall list'ning in mid Air suspend their Wings;
> No more the Birds shall imitate her Lays,
> Or hush'd with Wonder, hearken from the Sprays:
> No more the Streams their Murmurs shall forbear,
> A sweeter Musick than their own to hear,
> But tell the Reeds, and tell the vocal Shore,
> Fair *Daphne's* dead, and Musick is no more!
>   Her Fate is whisper'd by the gentle Breeze,
> And told in Signs to all the trembling Trees;
> The trembling Trees, in ev'ry Plain and Wood,
> Her Fate remurmur to the silver Flood;
> The silver Flood, so lately calm, appears
> Swell'd with new Passion, and o'erflows with Tears;
> The Winds and Trees and Floods her Death deplore,
> *Daphne,* our Grief! our Glory now no more!
>   But see! where *Daphne* wondring mounts on high
> Above the Clouds, above the Starry Sky.
> Eternal Beauties grace the shining Scene,
> Fields ever fresh, and Groves for ever green!
> There, while You rest in *Amaranthine* Bow'rs,
> Or from those Meads select unfading Flow'rs,
> Behold us kindly who your Name implore,
> *Daphne,* our Goddess, and our Grief no more!

In this passage Pope echoes a number of poets, including Dryden but draws most heavily on Oldham. 'Odours', 'perfumes' and 'incense' are interchangeable. Dr Johnson regretted the absurdity of the zephyr lamenting in silence. 'Rich', 'fragrant' and 'balmy' are gradus epithets, 'mounting' and 'gentle' are old commonplaces. 'Remurmur' (take from Dryden) and 'select' are inappropriate. The 'trees – breeze' rhyme is condemned by Pope himself in the *Essay on Criticism*. The rhymes throughout, as in all Pope's poems, are almost infallibly predictable. Some may consider it an advantage; I find it monotonous. Reading the passage as a whole, can anyone seriously speak of new life breathed into old commonplaces, or of brilliant versification as a substitute for poetic substance?

One of the most attractive and melodious passages in the *Pastorals* is the lament of Aegon for Doris in *Autumn*. It contains much graphic imagery, some of it original, and is suffused by that pleasing melancholy which reminds some critics of Virgil and Mozart. The *Pastorals* are here seen at their best, and it is possible to appreciate what the apprentice poet made of his materials. These are drawn from translations of Virgil's *Eclogues* by Dryden, John Caryll, and Stafford; Dryden's translation of Ovid's *Dido to Aeneas*; Milton's *Comus*; Garth's *Dispensary*, and Walsh's *Eclogues*. The two obvious blemishes are the unfortunate reference to the beneficent influence of Arcturus on the ripe grain (the star Arcturus was a bringer of storm and rain) and the bathos of

> The Shepherds cry, 'Thy Flocks are left a Prey —'
> Ah! what avails it me, the Flocks to keep,
> Who lost my Heart while I preserv'd my Sheep.

But the ingenuity with which Pope has melted together his various sources must be acknowledged. This can best be appreciated by studying the copious annotations in the Twickenham edition. With their help it is possible to reprint the lines, italicizing the words and phrases which Pope took directly (sometime with minor modification) from the sources listed above, but omitting Pope's own few italics. The passage thus appears as in the main a mellifluous blend of paraphrase and direct quotation from appropriate sources in Pastoral literature, with minimal touches drawn from personal observation either of nature or of graphic art.

> Resound ye Hills, resound my mournful Strain!
> Of *perjur'd* Doris, *dying* I *complain;*
> Here where the Mountains less'ning as they rise,
> Lose the low Vales, and steal into the Skies.
> While *lab'ring Oxen,* spent with Toil and Heat,
> In their *loose Traces* from the Field retreat;
> *While curling Smokes from Village-Tops* are seen,
> And the fleet *Shades* glide o'er the dusky Green.

Resound ye Hills, resound my mournful Lay!
Beneath yon Poplar oft we past the Day:
Oft on the *Rind* I carv'd her Am'rous *Vows*,
While She with *Garlands hung* the bending *Boughs*:
The *Garlands* fade, the *Vows* are worn away;
So dies her Love, and so my Hopes decay.
   Resound ye Hills, resound my mournful Strain!
Now bright Arcturus glads the teeming Grain,
Now Golden Fruits on loaded branches shine,
And grateful Clusters swell with floods of Wine;
Now blushing Berries paint the yellow Grove;
Just Gods! shall all things yield Returns but Love?
   Resound ye Hills, resound my mournful Lay!
The Shepherds cry, 'Thy Flocks are left a Prey —'
Ah! what avails it me the Flocks to keep,
Who lost my Heart while I preserv'd my Sheep.
Pan came and ask'd, *what Magick* caus'd my Smart,
Or what *Ill Eyes* malignant glances dart?
What Eyes but hers, alas, have Pow'r to move!
And is there *Magick* but what dwells in *Love*?
   Resound ye Hills, resound my mournful Strains!
I'll fly from Shepherds, Flocks and flow'ry Plains. —
From Shepherds, Flocks, and Plains, I may remove,
Forsake Mankind, and all the World – but Love!
I know thee Love! on foreign *Mountains bred*,
Wolves gave thee suck, and *savage Tygers fed*.
Thou wert from *Aetna's burning Entrails torn*,
Got by fierce Whirlwinds, and in Thunder *born*!
   Resound ye Hills, resound my mournful Lay!
Farewell ye Woods! adieu the Light of Day!
One *Leap* from *yonder Cliff* shall *end my Pains.*
No more ye Hills, no more resound my *Strains*!
   Thus sung the Shepherds till th'Approach of Night,
The Skies yet blushing with departing Light,
When falling Dews with Spangles deck'd the Glade,
And the *low Sun* had *lengthen'd* ev'ry Shade.

All the words and phrases in italics in the above lines represent echoes noted in the Twickenham edition; but it seems certain that Pope also took hints from *Lycidas*, which is, however, not there noted as a source. Nor has the Twickenham editor recorded the echo from *Paradise Lost,* I, in the phrase 'Aetna's burning Entrails'.

2 An Essay On Criticism

'The life of a Wit,' as Pope remarked in the preface to the 1717 edition of his poems, 'is a warfare upon earth.' Pope's warfare began from the moment he appeared in print. Those first steps in the literary world which he regarded as of such crucial importance did not go as well as he had hoped. Having taken them under such favourable auspices, he felt entitled to expect a favourable reception in the larger world of the coffee-houses and the periodicals. Whether or not the *Pastorals* were begun as the amusement of a sickly adolescent can never be certainly known. The ill-health consequent upon his contraction of spinal tuber-culosis soon after the age of twelve, and the sedentary nature of his life as a student denied a normal schooling, were causally interconnected, though the strands, physiological and temperamental, which composed the fabric of his existence can never be separated. He was at once spoilt and deprived, and the ambition to excel, to amount to something in the world, was built into all his activities from the start.

He saw his *Pastorals*, then, as a means of obtaining recognition. They were not recognized, and of this Ambrose Philips was in part the inno-cent cause. Philips' *Pastorals* were printed first in the *Miscellany* published by Tonson in 1709 in which Pope's *Pastorals* were the con-cluding item. There was no intention to slight the new author, but Pope felt slighted. His *Pastorals* attracted far less attention than Philips', which were more in line with the literary taste of the day. They reflected the interest in the native English tradition which looked back to Spenser, as distinct from the neo-classical ideals which belonged more to the seventeenth than to the eighteenth century. Collections of old English ballads were already being made, and Addison was soon to express his enthusiasm for *Chevy Chase*. Pope was out of sympathy with popular literature. Philips' *Pastorals* look stilted enough now, but they have a certain naïve freshness lacking in Pope's. It is easy enough, in the light of the subsequent achievements of the two poets, to sympa-thize with Pope; but it is by no means certain that to prefer Philips in 1709 was critically obtuse. Pope's disappointment over the reception accorded to him was exacerbated when in 1713 there appeared in Steele's paper, *The Guardian*, five essays on pastoral poetry which omitted to mention him but quoted freely from Philips. This was Pope's opportunity. He contributed a sixth essay to the series, unsigned, in which he quoted freely from his own *Pastorals* and made fun of Philips', while ironically pretending to prefer them. It has been maintained, on the one hand, that Pope's motive in this essay was personal enmity, and, on the other, that he was at least partly concerned with literary values. There can be little doubt, however, that his main concern was to draw attention to his own work. In this he was setting himself an example which he frequently followed.

In this way Pope embarked on his first literary quarrel. He never ceased to harry the enemy whom chance had provided, and Philips hit back. '[Pope's] malignity to Philips,' says Johnson, 'whom he had first made ridiculous, and then hated for being angry, continued too long.' In *A True Character of Mr. Pope*, 1716, ascribed at the time to Charles Gildon, but now regarded as the work of John Dennis, Pope is accused of double-dealing: Pope 'attempted to undermine Mr. *PHILIPS* in one of his *Guardians*, at the same time that the *Crocodile* smil'd on him, embrac'd him, and called him Friend . . .' There may well be some justice in this, since Pope was at the time in the process of transferring his allegiance from the Whigs to the Tories while remaining on good terms with both sides. A characteristic attack by Pope on Philips is the character of 'Macer', in which Philips is ridiculed for a literary practice of which Pope himself was guilty – that of advertising for contributions to miscellanies to supplement his own insufficient contributions. The idea that Pope waged unremitting war against Philips on account of his bad writing, and out of concern for literary standards, is fictitious; privately he expressed admiration for some of Philips' work, but he believed himself the victim of a conspiracy by the Addison circle to discredit him and deny him his deserts. The repeated sniping at the Addison circle was part of the 'warfare upon earth' by which the work and reputation of Pope were kept in the public eye.

Another of Pope's early enemies was the dramatist and critic, John Dennis. The origin of the quarrel is in some doubt. Pope wrote *An Essay on Criticism* in 1709, when he was twenty-one and Dennis fifty-two. Dennis was considered the ablest critic of the day, but he had recently had ill success as a dramatist. According to Norman Ault, Dennis, a highly irascible man, must have quarrelled with Pope in some coffee-house encounter. According to Dennis' own account, he had never met Pope. Bowles believed that Pope went out of his way to attack Dennis because the senior critic had ignored his *Pastorals*. I have seen no evidence to refute this suggestion, which seems to me reasonable. The fact that the year in which his *Pastorals* appeared, failing to make much of a hit with the critics, saw him direct his interest to the subject of criticism is surely significant. At all events when the *Essay* was published in 1711, it contained not merely one direct personal reference to Dennis as the irascible author of a failed tragedy, *Appius and Virginia*, as is sometimes stated, but a number of snide references to critics which readers might readily apply to Dennis. The overt reference to Dennis is in the following lines:

> Fear not the Anger of the Wise to raise;
> Those best can *bear Reproof*, who *merit Praise*.
> 'Twere well, might Criticks still this Freedom take;
> *But Appius* reddens at each Word you speak,
> And *stares Tremendous*! with a *threatening Eye*,
> Like some *fierce Tyrant* in *Old Tapestry*!

Sherburn calls this 'incautious'. It is more likely to be a piece of calculated effrontery. It seems to us mild enough, but in all the circumstances Dennis' anger is understandable. He immediately published his *Reflections . . . upon a late Rhapsody, call'd An Essay upon Criticism*. '. . . I not only found myself attack'd without any manner of Provocation on my side, and attack'd in my Person, instead of my Writings, by one who is wholly a Stranger to me, and at a time when all the World knew that I was persecuted by Fortune . . .' He goes on to accuse Pope of slyness and hypocrisy while professing candour, truth, friendship, and humanity. It is clear that Dennis has a chip on his shoulder and betrays the natural envy of a struggling and not too successful middle-aged author for a young man whom he believes to have attracted more attention in some literary circles than his work merits. A good deal of Dennis's *Reflections* is mere abuse of Pope's *Essay*, but there is a certain amount of just censure. Pope later silently emended the *Essay* at several points in conformity with Dennis's strictures. Dennis gives the *Essay* a full critical treatment, reserving his notorious and cruel personal attack on Pope for his final paragraph. 'As there is,' he writes, 'no Creature in Nature so venomous there is nothing so stupid and so impotent as a hunchback'd Toad.' Commenting on the *Reflections*, Sherburn says, 'No more cruel review ever greeted a young beginner.' The cruelty is undeniable, the circumstances understandable. What is important is the history of Pope's reactions to it. He had 'incautiously' declared war in a manner which made it very likely that the middle-aged critic would respond. That Dennis's response would be disproportionately violent and cruel was perhaps a calculated risk. Had Dennis's temperament been different, he would no doubt have laughed off the young beginner's attack. But he was without a sense of humour, at least so far as his own affairs were concerned, and Pope must have known this. To nickname Dennis by the title of his failed play may well have seemed as cruel as to refer to Pope's physical handicap. Moreover, it must be remembered that Dennis took Pope's reference to his blush of anger and apoplectic stare as an attack on his person. Spence later questioned Pope about his reactions.

> Spence: 'Did you never mind what your angry critics published against you?' – Never much: – only one or two things, at first. – When I heard, for the first time, that Dennis had written against me, it gave me some pain: – but it was quite over as soon as I came to look into his book, and found he was in such a passion.

At all events Pope was quick to realize the capital value of such an attack as Dennis's. Any ambitious young writer knows that defamation is better than neglect. In 1706 he had written to his friend Caryll that 'to be uncensured and to be obscure is the same thing'. Pope had stung the eminent critic to a reprisal, and this may well have been his prime object. Shortly after the appearance of Dennis's *Reflections* Pope wrote to Caryll, the Roman Catholic country gentleman for whose tolerant and placatory views he was always at pains to profess respect:

> I shall never make the least reply to him, not only because you advise me, but because I've ever been of opinion that if a book can't answer for its self to the public, 'tis to no sort of purpose for its author to do it.

For two years Pope kept his word to Caryll; but in 1713 Dennis printed a critical attack on Addison's tragedy of *Cato*. Dennis later said that Lintot published this at the instigation of Pope in order to make trouble. Sherburn says this was false, but elsewhere he calls Dennis honest, and certainly there is a directness about all that Dennis writes, crude as much of it is. At all events Pope, in order to ingratiate himself with Addison, whom he was then courting, took up the cudgels on his behalf, and attacked Dennis in an anonymous prose pamphlet, *The Narrative of Dr. Robert Norris*. Dr Norris was a quack curer of lunatics, here represented as attending on Dennis, the details of whose confinement to his bedchamber are drawn with gloating squalor. In the main the pamphlet makes tedious reading, and exceeds in cruelty Dennis's attack on Pope, because it is cold-blooded. It is an imitation of Swift's Bickerstaff pamphlets against Partridge. Pope lied to Caryll about its authorship, and Addison disowned it. Thackeray calls it 'a vulgar and mean satire'. Pope continued to pursue Dennis with lampoon and pamphlet, and Dennis replied in kind. The warfare was unremitting. The two men once made peace, but Pope broke it. The most virulent of his lampoons against the critic, then aged seventy-two, was printed anonymously in 1729:

Shou'd D —— s print how once you robb'd your Brother,
Traduc'd your Monarch, and debauch'd your Mother;
Say what revenge on D —— s can be had;
Too dull for laughter, for reply too mad?
Of one so poor you cannot take the law;
On one so old your sword you scorn to draw.
        Uncag'd then let the harmless Monster rage,
Secure in dullness, madness, want, and age.

Whether Pope's anonymous prologue to a benefit performance for the dying Dennis is to be taken at its face value is a matter of opinion. In it he refers to Dennis's old age, his blindness and his poverty. Some critics judge this to be ironical and question Pope's sincerity. To my mind there is a tone of relish and of equivocation in the lines:

As when that Hero who in each Campaign
Had brav'd the *Goth,* and many a *Vandal* slain,
Lay Fortune-struck, a Spectacle of Woe!
Wept by each Friend, forgiv'n by ev'ry Foe:
Was there a gen'rous, a reflecting Mind,
But pities *Belisarius,* Old and Blind?
Was there a Chief, but melted at the Sight?
A common Soldier, but who clubb'd his *Mite?*

It is worth while pausing to consider the nature of this characteristic quarrel, because it is now fashionable to deny the personal quality in Pope's vendettas and attribute them to a high-minded concern for literary values. The fact is that the two men had much in common, and the effect of Pope's inclusion of Dennis among his 'Dunces' has obscured Dennis's true qualities as a critic for over two hundred years. He was not a great critic, but in some respects he was a good one, maintaining throughout a long literary struggle the same standards and principles as are claimed for Pope. Much of his work had lost its original interest, but he does not deserve the virtual total neglect into which he fell. His works contain many tedious pages and much clumsy writing, but in his concern for neo-classical values and for a moral approach to literature he was on Pope's side. Like Pope, he admired Boileau and deplored the influence of Italian opera on popular taste. Dennis was above all serious, and thus became the butt of wits. Even Ayre, Pope's biographer and eulogist, has a word to say for Dennis – 'a Poet, and the greatest Critick of this Age'. In his earlier days he was considered a worthy associate for Congreve and Dryden.

Dennis is outspoken and unequivocal in his condemnation of plagiarism, about which he adopts a severely moral position, quite opposed to that of Walsh and his followers. In 1712 he wrote in *The Spectator*:

> . . . a Plagiary in general is but a scandalous Creature, a sort of a spiritual Outlaw, and ought to be treated as such by all the Members of the Commonwealth of Learning . . . how infinitely base is it . . . to deprive an Author of any thing that is valuable in him . . .? 'Tis only a Man's Thoughts and Inventions that are properly his: being alone things that can never be alienated from him, neither by Force nor Persuasion . . . and tho' another may basely usurp the Honour of them, yet they must for ever rightfully belong to their first Inventor . . . But Authors for the most part, and especially Poets, have nothing that can so much as be call'd their own but their Thoughts. 'Tis for those alone, and the glory which they expect from those, that they entirely quit their Pretensions to Riches . . . and therefore to endeavour to deprive them of those is exceedingly inhuman.

In his essay on *The Grounds of Criticism in Poetry*, 1704, Dennis shows himself to be a dedicated but somewhat clumsy literary theorist, wholeheartedly concerned for the future of English poetry, which he believed to have fallen from a state of grace. His design, he says, is 'to restore Poetry to all its Greatness, and to all its Innocence'. He goes on to say that poetry is utterly fallen throughout Europe, 'and upon its last Legs in *England*'. Dennis asserts passionately the indissoluble connection between poetry and virtue: '. . . Piety and Virtue was not only the first Original, but . . . has been, is and will be the only solid Basis, nay and the very Life and Soul of the Greater Poetry.' Then, somewhat illogically, he ascribes the fall of English poetry to neglect of the 'rules' as derived from the ancients; yet poetic genius is an inspired gift of God. Through a knowledge of rules we arrive at order, which is essential to the right management of all affairs. Dennis is unable to work out the interconnections between personal morality and his theory of order, between inspired genius and the application of artistic rules; but if his critical vision is a somewhat blurred one, he must be given credit for holding this vision passionately in an age of sophistication and cynicism. Despite repetition and circumlocution, he makes a brave effort to discover the aim and purpose of poetry and to relate it to the highest ideals of 'making mankind better and happier'.

> The final End of Poetry is to reform the Manners: As poetry is an Art,
> Instruction must be its final End . . .

Despite his confusion Dennis has a real idea of greatness in poetry,
where we wish to find 'that Spirit, that Passion and that Fire which so
wonderfully please'. With much of this Pope would, in theory at least,
have concurred. Indeed, his modern admirers credit him with putting
just such ideals into practice. Why, then, did he quarrel so bitterly, so
unrelentingly with the critic who held them? The reason is briefly, I
suggest, that Pope had little interest in the health of literature and
society in the abstract; he was too egocentric, too single-minded in the
cultivation of his own fame. Unlike Dennis, he held a competitive view
of the literary life. No doubt the older man was lacking in generosity,
and his critical assessments of Pope's work were coloured by personal
prejudice; nevertheless, he had aesthetic as well as personalistic objections to the writings he criticized. He gave Pope credit for smooth
versification (the 'correctness' enjoined by Walsh), but for little else. It
is clear that he found Pope's whole outlook and temperament too antipathetic to allow much room for admiration of his poems. For this, and
for the violence and directness of his attacks in articles and pamphlets,
Pope never forgave him.

That Pope's *Essay on Criticism* was not the sort of thing to appeal to
a man of Dennis's views, even apart from its references to himself,
can be partly explained if we accept the description of it given by
Brower.

> The *Essay on Criticism* has the bounce and go of verse by a terribly
> bright young man who has recently acquired all the 'right ideas', which
> he gets off with dazzling verbal skill and cheerful superiority.

As with all Pope's major poems, opinions as to the merits of the *Essay*
vary widely. Johnson and Hazlitt both admired it. The latter considered
it original. Sherburn is near the truth when he says that Pope 'was not
beguiled by any itch of originality: his method was scientific and induc-
tive: the experience of the past could be codified into guiding rules and
could show the proper temper and behaviour for the critic'. Lady Mary
Wortley Montagu, as reported by Spence, had no illusions about the
originality of the *Essay* and states bluntly the reactions of a contemporary

> I admired Mr. Pope's Essay on Criticism at first, very much, because I
> had not then read any of the ancient critics and did not know that it
> was all stolen.

So much for the view that Pope's contemporaries automatically appreciated learned references: Lady Mary was, by the standards of her time, a well-read woman. Undoubtedly the earliest readers were dazzled by the precocious sprightliness of the poem, but nobody took the critical ideas expressed in it very seriously. Leonard Welsted, another lifelong opponent of Pope whose work has been unduly neglected because of his inclusion in the *Dunciad,* expresses a more than personalistic disapprobation for the *Essay* in his *Dissertation concerning the Perfection of the English Language, the State of Poetry, &c.* Published in 1724 and addressed to his patron, the Duke of Newcastle, it is worthy of attention as having some originality, and as showing that critical ideas now considered 'Romantic' circulated in the heyday of Augustan neo-classicism. Welsted does not name Pope's *Essay,* but everyone must have known that he had it in mind. He disparages 'rules' for writing, and attacks modern attempts to compose an *Ars Poetica,* as 'nothing but a pert insipid heap of commonplace'. He goes on:

> nor do any, nor all of them put together, contribute in any considerable degree, if they contribute at all, towards the raising or finishing a good genius. The truth is, they touch only the externals or form of the thing, without entering into the spirit of it; they play about the surface of Poetry, but never dive into its depths; the secret, the soul of good writing, is not to be come at through such mechanic Laws; the main graces, and the cardinal beauties of this charming art, lie too retired within the bosom of Nature, and are of too fine and subtle an essence, to fall under the discussion of Pedants, Commentators, or trading Criticks, whether they be heavy Prose drudges, or more sprightly Essayers in Rime. These beauties, in a word, are rather to be felt than described. . . . What instruction shall convey to him [a writer] that flame, which can alone animate a work, and give it the glow of Poetry? And how, or by what industry, shall be learned, among a thousand other charms, that delicate contexture in writing, by which the colours, as in the rainbow, grow out of one another, and every beauty owes its lustre to a former, and gives being to a succeeding one?

As with Dennis there is much in Welsted with which Pope could have agreed, if temperamental and personal differences during this period had made it possible to hold a serious literary debate; but non-literary allegiances were too strong. Religion and politics divided men who might have had much to give each other: even without such differences Pope scarcely ever forgave a fellow-writer who did not acknowledge his supremacy. An attack on Pope by Welsted and James Moore-Smythe entitled *An Epistle to Mr. A. Pope,* 1730, refers to Charles

Gildon, one of Addison's Whig circle at Button's, and adds an amusing footnote:

> Charles Gildon, dismissed from the Duke [of Buckingham]'s pension and favour, on account of his obstinacy in refusing to take oaths to Pope's supremacy.

In the battle of wits in which he engaged on many fronts Pope's superior wit usually, but not always, triumphed. He immortalized and eclipsed Welsted in the *Dunciad* in one neat line, as unfair as it is effective:

> *Flow Welsted, flow! like thine inspirer, Beer,*

of which line Welsted's posthumous editor, John Nichols, wrote in 1787: 'The ridicule attached to his supposed "Inspirer" has had the effect of a magic spell, in depressing what to WELSTED himself seems to have been matter of little concern' – that is, his reputation; for Welsted was essentially modest and unassuming. I know of no evidence that Welsted had a particular addiction to beer. He was in fact a wine-drinker. The reference to beer was probably a veiled sneer, not at Welsted's taste, but at his poverty.

A very fair statement of the modern view of the *Essay on Criticism*, as well as an example of the continuing power of Pope's poems to evoke controversy among his readers – and even an ambivalent attitude in the mind of a single reader – is made in *The Times Literary Supplement* for 29 December 1961 by the anonymous reviewer of the Twickenham edition. After calling the *Essay* 'outrageously and exquisitely clever' the writer goes on:

> It is not that its critical content is in any clear sense original. It is rather a capsule which contains, in a mere 700-odd lines, the essence of Dryden's liberal neoclassicism recast in bold and well-fashioned rhyming slogans. The matter is 'all stolen', as Lady Mary Wortley Montagu rudely put it. More seriously, it is disfigured by Pope's characteristic evasiveness and repellent self-pity. His original contribution to Augustan criticism is slight. In his early career, as in the *Essay* and in the 1717 preface . . . critical statements are either truistic, or derivative (usually of Dryden), or disingenuously dismissive, as of a young man anxious to forestall attacks upon his own works.

With considerable perspicacity the reviewer elaborates his charge of 'evasiveness':

The *Essay* is marvellously finished, but it does not ring quite true in itself, and it does not ring true at all when we consider Pope's later career. . . . Duplicity is his *forte*; for though he inherited a useful fund of question-begging neoclassical terms like 'nature' and 'art', no other Augustan critic so exalts the possibilities they offered in exquisite evasion.

Is it fair to suggest that Pope's evasiveness is catching? The *Essay on Criticism*, it seems, is 'exquisitely clever', but what value does the reviewer place on exquisite encapsulation of critical commonplaces? Nevertheless, the point about Pope's evasiveness in the *Essay* is a good one. Pope was evasive because he was unoriginal. He had no critical principles of his own to put forward, and was concerned above all to impress his readers with a dazzling show of verbal pyrotechnics. The *Essay* is in fact a piece of versification in a very literal sense: the whole thing was first drafted in prose. The sources from which ideas and hints were derived fall into four groups: the ancients (mainly Horace, Cicero, Quintilian, Petronius, and Longinus); Renaissance critics such as Montaigne, Bacon, and Vida; seventeenth-century French critics (La Bruyère, Rapin, St Evremond and, above all, Boileau); and a host of Restoration and contemporary English poets, philosophers and critics – among whom are Waller, Davenant, Denham, Rochester, Suckling, Roscommon, Locke, Sprat, Temple, Prior, Garth, Dennis, Gildon, Atterbury, and Wycherley; and – the greatest single influence – Dryden.

A characteristic example of Pope's method is offered by the following two couplets:

> In search of *Wit* these lose their *common Sense*,
> And then turn Criticks in their own Defence.
> Each burns alike, who can, or cannot write,
> Or with a *Rival*'s or a *Eunuch*'s spite.

This is an ingenious conflation of elements from Dryden and Rochester:

> The Blockhead stands excus'd, for wanting Sense;
> And Wits turn Blockheads in their own defence.
>   (Dryden, *Prologue to Amphitryon*)

> They write Ill, and they who ne'er durst write,
> Turn Critiques, out of meer Revenge and Spight.
>   (Dryden, *Prologue to the Second Part of the Conquest of Granada*)

'Twas Impotence did first this Vice begin,
Fooles censure Wit, as Old men raile of Sin,
Who envy Pleasure which they cannot tast ...
(Rochester, *Epilogue to Circe*)

The *Essay* has been admired for slickly mnemonic couplets like the
following:

Be *Homer*'s Works your *Study,* and *Delight,*
Read them by Day, and meditate by Night,

but how much of the credit should go to Pope and how much to his
sources? For Pope had read Roscommon's translations of Horace's
Ars Poetica:

Consider well the *Greek* Originals,
Read them by Day, and think of them by Night

and Tate and Brady's version of Psalm I:

But makes the perfect Law of God
his Business and Delight;
Devoutly reads therein by Day,
and meditates by Night.

Pope was not above stealing from Tate and sneering at him in the
Dunciad.

Of the twenty passages from the *Essay* cited in the *Oxford Dictionary
of Quotations* only three, according to the Twickenham edition are
without sources in the words or thoughts of earlier writers. Two of these
are in no way remarkable; the other is the favourite tag,

To Err is *Humane*; to Forgive, *Divine.*

Despite its appearance of transparency, perhaps this line conceals an
element of equivocation: does the future author of the *Dunciad* mean
that forgiveness is God's business, not man's?

One of the most frequently admired passages is that on onomatopoeia:

True Ease in Writing comes from Art, not Chance,
As those move easiest who have learn'd to dance.
'Tis not enough no Harshness gives offence,
The *Sound* must seem an *Eccho* to the *Sense.*
Soft is the Strain when *Zephyr* gently blows,
And the *smooth Stream* in *smoother Numbers* flows;

> But when loud Surges lash the sounding shore,
> The *hoarse rough Verse* shou'd like the *Torrent* roar.
> When *Ajax* strives, some Rock's vast Weight to throw,
> The Line too *labours,* and the Words move *slow*;
> Not so, when swift *Camilla* scours the Plain,
> Flies o'er th'unbending Corn, and skims along the Main.

Brower may be right in saying that the eighteenth century was readier than later readers to accept the *Essay on Criticism* as a poem: 'Being thoroughly familiar with what was being said, they could relax and enjoy Pope's marvellous "feat of words" as he led them through familiar intellectual scenes.' (As we have seen, however, Lady Mary Wortley Montagu's relaxed enjoyment of the *Essay* occurred before, not after, she became familiar with its sources.) As a piece of intellectual high spirits on the part of a young man adapting quotations from Vida, Boileau, Milton, Roscommon, Dryden, and Garth, the lines on onomatopoeia are entertaining enough. But was the eighteenth century really any more impressed than we are by platitudes like 'True Ease in Writing comes from Art, not Chance' and 'The *Sound* must seem an *Eccho* to the *Sense*'? Who ever said that ease in writing came by chance? As for the fuss about onomatopoeia, it seems to evidence a very superficial view of poetry. For the fact is that the English language (whatever may be said of Greek and Latin) is such that it is impossible to attend closely to meaning without attending to sound. Indeed, sound is part of sense. This was known instinctively by the Elizabethans. The Twickenham editor quotes a line from Garth's *Dispensary,* 'The Surges gently dash against the Shoar', presumably as a bad example, but the line is bad, not because it sounds wrong, but because it is nonsense.

Pope is so often praised for the limpidity of his verse that readers are inclined not to notice how often he is obscure in thought and unnatural in expression. It is difficult at first glance to find any meaning, for instance in the couplet

> *Art* from that Fund each *just Supply* provides,
> Works *without Show,* and *without Pomp* presides.

'Fund' here means the inexhaustible resources of Nature. The word-order is so twisted that it is not immediately obvious that 'Works' is a verb dependent on 'Art'. When this is realized, one at first imagines that there is some real antithesis in the second line, but this proves to be wrong; 'without Pomp presides' (a weak rhyme for 'provides') adds nothing to what is said in 'Works without Show'. In fact Dennis was right to condemn the couplet as merely an elaboration of the old commonplace *'Ars est celare artem'*, 'the common Subject that Pedants give their Boys to make Themes and Declamations upon'. Pope is doing no more than piously repeating the old commonplace which much of his writing, certainly the *Essay on Criticism,* entirely fails to live up to.

In the end intellectual high spirits weary when used, not to explore unfamiliar paths, to discover new truths, but to display the writer's wit and wide reading; platitudes and commonplaces bore us. On the other hand, you may find mental exhilaration in studying the dexterity with which a writer adapts the words and sentiments of others to make a mellifluous compound. You may find the old commonplaces inspired with new life. My own feeling is that, if you admire the *Essay on Criticism,* it may be because Pope's virtuosity has succeeded in blinding you to the emptiness and derivative quality of most of what he says. It is hard to believe that, in a passage like the following the references to Virgil, Vida, Cowley, Sheffield, and Dryden were considered by all of Pope's readers a sufficient compensation for the irrelevance of their content and the empty rhetoric of their expression:

> Hail *Bards Triumphant* ! born in *happier Days;*
> *Immortal* Heirs of *Universal* Praise !
> Whose Honours with Increase of Ages *grow,*
> As Streams roll down, *enlarging* as they flow !
> Nations *unborn* your mighty Names shall sound,
> And Worlds applaud that must not yet be *found* !
> Oh may some Spark of *your* Coelestial Fire
> The last, the meanest of your Sons inspire,
> (That on weak Wings, from far, pursues your Flights;
> *Glows* while he *reads,* but *trembles* as he *writes*)
> To teach vain Wits a Science *little known,*
> T'*admire S*uperior Sense, and *doubt* their own !

3 The Rape of the Lock

Pope's literary career falls into three main periods: that of the pastoral and descriptive poems, the 'heroi-comical' *Rape of the Lock,* the so-called 'romantic' poems, and a number of translations and adaptations; next, the period of the Homer translations and the edition of Shakespeare; and finally, that of the *Essay on Man,* the *Dunciad,* the Horatian epistles and satires. The first period ended with the first collected edition of the poems in 1717, by which time the publication of the *Iliad* translation had begun. The most considerable work in this volume was *The Rape of the Lock,* first printed anonymously in 1712 as a poem in two cantos and subsequently much enlarged, to appear in 1714 in five cantos. Like all Pope's major poems, it was undertaken either as a tribute to, or at the suggestion of someone he wished to please. The original occasion of the *Rape* was a request by his benefactor, John Caryll, to write a poem making fun of a quarrel between two ancient Catholic families; the quarrel had broken out when Lord Petre formerly Caryll's ward, had offended Arabella Fermor by snipping off one of her ringlets. Pope later said that the lady was at first pleased with the poem, and that it had done much to reconcile the two families After its first appearance in print, however, the lady took offence a innuendoes and indecencies pointed out by friends; but Pope endea voured to pacify her in a dedication to the enlarged edition of 1714 He later stated that this edition sold 3,000 copies in four days, and tha two further editions were called for by the end of the year. The perio was one of political unrest, culminating in the Jacobite rising of 1715 In the spring of that year Pope exploited the situation by publishing under the assumed name of Esdras Barnvelt, a *Key to the Lock,* whic pretended to prove that Pope's poem was a dangerous political satir This clever hoax, described by Sherburn as 'delicious burlesque', wa an astute piece of self-publicity. More than one critic has remarked o Pope's skill and pertinacity as a publicist for his own work. The *Key t the Lock,* published at the age of twenty-seven, is his first considerab essay in the art of self-advertisement.

Despite the immediate success of the *Rape,* it seems not to hav attracted much critical attention in the press during Pope's lifetime. The *Spectator* Addison damned it with faint praise; in a play, *A Ne*

Rehearsal, 1714, Gildon made a general attack on Pope in the character of Sawney Dapper (perhaps a reference to the coxcomb Dapperwit in the *Rape*) as ' a young poet of the modern stamp, an easy versifier, and a contemner secretly of all others'. Dennis wrote a pamphlet against the *Rape,* but withheld publication for fourteen years, until Pope broke their truce by attacking Dennis in the *Dunciad.* There is not much substance in Dennis's pamphlet; serious as it is in its censure of the *Rape* for lack of moral purpose, it is unduly weighted by personal prejudice, and Dennis had not Pope's gift for making malice sound like truth.

The *Rape* appears to have evoked no other printed criticism during Pope's lifetime. In the chorus of praise which began to be heard after his death Warton's was one of the earliest voices and set the tone for later critics. He mentions all of Pope's principal sources, but considers that Pope improved on some of them, notably Vida and even Shakespeare. Writing in 1959, Brower remarks:

> In the dramatic image of the *Rape of the Lock* Pope created a native Augustan myth, as later readers have instinctively and perhaps naïvely demonstrated, by taking the poem for the stock symbol of the 'Age of Queen Anne'.

This conception of the *Rape* evidently originated with Warton, who, it will be remembered, said that it is 'the best satire extant; . . . it contains the truest and liveliest picture of modern life'. He also anticipated the attitude of Romantic critics who see in the *Rape* more imagination than is evident elsewhere in Pope. Nevertheless his praise is not unqualified:

> It is in this composition, Pope principally appears a poet; in which he has displayed more imagination than in all his other works taken together. It should however be remembered, that he was not the first former and creator of those beautiful machines, the sylphs; on which his claim to imagination is chiefly founded. He found them existing ready to his hand; but has, indeed, employed them with singular judgment and artifice.

Johnson found the *Rape* 'the most attractive of all ludicrous compositions'; but it was left to the Romantic generation to accord the poem extravagant and unconditional praise. On this point even Bowles and Byron were united. Bowles, in the course of a eulogistic account, called it wholly original, and Byron thought it 'sublime'. 'Do you wish,' he asks, 'for invention, imagination, sublimity, character? seek them in the Rape of the Lock.' Hazlitt's well-known enthusiasm for the 'filligree' aspect of the poem is worth some attention, since, like Byron's remarks, it well illustrates the vagueness of much Romantic criticism. He says, 'It is admirable in proportion as it is made of nothing.' He compares the poem to a spider's web. 'It is made of gauze and silver spangles.' Everything glitters. 'Airs, languid airs, breathe around; . . . No pains are spared, no profusion of ornament, no splendour of poetic diction, to set off the meanest things. The balance between the concealed irony and the assumed gravity, is as nicely trimmed as the balance of power in Europe. The little is made great and the great little. You hardly know whether to laugh or weep. It is the triumph of insignificance, the apotheosis of foppery and folly. It is the perfection of the mock-heroic!' There is nothing like this sort of writing for blinding a reader's judgement. 'Perfection' is a word which should be used with caution. I have already referred to an obvious imperfection in one of the very passages Hazlitt quotes in illustration – the description of Belinda and her ringlets at the beginning of Canto II. The Twickenham editor also points out what he calls an 'oversight' by Pope – the use of the epithet 'graceful' twice in six lines. Nor can the line 'And, like the sun, they shine on all alike' be considered flawless. The passage is not 'made of nothing'; it is made, to a considerable extent, of the kind of multiple references, overt or concealed, that we meet with everywhere in Pope's poems – in this case to Virgil, Chaucer, Shakespeare, Shadwell, and Dryden, among others.

Post-Romantic criticism has been inclined to greater caution in its assessment of the *Rape*. Stephen finds it 'admirable after its kind', but deplores its sneering attitude to women. Sutherland admires its 'lovely absurdities'. Dobrée's account of the poem stresses the mock-heroic aspect and seems aimed at proving that it is light verse. Tillotson, while praising the poem, considers it to be one of the poems by which Pope is not to be judged. 'Historical study,' he asserts in his Preface to the Twickenham edition of the *Rape*, 'is obligatory for any student of Pope.' Some readers, both in Pope's time and later, have diagnosed in the poem anti-religious as well as misogynistic tendencies. Wilson Knight, on the other hand, claims that 'the poem is not iconoclastic but holds a warm humanism'. Throwing moderation out of the window he refers to a passage in the *Rape* as being 'done with a glorious sense of the trivial sublimated to the heroic stature'; and with characteristic panache, 'Shakespeare,' he says, 'gives us drama and Milton epic, and Pope builds from both in *The Rape of the Lock*'. Stephen, however, considered that Pope vulgarized Shakespeare in his delineation of the sylph Ariel.

The poem has proved very popular among modern American critics

I have already discussed Brower's encomium on the *Rape* as a 'native Augustan myth', and it should also be noted that he admires the prefatory dedication to Arabella Fermor as 'a perfect example of the virtue he recommends' – that is, moderation and good humour. It is also an example of patronizing superiority to women. Root, as we have seen, appears to be back in the 'fillagree' age of rapturous question-begging in his praise of 'the nice craftsmanship of a watchmaker' and the superlative assessment quoted on an earlier page: 'On any principle of criticism it is a great masterpiece of poetic art, one of the permanent achievements of English poetry.' This is the kind of writing which has got evaluative criticism into bad odour.

It was Austin Warren who definitively discredited the 'fillagree' attitude and pointed a new direction for critical discussion of the *Rape* in twentieth-century terms. True, he is not wholly free from the question-begging epithet to which all critics sometimes have recourse, even when they deprecate it. To refer once again to a passage quoted earlier

> Zeugma, the joining of two unlike objects governed by a single verb, is of course a form of pun; yet this verbal play constitutes one of Pope's most poetical resources in the *Rape* . . .

One of the examples he quotes is the line:

> Or stain her Honour, or her new Brocade.

Other examples come to mind, for instance:

> When Husbands or when Lap-dogs breathe their last

It is difficult to see what is especially 'poetical' about this device, used as it generally is to underline a sneer. However, Warren is more guarded in his appreciation of the *Rape* than some of his compatriots. Indeed, it is not easy to be quite sure about what value he places on it.

> What keeps it from being that filigree artifice which the romantics saw (and praised) is its playing with fire, especially the fires of sex and religion. Though Pope was scarcely a 'good Catholic', his parents were devout; and he is writing of an 'old Catholic' society; and many of his effects involve the suggestion of blasphemous parallels: the linking of English folklore and the Lives of the Saints . . .

I doubt if even a good Catholic would have considered this blasphemous. Pope had no real interest in folk-lore. What he knew of it was borrowed from Shakespeare. But there was nothing new, and certainly nothing blasphemous, in linking religion with folk-lore; it had been done ever since the conversion of Britain. Many good Catholics in

Pope's time could still enjoy Bishop Corbet's *The Fairies' Farewell; or God-a-Mercy Will:*

> By which we note the Fairies
> Were of the old profession;
> Their songs were Ave Maryes,
> Their daunces were procession.

Warren goes on:

> What, for religion, is got by parody parallel is, for sexual morality, managed by insinuation.

He is on surer ground here. He might indeed have pointed to the title of the poem as a sexually suggestive pun, and to the Baron's seizure of the lock as a sexually symbolic act. It is evident from Pope's essay on pastoral poetry that he was aware, as no doubt his contemporaries were, of the sexual innuendo in the image of a key in a lock.[1] Certainly it was the veiled indecencies in the poem which angered the Fermor family.

Warren's view of the poem sets the tone for the first full-length study, *Pope: The Rape of the Lock,* by J. S. Cunningham, 1961.

> An irrepressible jeu d'esprit, the poem is also a serious anatomy of 'polite' behaviour, and probes the ageless hurts and pretences of the sex war.

In an introduction to this monograph David Daiches adopts a position opposed to that of Tillotson who, in his introduction to the Twickenham edition, it will be remembered, regards a historical approach as 'obligatory'. Daiches deprecates biographical and other extraneous considerations and calls for clarification and evaluation. He maintains that 'How good is this work and why?' is the kind of question the student should ask himself. I do not know any method of evaluating a poem without going outside it. In a detailed exegesis three times as long as the poem itself, Cunningham's account is so illuminating and so enthusiastic as to make it almost unnecessary for the student to have any reactions himself. He appears to start from the premiss that the *Rape* is a masterpiece and therefore that any attitude other than admiration is out of the question. He believes that the aim of the poem is deflatory, praising Pope's satire for pointing out how the *beau monde* inflates triviality into a rite. What he fails to note is that Pope

[1] See the author's *The Everlasting Circle,* pp. 249–250 and Introduction (p. 22), London, 1960.

thoroughly enjoyed the social rite, lingering on it with almost the loving envy of a wallflower. The whole of Pope's life-style is that of a man eager to be at home in the fashionable world and enjoy the intimacy of beautiful women. Whatever we may think of the pruriency of the passages connected with Belinda, we cannot ignore its existence. The usual line of approach by modern critics to the *Rape* (as well as to the *Dunciad*) is that the tradition of serious epic having failed, Pope was obliged to turn his hand to burlesque epic. Pope told Spence that, had he not embarked on the translation of Homer, he himself would have attempted to write an original epic. His real reason for not doing so was that serious epic was impossible in an unheroic age, and Pope was not the man to attempt what he felt instinctively would not appeal to the fashionable reading public. As Cunningham points out:

> Mock-heroic was, then, an invaluable tactic for Pope. It turned to account his embarrassment with some features of epic itself and of the epic tradition . . .

I maintain, despite some critics' assertions to the contrary, that the effect of the mock-heroic, whatever Pope's intention, was to deflate serious poetry. Unless a critic is prepared to make some sort of comparative evaluation of epic and mock-epic, he exposes himself to the charge of considering burlesque as as good as the real thing.

Cunningham's monograph reproduces a number of current attitudes about Pope, for instance the anti-Arnold attitude. He deprecates what he calls Arnold's distinction between the poetry of imagination and that of ratiocination. But Arnold was far from being the first in this field; Warton, cited by Cunningham with approval, had made the same distinction. So, by implication, had Welsted, Pope's exact contemporary. It is a valid distinction, not to be obscured by attributing it to Arnold. Cunningham also admires Pope's versification, but is far too sophisticated to let himself be thought to regard it as being an end in itself.

> But however much his poetry compels *awareness* of its skills, Pope in the long run defies discussion in terms of mere verse technique; indeed, these terms were for long the faint praise used to damn him as an accomplished metronome. The metrical skills *are* vital: fastidious without seeming laboured, dexterous with a seemingly nonchalant sureness of touch. But in talking of Pope's couplets at their best, we should think not only of his *fitting* material *into* the metrical form but also of an intimate formative interplay between the two, each reacting upon the other. The couplet

can be as intimately tied, and as subtly responsive, to a creative intelligence, as forms apparently much 'freer', like mature Shakespearean blank verse.

This is to have your cake and eat it. Leaving aside the question of how good poetry is which 'compels awareness of its skills' – *Ars est celare artem* is a maxim Pope never learned – we may note that Cunningham seems to be saying, 'Pope's verse is marvellous, of course, but this isn't important'. We may note, too, the by now familiar investiture of Pope with the Shakespearean halo. What does *'apparently* much "freer"', *like* mature Shakespearean blank verse' imply, if not that the *Rape* is in the same class as *Antony and Cleopatra*?

Much of Cunningham's study is taken up with detailed illustration of Pope's verbal dexterity, but the main effect of this is to demonstrate the basic monotony and repetitiveness of the mock-heroic mode, with its excessive reliance on bathos and deflation. Dennis was no doubt exaggerating when he said that the *Rape*, though described as 'heroi-comical', has not a single jest in it, but it is true that one particular jest – the antithetic deflatory zeugma – is repeated a great many times. However, Cunningham is not without such higher resonances as the anti-romanticism of modern criticism permits. Writing of the conclusion to the poem, he says:

> In the teeth of this series of discrepancies the last paragraph earns its genuine resonance. That it does so is partly owing to Pope's use of the sun image, which has been, in varying ways, associated with Belinda throughout. . . . Fragile as precious china, transient as daylight, her natural element, Belinda's beauty is given its fitting homage, in a confluence of romantic exaggeration and epic sonority . . .

If this study has the effect of sending readers back to Pope's text, it has its educational value. But it seems to me that Cunningham turns a blind eye to a number of defects in the *Rape* – its self-proclaiming virtuosity as a *tour de force,* its ostentation of classical reading, its sneering patronage of women, the assumed right of a man in a man's world to be smutty about them.

A further feature of the *Rape of the Lock* which I believe, as a matter of cardinal principle, to detract from its value as poetry is the lack of originality. Some critics, it is true, so far from regarding this as a defect, consider it a virtue, since they set no store on originality and prefer a multiplicity and variety of literary reference. There is a tendency in anti-historical criticism to ignore the concealed borrowing with which the whole texture of the *Rape* is interwoven, and point with delighted approval to those which the average reader is intended to detect – the conscious burlesque echoes of Homer, Virgil, or Milton. For instance, in the much praised passage at the end of Canto III describing the snipping of the lock, the Baron's scissors accidentally cut a 'wretched sylph' in half. Then occurs the line:

> But Airy Substance soon unites again.

In his own notes Pope points out the parallel with *Paradise Lost,* VI, 330, in which Satan's 'airy substance' reunites after being wounded by the sword of Michael. I do not know by what canon of criticism this is to be considered a happy stroke, unless we are supposed to admire mere cleverness and a 'pert' facility in sending up the classics. We are expected to approve the ease with which an unheroic age compensates for being unable to write heroic poetry, epic or religious, by making fun of it. It is a matter of taste.

Those who insist, however, on an historical approach pay more attention to the unoriginality of the poem. The Twickenham editor, after a discussion of Boileau's *Lutrin* and Garth's *Dispensary,* two of the major sources for Pope's mock-epic, comments, 'When Pope came to write his poem he had little left to invent'. Boileau's poem, which he claimed to be original, was, for the succeeding age, a prototype for a kind of social satire which enjoyed a considerable vogue. Until the appearance of the *Rape,* Samuel Garth's *The Dispensary,* 1699, was the most popular English example of the *genre.* 'A comparison with Garth,' the Twickenham editor declares, 'enforces Pope's superiority.' It is a comparison which the ordinary reader finds it hard to make, because Garth has long been out of print and is disregarded. His name does not appear in any but specialized bibliographies, and nothing of his is given in the Oxford books of English verse. But Pope was proud to recall his praise and willing to borrow from him repeatedly.

> To die, is landing on some silent shore,
> Where billows never break, nor tempests roar:
> Ere well we feel the friendly stroke, 'tis o'er.
> The wise through thought th'insults of death defy;
> The fools, through blest insensibility.
> 'Tis what the guilty fear, the pious crave;
> Sought by the wretch, and vanquished by the brave.
> It eases lovers, sets the captive free;
> And, though a tyrant, offers liberty.

Written before the death of Dryden, this is surely excellent verse, as lively and pointed as much in Dryden or Pope. As a whole *The*

Dispensary is quite as lively, if not as light, as the *Rape* and is quite unjustly forgotten. Although it owes much to Boileau's poem, it is more original than Pope's. It concerns the dispute between the Royal College of Physicians and the apothecaries about the dispensing of free medicine for the poor – a satire, as it were, in favour of a national health service. Of wider social interest than the *Rape,* it has a good-humoured largeness of conception, but there is abundance of light and effective satire. The topical interest in the portraits of the doctors and apothecaries must have been considerable.

> All night the sage in pensive tumult lay,
> Complaining of the slow approach of day;
> Oft turned him round, and strove to think no more
> Of what shrill Colon said the day before.
> Cowslips and poppies o'er his eyes he spread,
> And Salmon's works he laid beneath his head.

It is sheer prejudice to claim that Pope wrote better than this, though in the *Dunciad*, written nearly thirty years after *The Dispensary*, he perfectly caught Garth's manner. Small wonder that some of his contemporaries regarded him as a sedulous ape.

> Nigh where Fleet ditch descends in sable streams,
> To wash his sooty Naiads in the Thames.

This too is Garth, though anyone would take it for Pope. In Garth's Canto VI there is also a mock-Virgilian description of a visit to Hades by Celsus, under the guidance of Health, to consult dead doctors. Here are a few lines from the account of the home of Chaos:

> Here his forsaken seat old Chaos keeps;
> And, undisturbed by form, in silence sleeps;
> O grisly wight, and hideous to the eye,
> An awkward lump of shapeless anarchy.

Apart from Garth and Boileau, Pope's major sources are *Le Comte de Gabalis* by the Abbé Villars, from which he took the idea of the sylphs, deriving details as to their behaviour from *A Midsummer Night's Dream* and *The Tempest*; and Vida's *Sacchia*, from which he imitated the description of the game of ombre. Among other sources too numerous to list in full are: the Classics in translation (Homer, Virgil, Horace, and Ovid); Florio and Spenser; the Vulgate; Racine; Milton, Davenant, Waller, Denham, Sedley, Dennis, Dorset, Ambrose Philips, Eusden, Prior, Pomfret, Addison, and Blackmore; the *Spec-*

tator and *Guardian*. It will be noted that Pope did not scruple to borrow from writers he afterwards pilloried in the *Dunciad*, such as Blackmore, Eusden, Philips, and Dennis. But in mock-heroic anything goes.

The joke about husbands and lapdogs ('When Husbands or when Lap-dogs breathe their last') is at least as old as Juvenal and had made its most recent appearance in *The Tatler*. But the closest parallel to Pope's line occurs in Farquhar's *Sir Harry Wildair*, 1701:

> Shall I tell you, the Character I have heard of a fine Lady? A fine Lady can laugh at the Death of her Husband, and cry for the Loss of a Lap Dog . . .

To Pope's readers the joke, therefore, was evidently something of a chestnut, though 'ne'er so well expressed'. Another well-polished chestnut in the popular:

> The hungry Judges soon the Sentence sign,
> And Wretches hang that Jury-men may Dine.

This 'hungry judge' appears in the plays of Congreve and Wycherley. But the most persistent resonance to be heard in the *Rape* is probably that of classical poetry in the language and accents of Dryden.

> Then prostrate falls, and begs with ardent Eyes
> Soon to obtain, and long possess the Prize:
> The Pow'rs gave Ear, and granted half his Pray'r,
> The rest, the Winds dispers'd in empty Air.

In the first couplet Pope 'cleverly adapts', to quote the Twickenham editor, Dryden's translation of the *Aeneid*:

> Him, the fierce Maid beheld with ardent Eyes;
> Fond and Ambitious of so Rich a Prize.

And the second couplet is a conflation from two sources – Dryden's *Aeneid*:

> *Apollo* heard, and granting half his Pray'r,
> Shuffled in Winds the rest, and toss'd in empty Air

and Dryden's *Metamorphoses* of Ovid:

> This last Petition heard of all her Pray'r,
> The rest dispers'd by winds were lost in Air.

There is, however, no denying the attractiveness of the *Rape* as a piece of *vers de société*, provided the reader is not in search of original

ideas or expression, and provided he finds deflatory writing amusing.
It has had its admirers for two hundred and fifty years. Pope's touch
is light, and we are not meant to take the poem very seriously. It is
when critics are solemn about it that we feel justified in regarding them
as guilty of over-estimation. I doubt if the *Rape* really has much to do
with the fires of sex and religion. In a serious poem about sex warfare
both sexes would be given a hearing. In the *Rape* the men are carica-
tures, but the poem is preached at women in a tone which is alternately
sneering and patronizing. This will pass only if we do not read too
much into the poem. But Cunningham, writing of Clarissa's speech near
the beginning of Canto V, remarks:

> Clarissa's speech undoubtedly carries the 'moral' of the poem, touching
> some of its deepest chords, while at the same time exhibiting the radical
> limitations of even this degree of maturity in the society in which it is so
> firmly set.

The question is, how deep are these deepest chords? Here is the speech.
It is worth looking at, as it well illustrates the undeniable attractiveness
of Pope's writing in what might be called his mature youthful manner,
despite its limitation and superficiality:

> Say, why are Beauties prais'd and honour'd most,
> The wise Man's Passion, and the vain Man's toast?
> Why deck'd with all that Land and Sea afford,
> Why Angels call'd, and Angel-like ador'd?
> Why round our Coaches crowd the white-glov'd Beaus,
> Why bows the Side-box from its inmost Rows?
> How vain are all these Glories, all our Pains,
> Unless good Sense preserve what Beauty gains:
> That Men may say, when we the Front-box grace,
> Behold the first in Virtue, as in Face!
> Oh! if to dance all Night, and dress all Day,
> Charm'd the Small-pox, or chas'd old Age away;
> Who would not scorn what Huswife's Cares produce,
> Or who would learn one earthly Thing of Use?
> To patch, nay ogle, might become a Saint,
> Nor could it sure be such a Sin to paint.
> But since, alas! frail Beauty must decay,
> Curl'd or uncurl'd, since Locks will turn to grey,
> Since painted, or not painted, all shall fade,
> And she who scorns a Man, must die a Maid;
> What then remains, but well our Pow'r to use,
> And keep good Humour still whate'er we lose?

> And trust me, Dear ! good Humour can prevail,
> When Airs and Flights, and Screams, and Scolding fail.
> Beauties in vain their pretty Eyes may roll;
> Charms strike the Sight, but Merit wins the Soul.

This is a deftly versified account of the then fashionable prudential morality of Montaigne, Locke, and Shaftesbury, enjoining on young women the virtues of good sense and good humour. The literary echoes – mainly from Dryden, Hopkins, and Pomfret – come less thickly than in many other passages of equal length. But the deepest chord here sounded seems to be the desire of women to get themselves husbands and the desire of men to have good-natured wives. The best I can do to express my feeling about this as poetry is to put beside it some well-known – perhaps too well-known – lines on a similar theme by a poet entirely forgotten in Pope's day. If Pope is gossamer, I do not know what to call Herrick.

> Sweet, be not proud of those two eyes
> Which Star-like sparkle in their skies;
> Nor be you proud, that you can see
> All hearts your captives; yours, yet free;
> Be you not proud of that rich haire,
> Which wantons with the Love-sick aire;
> When as that Rubie, which you weare,
> Sunk from the tip of your soft eare,
> Will last to be a precious Stone,
> When all your world of Beautie's gone.

According to Ayre, the *Rape* 'was wrote to expose the little unguarded Follies of the Fair Sex'. This phrase is taken from Pope's own dedication to the 1714 edition addressed to Arabella Fermor, to whom his tone is well-bred, hypocritical, and patronizing. It is also addressed to the public, who are informed that Pope printed the poem in the first place only because 'an imperfect copy [had] been offer'd to a Bookseller'. There is no reason to think this touch of self-inflation is true, or that the professions of self-depreciation are sincere. The dedication is of no importance except in so far as its tone towards women is that which is implied throughout the poem. This tone is one of cynical gallantry, based on the treatment of women as intellectually inferior to men, as morally frail, as worthy of attention only if they are pretty and attractive to men; the loss of virginity is comparable with the breaking of china. Tillotson quotes with approval Warburton's comment, 'the fine satire on the female estimate of human mischances', on the lines:

> Or whether Heav'n has *doom'd* that Shock must fall.
> Whether the Nymph shall break Diana's law,
> Or some frail China Jar receive a Flaw,
> Or stain her Honour, or her new Brocade,
> Forget her Pray'rs, or miss a Masquerade,
> Or lose her Heart, or Necklace at a Ball;

Warburton is as cynical about women as Pope. Vanity, snobbery, prudery, affectation are the marks of a woman. She is acceptable only if she combines good sense and good humour with good looks. All this would not matter if Pope himself had any standards other than those of the contemporary *beau monde*. The *Rape is* a satire – it has been claimed to be great satire and a microcosm of Augustan society – but its social criticism is invalid because Pope cannot detach himself from the values he criticizes. Much of Pope's social satire is invalid for the same reason; as De Quincey observed, he has no real quarrel with society. His quarrels are with individuals, and his satire is always at its most energetic when he is attacking an individual. The description of the Cave of Spleen in Canto IV is amusing enough, and expresses in verse the current male attitudes towards women which found their way into *The Spectator* and *The Tatler*, those productions of the exclusively male London clubs. But the verse seems to receive an extra charge from something personal in Pope's malice.

> Two Handmaids wait the Throne: Alike in Place,
> But diff'ring far in Figure and in Face.
> Here stood Ill-Nature like an ancient Maid,
> Her wrinkled Form in Black and White arrayed;
> With store of Pray'rs, for Mornings, Nights, and Noons,
> Her Hand is fill'd; her Bosom with Lampoons.
> There Affectation with a sickly Mien
> Shows in her Cheek the Roses of Eighteen,
> Practis'd to Lisp, and hang the Head aside,
> Faint into Airs, and languishes with Pride;
> On the rich Quilt sinks with becoming Woe,
> Wrapt in a Gown, for Sickness, and for Show.
> The Fair-ones feel such Maladies as these,
> When each new Night-dress gives a new Disease.

It is as if in the sex war Pope is himself taking sides against women. Within the limitations which this imposes it is possible to enjoy many isolated passages from the *Rape*. For instance:

What guards the Purity of melting Maids,
In Courtly Balls, and Midnight Masquerades,
Safe from the treach'rous Friend, the daring Spark,
The Glance by Day, the Whisper in the dark;
When kind Occasion prompts their warm Desires,
When Music softens, and when Dancing fires?
'Tis but their sylph, the wise Celestials know,
Tho' Honour is the Word with Men below.

It has often been remarked that Pope cannot sustain an impulse for long and that his energy comes in fits and starts. The spasmodic quality of the writing in the *Rape* seems to me partly to arise from the fact that Pope does not really believe in his burlesque – not enough, at least, to sustain the drama. This is connected, of course, with the patchwork quality of the writing – one passage derived from Homer, the next from Virgil, the next perhaps some versified lines from *The Tatler*. The high moment in the *Rape* is the severing of the lock towards the end of Canto III. The tone of this passage, a mere eight lines, is one of tense and even tragic drama. It concludes:

> The meeting Points the sacred Hair dissever
> From the fair Head, for ever and for ever!

There is, however, no feeling in this; the inspiration is purely verbal. Pope does not appear to care about the loss of the lock, as he must do if the burlesque is to be sustained and the excitement genuine. For within four lines the suspense has been snapped. Immediately after the couplet just quoted comes:

> Then flash'd the Lightning from her Eyes,
> And Screams of Horror rend the'affrighted Skies.
> Not louder Shrieks to pitying Heav'n are cast,
> When Husbands or when Lap-dogs breathe their last...

The tension is snapped for the sake of a clever sneer, a mere zeugma; and the atmosphere is dissipated in a collection of echoes from Cowley, Farquhar and others in order to show off the epigrammatic brilliance of a parodist. It is the wanton mischief of a boy pricking a balloon he has just blown up. You may say it is all good fun; the thing is mere burlesque. But even the mock-heroic has its laws. The basic weakness in Pope is well-illustrated by a contrast with Chaucer's *Nun's Priest's Tale*, a masterpiece of the *genre*, where the seizure of Chantecleer is followed by an immense sustained outburst of noise and action continued for over sixty lines. No doubt it is a mistake to take *The Rape of the Lock* too seriously, but after all it was thought by some critics in Pope's century to be his best poem, and in our century it has been called 'a great masterpiece of poetic art, one of the permanent achievements of English poetry'.

4 Eloïsa to Abelard
Elegy to the Memory of an Unfortunate Lady

Having considered Pope's earliest poems and his first major satire, I want now to turn to the so-called 'romantick' poems. Both *Eloïsa to Abelard* and *Elegy to the Memory of an Unfortunate Lady* first appeared in the collected *Works* of 1717. Both poems represent something new in Pope's writing and also something with which we are already familiar. They are concerned with the romantic, the 'picturesque'; they are also carefully adapted from other and similar works to produce pieces that would be both popular and revealing of Pope's ability to write in any of the classical genres. They are carefully written to please and impress his public, and these overtly emotional poems reveal as clearly as any in his canon, Pope's absolute dependence on other writers for the sources of his inspiration, let alone his expression. Nevertheless, Quennell has called *Eloïsa to Abelard* 'the most poignantly personal poem that he had yet composed and published', and says that 'despite their Gothic details and stately Augustan framework, his verses reflect the agonised confusion of an individual human heart'.

Thus both *Eloïsa* and the *Elegy* have a certain autobiographical significance. How precisely this can be defined is a matter for dispute. The two women concerned are Martha Blount and the fascinating and intelligent Lady Mary Wortley Montagu. Martha Blount and her sister Teresa lived with their widowed mother and unmarried brother and were part of that closely-knit fraternity of Catholic gentlefolk in Berkshire with whom the Pope family was familiar. Pope himself seems initially to have been in love with both of the sisters simultaneously. It was however towards Martha – called 'Patty' by her friends – that his affection finally veered. The relationship is a significant one since it helps us to discover what the poet's attitude to women really was. As I have already shown, the *Rape of the Lock* reveals, under its literary commonplaces a distinctly condescending approach to women. If Pope has been praised for the familiarity with the female world that is shown in his poems, it is partly because he was able to watch them as a privileged and indulged exile. He could be treated as a potentially serious lover could not be treated. The result was that his affection became distorted. In his letters and poems to Martha, as in his other conduct with

women, we find a curious blend of smut and sentimentality which is
deeply disquieting. Martha herself, though for a while she was an ideal,
was not averse to the occasional improper reference in her letters to
Pope. Indeed, she often emerges as a sympathetic character, quick-
witted, 'blest with Temper' and, above all, sufficiently secure to treat
Pope without scorn or pity. If some of her letters to him were a 'delight
to me beyond all expression' he could, nevertheless, be bitter about his
enforced position. In his *Epistle* to her there are some suppressed lines
describing his visits to brothels in her absence, of which one line reads:

> And if poor *Pope* is cl—pt, the Fault is yours.

However, we cannot polarize the relationship as simply as this. There
was genuine tenderness on Pope's side, as this letter, written from Stowe,
reveals:

> All the mornings we breakfast and dispute; after dinner and at (nig)ht,
> Musick and Harmony; in the Garden, Fishing; No Politicks (and) no
> Cards, nor much Reading. This agrees exactly with (m)e, for the want
> of Cards sends us early to bed. I have no Complaints, but that I wish for
> you and can't have you. I will say no more – but that I think of you and
> for you, as I ever did, and ever shall, present or absent. I can really
> (forge)t every thing besides.

On the other side too, Martha could be a prude. Warton speaks of
Pope's lifelong attachment to her and of her 'affectation and ill temper'
which 'gave him many hours of uneasiness and disquiet'. 'When she
visited him in his very last illness, and her company seemed to give him
a fresh spirit, the antiquated prude could not be prevailed on to stay
and pass the night at Twickenham, because of her reputation.' However, Pope made her his residuary legatee.

If Pope's relations with Martha Blount continued on and off throughout his life in this complicated, unsatisfied way, Lady Mary, who was
his greatest love, became his bitterest enemy.

Forceful, intelligent, and, before catching smallpox, a rather beautiful woman, Lady Mary was doubtless flattered by Pope's love. Like
many women of her stamp, she often found it difficult to get on agree-
ably with her own sex, while many of the men she found about her were
below her intellectual level. She lost her mother during her early childhood and was first brought up by her grandfather and then by Lord
Dorchester. In later life she was to have vivid recollections of her childhood – indeed, much of her life was passed in memorable circumstances. When she was about seven her father took her to a meeting

the Kit-Cat Club. Here she 'went from the lap of one poet, or patriot, or statesman, to the arms of another, was feasted with sweetmeats, overwhelmed with caresses, and, what perhaps already better pleased her than either, heard her wit and beauty loudly extolled on every side'. A precocious, attractive little girl – her *Entire Works* had been produced before she was fourteen – she taught herself an appreciation of literature. Her father, working his way up the hierarchy, allowed her to experience the benefits of her rank. Her first important affair – a clandestine one – ended in a marriage to the dull Edward Wortley, a Member of Parliament and a friend of Addison and Steele.

It is not clear when she first met Pope, but he mentions her in a letter to the Blounts written on 23 July 1715. Pope was twenty-seven she a year younger and, while still writing, she was also engaged in furthering the career of her husband and herself by fascinating the new court. In the autumn of that year Pope, Gay, and Lady Mary collaborated in a series of satirical *Town Eclogues*. It was in that December that Lady Mary contracted smallpox, but if the disease blemished her looks it did not destroy her energy.

However, before discussing Pope's relationship with Lady Mary in greater detail, it is necessary to say something about the publication of the *Town Eclogues*. This incident is possibly the most disgusting in the whole of Pope's career and reveals how far his claim to be the moralist of his age can be taken seriously. It also shows that his concern for literary standards was rooted in his own crippled psychology and that it had little to do with a love of letters.

The manuscripts of the *Town Eclogues* were picked up by the Grub Street publisher Curll, who produced them under the title of *Court Poems*. He claimed that the works had been found in Westminster Hall after the trial of the Jacobite Lord Winton and gave hints as to who the writers were, these included 'the Judicious Translator of Homer'. His action was, of course, despicable. Pope's reaction however shows paranoia rather than a desire to clear his name. He and Lintott lured Curll out for a drink and dropped an emetic, possibly mixed by Dr Arbuthnot, into the poor man's sack. So far so cruel, though it is to be remembered that there were no libel laws at this time. However, Pope's revenge was by no means complete. He hastened home and prepared some pamphlets, the title of the first being *A Full and True Account of a Horrid and Barbarous Revenge by Poison on the Body of Mr. Edmund Curll, Bookseller*. The effects of the emetic are recounted with Rabelaisian energy and fantastic detail. Curll is shown making his will, summoning his hacks and being in 'the greatest adversity that ever befell my poor man since he lost one testicle at school by the bite of a black boar'. Pope later told Caryll that he 'contrived to save the fellow a beating by giving him a vomit'. This is perfectly true, Pope could not have beaten Curll, who was a big man. Where Pope did lie however was in telling Caryll that the pamphlets were written by 'a Late Grub-street author', a deceit as revealing as any in Pope's career.

Pope was clearly fascinated by Lady Mary – her mind, her looks, her wit. That he made a considerable emotional investment is clear from the virtually paranoid hatred which he lavished on her after their quarrel. He called her a whore and claimed she had the pox. The latter is a fact or a fiction that we owe to Pope alone. What is significant about this is that he nowhere blames himself for loving such a woman. But the image that his hatred fashioned was as fictitious as that which his love fostered. He once wrote to her that no one 'knows you better'. In fact his knowledge was slight. Ignoring her own, head-strong character, he tried to make her his intellectual mistress. 'You may easily imagine,' he wrote, 'how desirous I must be of a correspondence with a person, who had taught me long ago that it was as possible to esteem at first sight as to love: and who has since ruined me for all the conversation of one sex, and almost all the friendship of the other.' He was soon to be able to indulge his myth of her in total freedom. Early in April 1716 her husband secured the position of Ambassador Extraordinary to the Sublime Porte. Lady Mary prepared to spend a number of years in Turkey. The affair was now to be continued in Pope's letters:

> Whether or no you will order me, in recompense, to see you again, I leave to you; for indeed I find I begin to behave myself worse to you than to any other woman, as I value you more. And yet if I thought I should not see you again, I would say some things here, which I could not to your person. For I would not have you die deceived in me, that is, go to Constantinople without knowing, that I am to some degree of extravagance, as well as with the utmost reason, Madam, your faithful and most obedient humble servant, A. Pope.

Of course the affair was ultimately an impossible one. Pope must have known this, despite the fact that he indulged himself, and despite the fact that Lady Mary, in letters at least, was fashionably compliant Pope's however was not a polite flirtation. It was a romantic, and to that extent a self-obsessed fantasy, which is the autobiographical aspect that is reflected in *Eloïsa to Abelard*. The impossibility is generalized, however, since Pope had interested Martha Blount in the poem and it seems that he suppressed a promised conclusion relating to her. As the *Twickenham* editor writes: 'if the history of the poem shows Pope veering from Martha to Mary, most of the personal undertone of the poem fitted each of them equally.'

Pope's immediate source for his poem was John Hughes's translation of a French version of Abelard and Eloïsa's letters. This French version had been considerably modernized and the lovers are presented in a very contemporary way. There was thus no need for Pope to wrestle with the medieval version since the most obvious idiosyncrasies had already been successfully removed for him. He could base his poem chiefly on the first letter, which gives a chronological view of the situation, but he also drew to a certain extent on some of the others. *Eloïsa to Abelard* is thus a versification of a book already extant. How close a version will be illustrated later.

The gothic and religious elements in the poem were not new. In 1678 Sir Roger L'Estrange had published a translation under the title *Five Love-Letters from a Nun to a Cavalier* and these proved sufficiently popular to provoke 'replies'. They were also twice translated into verse. The specific emotional situation of *Eloïsa to Abelard* was nothing new. This is not, of course, a criticism of Pope, but it well illustrates his good eye for what was selling and for what was popular. When we come to a detailed discussion of the poem, I hope to show that Pope's influence on the new Gothic vogue was not considerable. Nearly all of his most vivid images are versions of other poets' lines and not all of them are improvements.

It is however the form of *Eloïsa to Abelard* which is most significant. According to John Butt: '*Eloïsa to Abelard* and the *Elegy to the Memory of an Unfortunate Lady* are best understood as imitations, though more than mere imitations, of Ovid's *Heroical Epistles* and the elegies of Ovid and Tibullus.' Ovid's *Heroides* had been popular since the days of Chaucer. Dryden declared that they were 'generally granted to be the most perfect piece of Ovid' and they had been translated and travestied throughout the seventeenth and early eighteenth centuries. Dryden had declared Ovid unrivalled 'in the Description of the Passions' and found the best Ovid in the *Heroides*, Oldmixon had defined the heroical epistle thus:

> Passion and Nature are the distinguishing Character of such Epistles . . . the Sentiments shou'd be gallant and tender, the Language easie and musical, and nothing (shou'd) appear forc'd and affected.

Thus what was demanded was passion, elegance, and clarity. There were plenty of precedents; Drayton, Daniel, and Donne had all produced similar works; in 1713 the Countess of Winchelsea had produced her *Epistle from Alexander to Hephaestion in his Sickness*. However, as Tillotson says: 'With Pope's poem, the heroic epistle is brought back into its strictest Ovidian definition: the persons are historical, and the woman forsaken by the man.' Pope thus had no need to invent the form or the substance of his poem. All he needed to do was make his source book a little more dramatically heightened.

The form of the heroic epistle had been derived from Ovid, but the actual expression of emotion was to avoid what a number of critics considered was Ovid's sin of being too metaphysical, too particular in his means of expression. Rhetoric was to replace subtle psychology and by presenting only what is 'permanent' in human nature, give the work the automatic status of a classic. Tillotson's analysis of the background to the poem throws most of the weight of our appreciation on the rhetoric. The story, he says, was a familiar one and this gave the poet certain advantages, it also had the additional strength of being true. This is, in fact, a familiar situation, after all it is the basis of Shakespeare's Histories; Tillotson himself makes the comparison between *Eloïsa to Abelard* and drama. The deduction he makes from the familiarity of the story however is a *non-sequitur*:

> The reader, therefore, expects not to be told the story and persuaded of the passions, but to see a use made of the materials that are known, to see as good a letter as possible made out of them.

What, one might ask, are the letters to consist of if not the story and the passions? Tillotson's answer is 'the skill, the quality of the manipulation'. To a certain extent this is true. One thinks of the skill with which Chaucer and Shakespeare manipulated their familiar sources, but if those two writers offer us superb examples of their respective genres it is because they knew that passion and rhetoric must be one. Pope however is exempted from this:

> The reader will judge the letter as he judges a fugue on a given subject. Eloïsa becomes for him the 'artist', the intellectual master co-ordinating times, places, and moods, the 'artist' of emotion rather than the experiencer of it. The rhetoric is necessary because the skill must be shown. It is assuredly not a case of *ars celare artem*. Nature and known fortunes become surprising by means of Art.

Tillotson's comparison with a fugue is unfortunate since if a fugue is a development of a given theme, the best fugues never lose sight of the musical idea – both form and feeling. However, Pope frequently fails even by Tillotson's definition. Where is the shaping and co-ordinating skill of this platitude:

> Should at my feet the world's great master fall,
> Himself, his throne, his world, I'd scorn 'em all;
> Not *Caesar's* empress wou'd I deign to prove;
> No, make me mistress to the man I love. . . . ?

Similarly, if rhetoric implies an ability to shape harmonious phrases, what are we to make of this barbarous line

> The dear Ideas, where I fly, pursue. . . . ?

If *Eloïsa to Abelard* is 'assuredly not a case of *ars celare artem*' it is often a case of *vox et praeterea nihil*. However, for Tillotson: 'the art of the poem is as triumphant as figure-skating'.

This sort of rhapsodic criticism is characteristic of much that has been written about *Eloïsa to Abelard*. Wilson Knight has called it: 'probably the greatest short love poem in our language', a note which was set by Byron when he said 'If you search for passion, where is it to be found stronger than in the epistle from *Eloïsa to Abelard* . . .?' Warren compares the poem to Racine; Sutherland, more modestly, compares it to the drama of Nicholas Rowe. The greatest proportion of criticism seems to see the poem as full of personal pathos, some psychological complexity, and above all as an example of 'inspiration'. On this last point Cazamian writes:

> Never has Pope been nearer to true inspiration. The language itself bears the marks of an ardour which, on this occasion, at times, creates its form in untrammelled liberty.

With this in mind let us examine the first three paragraphs with the help of the *Twickenham* edition.

> In these deep solitudes and awful cells,
> Where heav'nly-pensive, contemplation dwells,
> And ever-musing melancholy reigns;
> What means this tumult in a Vestal's veins?
> Why rove my thoughts beyond this last retreat?   5
> Why feels my heart its long-forgotten heat?
> Yet, yet I love! – From *Abelard* it came,
> And *Eloïsa* yet must kiss the name.
>   Dear fatal name! rest ever unreveal'd,
> Nor pass these lips in holy silence seal'd.   10
> Hide it, my heart, within that close disguise,
> Where, mix'd with God's, his lov'd Idea lies.
> Oh write it not, my hand, – The name appears
> Already written – wash it out, my tears!
> In vain lost *Eloïsa* weeps and prays,   15
> Her heart still dictates, and her hand obeys.

> Relentless walls ! whose darksome round contains
> Repentant sighs, and voluntary pains:
> Ye rugged rocks ! which holy knees have worn;
> Ye grots and caverns shagg'd with horrid thorn !   20
> Shrines ! where their vigils pale-ey'd virgins keep,
> And pitying saints, whose statues learn to weep !
> Tho' cold like you, unmov'd, and silent grown,
> I have not yet forgot myself to stone.

It cannot be denied that these lines build up a reasonably powerful, melodramatic atmosphere. Let us examine, however, what they are built from. The opening couplet is a straight adaptation from Broome's *A Poem on the Seat of War in Flanders . . . Written 1710*:

> Ye gloomy Grots ! ye awful solemn Cells,
> Where holy thoughtful, *Contemplation* dwells.

In line 12 we have the first allusion to Hughes who wrote: 'Thou charming Idea of a Lover', and 'you . . . the dear Idea.' 'Dear Idea' is a bad enough phrase in prose, in verse it shows how dull Pope's ear could be. Lines 13 to 15 are a simple rephrasing of these from Crauford's *Ovidius Britanicus: Or, Love Epistles*:

> My trembling Hand cou'd not my pen contain,
> Nor all my Courage, falling Tears restrain;
> Or if I write, they wash'd it out again !

Line 16 is a reference to Hughes again: 'All I desire is such letters as the heart dictates, and which the Hand can scarce Write fast enough.' Line 20 is from *Comus*: 'By grots, and caverns shag'd with horrid shades.' Line 21 derives from one, or possibly both, of two quotations from Wharton: 'Where pale-ey'd griefs their wasting vigils keep,' which comes from his poem *Fear of Death*, or

> Where kneeling statues constant vigils keep,
> And round the tombs the marble cherubs weep.

Milton too has a 'pale-ey'd priest' in the *Nativity Ode*. The succeeding line is a reminiscence of Virgil, while line 24 is a mélange of echoes. We find this passage in Hughes: 'O Vows ! O Convent ! I have not lost my Humanity under your inexorable Discipline ! You have not made me Marble by changing my Habit.' The phrase 'Forget thyself to Marble' occurs in *Il Penseroso*. Thus in the first twenty lines there are at least nine direct references, besides a considerable number of possible allusions which I have not listed. Tillotson claims however that at one point at least these 'resonances' serve a crucial function:

From the literary point of view the conflict ['between religious vows and paganism'] is central: the poem is constructed around it. And it provides opportunity for those 'layerings' of effect which are so characteristic of Pope's methods of writing. It allows the Ovidian imitation to be parallel and divergent at the same time. For instance, Eloïsa's vision of the nun who calls her is imitated from that of Ovid's Dido who heard the same call when visiting the monument of the husband she had murdered:

> hinc ego me sensi noto quater ore citari;
> ipse sono tenui dixit 'Elissa, veni!'
> Nulla mora est, venio, venio tibi debita coniunx;

which in Sherburne's translation ran:

> me thought, I heard, foure times to say,
> With trembling voyce, *Eliza*, come away.
> I come, I come, thy once vow'd wife ...

Pope keeps the frame, even the translated words, but what was pagan has become Christian (the voice is that of a sainted nun) and just because of this Eloïsa is being shut again in her vocation.

Such a reading is valid, I think, only if we consider that the conflict between the sacred and the profane *is* really central to the poem. Obviously it is the dichotomy on which the situation is based, but how seriously is it explored? *Eloïsa to Abelard* has been called a great love poem, but the seriousness with which the religious aspects are explored is questionable. It has never been called a great poem of the religious life, or even of the failed religious life. It is the melodrama that is central to the poem and such resonances as Tillotson finds, if they work at all, are simply decorative. The poem is based on the attraction of observing a woman in agony, not on a true philosophical dilemma. This was realized by at least one contemporary, Ralph, who was consigned to the *Dunciad*, with apparently the desired results, as a consequence. Ralph also criticized the quality of the 'love' in the poem. So far as I know he is the only critic to have done so. There is an underlying selfishness, or self-obsession, in Eloïsa's complaints and Ralph, who was only a mediocre poet himself, makes this point clear, as well as a possible but unlikely reason for Pope's writing the poem:

> ... In *Prior's* verse
> *Henry* and *Emma* charm the finest Tastes;
> The racking *Trial*, the dissembled Guilt,
> The weeping Maid, her Sighs, her Tears, her firm
> Unbated Love, melt ev'ry soul and claim

A sympathizing Tear. – Sawney beheld
The Labour, heard the Praise; fair *Heloise* now
Employs his Thought, and furnishes his Rhyme;
Her tender wailings, and repentant Pangs
Her frantick Flame, oppos'd to *Emma's* Warmth
To *Emma's* Woe must shine; But Innocence
And Virtue were forgot, and tis the Nun,
The enamour'd raging, longing Nun, that gives
The Verse a Name: Extract her tender Thought
Her hot Desires, and all the rest will shrink
From Fame, like Parchment shriv'ling in the Blaze.

Eloïsa to Abelard represents Pope's attempt to write an heroic epistle
in the manner of Ovid, and the *Elegy to the Memory of an Unfortunate
Lady* is his approach to another important classical form – the Elegy.
In this his models were Tibullus, Propertius, and Ovid again, as well
as modern poets, especially Ben Jonson.

It is clear from a number of Pope's letters written before 1717 that
he wanted to write an elegy but that no occasion had occurred to
warrant one. Nor did it. That this caused Pope some embarrassment
is clear from the way in which he avoided the question. 'I think you
once gave me her history;' Caryll wrote, 'but it is now quite out of my
head.' Pope's reply does not exist. However, Ruffhead fabricated a
story and Warton wrote that 'If this *Elegy* be so excellent, it may be
ascribed to this cause, that the occasion of it was real. . . .' Clearly, it
was considered desirable that there should have been an actual bereave-
ment that upset the poet, and Pope must have realized that the lack of
such an occasion would be to his discredit. He carefully puts critics
off the scent by having these lines near the close of his poem:

> How lov'd, how honour'd once, avails thee not,
> To whom related, or by whom begot.

Seen in this way, the whole incident reveals once again Pope's habitual
deviousness. There was no dead body, what better way to hide this lack
then than by declaring that neither the parents nor the social circle of
the heroine were important, in other words dismiss the difficulty by sentiment? The elegy was an important form, Pope had not so far written
one and a work in the genre was clearly desirable as an inclusion in the
1717 volume – a book which was very carefully designed as a showcase, a
revelation of the number of styles in which the coming young poet could
write. In fact, the lines I have just quoted do not even make full sense
in the context of the poem, since the passage of satire about funerals

makes it very clear that the poet wishes that the whole of the unfortunate lady's house should suffer and through several generations.

There are two possible autobiographical sources, one of which may be taken as relating to the 'tragic' side of the poem and the other to its elegiac aspects. Pope and Caryll had been supporting two unfortunate ladies and were to continue to do so for a considerable time. These ladies were Mrs Weston and Mrs Cope. Both were separated from their husbands, indeed, Captain Cope had contracted a bigamous relationship and was living safely abroad. The other source is, naturally, Lady Mary, whose separation from Pope seemed like death. In their letters there are one or two indications that this metaphor might be the genesis of the poem. This is how she wrote to Pope on 16 January 1717:

> ... I think ... I ought to bid adieu to my friends with the same solemnity as if I were going to mount a breach, at least, if I am to believe the information of the people here, who denounce all sorts of terrors to me; and, indeed, the weather is at present such, as very few ever set out in. I am threatened at the same time, with being frozen to death, buried in the snow, and taken by the Tartars, who ravage that part of Hungary I am to pass. ... How my adventures will conclude, I leave entirely to Providence; if comically, you shall hear of them.

The journey she was undertaking was a very considerable and dangerous one and the risks are not necessarily exaggerated. The occasion of the poem cannot be defined any more closely than this. Pope, writes the *Twickenham* editor, 'wanted just enough "fact" to float the emotion'.

The *Elegy* is an exceptionally muddled poem. Superficially it appears profound, compassionate, and imaginatively rich. The last aspect I will deal with later, but an analysis of the construction of the poem shows how confused it is, despite Pope's assertion to Spence that 'most little poems should be written by a plan: this method is evident in Tibullus, and Ovid's Elegies, and almost all the pieces of the ancients'.

In the first ten lines Pope considers the question of the Roman Catholic condemnation of suicide and asks if heaven can show no mercy even for a suicide committed for the sake of love. He then asks why the unfortunate lady was fated to be ambitious beyond the range of ordinary mortals. Clearly her ambition originated in heaven. Having raised an important theological point Pope then drops it. He has juggled with one idea and extracted a certain amount of sentiment from it. He then, in a rather pointless digression, picks up the idea of fate and wonders whether this brought about her early death simply because of her spiritual superiority. Lines 29–46 then steer the poem away towards satire. The false guardian is attacked for being responsible for the lady's death, and then Pope brings in the particularly savage wish that not only the guardian but all his female descendants should die so that bystanders can jeer at their hard hearts. This is savagely nonsensical since these descendants had nothing to do with the unfortunate lady's death. It is however in lines 47–75 that the greatest confusion occurs. Pope asks what can atone for the lady's obscure and dishonourable funeral. Apparently she *was* both mourned and honoured and was indeed saved from the insincere mourning of her friends in this way. Why this should be considered a hardship it is difficult to say. Sentimentality and the familiar trope of insincere mourning seem to be at odds here. Pope has created two opposed effects. The lady's tomb is beautifully decked with flowers, and both nature and the angels mourn her. So, though in a nameless grave, a woman rests in peace who possessed worldly honours. The previous love and honour she evoked now avail her nothing however. One wonders why this matters if angels mourn her. What Pope is trying to do, but without success, is to effect a transition from the idea that she has a reward, despite being rejected – a reward which, as we have seen, is a very satisfying one – to the rather obvious notion that:

> A heap of dust alone remains of thee;
> 'Tis all thou art, and all the proud shall be.

Pope's attempt to combine the idea of salvation and reward and that of *contemptus mundi* is singularly ham-fisted. As in *Eloïsa to Abelard*, the *Elegy* ends on a personal note. Poets, like the objects of their song, must themselves perish – even Pope himself. Such is the tone that has been built up that Pope cannot bring off this inescapably mundane idea. This required the lyric grace of Herrick:

> But die you must (faire Maide) ere long,
> And He, the maker of this song.

I have given some idea of the construction of this poem since I want to illustrate that Pope's powers in this direction were not particularly strong. The rational, the intellectual argument simply does not hold water. It sounds impressive, but falls to pieces under scrutiny. None of the questions that he raises in the first part do any more than give to the problem a spurious air of philosophizing while, in the second part, his keenness to include all the tropes of the form has resulted in a confusion that virtually amounts to a sequence of contradictions.

This poem, then, contains little that is original. Again, with the help of the *Twickenham* edition, let us examine a passage:

But thou, false guardian of a charge too good,   30
Thou, mean deserter of thy brother's blood !
See on these ruby lips the tender breath,
Those cheeks, now fading at the blast of death:
Cold is that breast which warm'd the world before,
And those love-darting eyes must roll no more.
Thus, if eternal justice rules the ball,   35
Thus shall your wives, and thus your children fall:
On all the line a sudden vengeance waits,
And frequent hearses shall besiege your gates.
There passengers shall stand, and pointing say,
(While the long funerals blacken all the way)   40
Lo there were they, whose souls the Furies steel'd,
And curs'd with hearts unknowing how to yield.
Thus unlamented pass the proud away,
The game of fools and pageant of a day !

Line 29 is a recreation of Dryden's translation of the *Amores*: 'But thou dull Husband of a Wife too fair' while line 33 is found in both Spenser and Donne. 'Love-darting eyes' (34) is taken from *Comus*. The famous and much admired line 38 has a number of analogues in Dryden's translations:

> The Streets are fill'd with frequent Funerals;
> > (*Aeneid ii.* 491)
> And Litters thick besiege the Donor's Gate;
> > (Juvenal *Satire* I 182)

and:

> Sad Pomps, a Threshold throng'd with daily Biers.
> > (Juvenal *Satire* X 386)

Line 41 derives from Homer; in Pope's translation it reads:

> The Furies that relentless Breast have steel'd,
> And curs'd thee with a Heart that cannot yield.

Thus here again we see Pope the mosaicist reconstituting his poem with lines borrowed from other works. The opening of the poem itself is of course taken from Jonson and it cannot be claimed that Pope improves on Jonson's gentle romanticism. Here is Pope:

> What beck'ning ghost, along the moonlight shade
> Invites my step, and points to yonder glade?

And here is Jonson (*Elegie on the Lady Jane Pawlet*):

> What gentle ghost, besprent with *April* deaw,
> Hayles me, so solemnly, to yonder Yewgh?
> And beckning wooes me . . .?

Tillotson has again come up with an ingenious vindication of the frequent 'borrowings' in this poem. I will quote it if only to show how far the critics are prepared to cover Pope's traces:

> Particularly evident are the patches of diction and imagery that are derived from Elizabethan sonnets and from the panegyrics of the metaphysical poets of the seventeenth century. It is by such short-hand means that Pope persuades the reader that it is not merely Mrs. X who is dead, but a goddess, the ideal of a hundred poets.

One questions a critic when he can praise a poet for using 'short-hand means' – I would prefer to call them underhand. A 'short-hand' Beatrice, a 'short-hand' Laura? So much for literary values.

5 The Translations
The Edition of Shakespeare

Pope's earliest translations date from the beginning of his career. After he was twelve, during the time that he set himself to study, like many of his contemporaries at school, he produced versified renderings of the classics. There are some early translations of Homer, Statius, and Ovid. The translations reprinted in the 1717 volume, however, are adaptations of Chaucer. There is the *Merchant's Tale*, here called *January and May*, which 'was done at sixteen or seventeen Years of Age', an adaptation called *The Wife of Bath her Prologue*, and a rendering of parts of the second and third books of Chaucer's *House of Fame*.

Dryden had translated Chaucer, rather freely, and no doubt this was one of the reasons why Pope set about the task. Dryden had confined his choice 'to such tales of Chaucer as savour nothing of immodesty' and he had specifically kept away from the Wife of Bath's *Prologue*. This, as we have seen, is one of the pieces that Pope selected. One may well ask why this was, since both this work and the *Merchant's Tale* are examples of Chaucer's bawdy. The *Twickenham* editor explains this on the grounds that both pieces are concerned with marriage — a popular theme – and that both pieces are comic, and Chaucer was regarded at this time chiefly as a comic poet. The latter is not strictly true: Dryden, as is well known, had found 'God's plenty' in Chaucer, even if he did not choose to render all of it. We know that he was moved by the story of Palamon and Arcite, and Pepys persuaded him to translate the portrait of the Parson from the *General Prologue*. In addition, Warton wished that Pope 'had exercised his pencil on the pathetic story of the Patience of Griselda, or Troilus and Cressida . . .' Thus, if the appreciation of Chaucer was not wholly scholarly – there was no really adequate text – the whole range of his production was nevertheless known. It is possible that Pope took his cue from Dryden himself about translating these two works. The older poet had written: 'If I had desired more to please than to instruct, [these] would have procured me as many friends and readers, as there are *beaux* and ladies of pleasure in the town.' Pope took the hint and deliberately translated what Dryden regarded as scurrilous. Such a piece of self-advertising would have brought the young poet into the public eye. In fact, because the poems are adaptations rather than literal translations, the bawdy passages are not given their full weight. This, naturally, has disastrous consequences.

The verse of these pieces is not particularly distinguished, though it must be remembered that they are apprentice work. However, the excuse for such translations in the first place was that Chaucer's versification was considered rough – the proper rules for scanning him had not yet been fully rediscovered – and the poet was the victim of what he feared at the end of *Troilus and Criseyde*, that people would 'mysmetre for defaute of tonge'. In addition, it was considered that his power of construction was sometimes lacking. To quote Dryden again:

> Chaucer, I confess, is a rough diamond, and must first be polished, ere he shines. . . . living in our early days of poetry, he writes not always of a piece; but sometimes mingles trivial things with those of greater moment. Sometimes also, though not often, he runs riot, like Ovid, and knows not when he has said enough.

Thus it was considered that an elegant rephrasing and a certain readjustment of the text were called for. Even Horace Walpole, despite his love of the medieval, preferred to read Chaucer in eighteenth-century versions.

The *Twickenham* editor writes of Pope's version of the *Merchant's Tale* that 'in making his modernization Pope loses much of [Chaucer's] imperturbably honest human actuality of person, speech and even incident. He makes the story shrink back into something more like a *fabliau*, a neatly told story with a point'. This is, in fact, the most damning criticism that could be made, since if Chaucer was experimenting with literary genres, the elements that Pope is held to have rejected are just those with which Chaucer was most concerned. Where Pope gains, it is maintained, is in introducing satire. Can it honestly be said that Pope improves on Chaucer here?

> Sir, I have liv'd a Courtier all my Days
> And study'd Men, their Manners, and their Ways;
> And have observ'd this useful Maxim still,
> To let my Betters always have their Will.

This is the original:

> For brother mine take of me this motife,
> I haue been now a court man all my life,
> And God wot, though I now vnworthy bee,
> I have stonden in full great degree

Abouten Lords in full great estate:
Yet had I neuer with none of them debate,
I neuer hem contraried truly.

And the loss of true poetry can be illustrated by one other line. The
original of 'Like empty Shadows, pass, and glide away' is 'That passen
as a shaddow on a wall'.

The *Twickenham* editor's comment on *The Wife of Bath her Prologue* is a similar condemnation of Pope:

Pope sacrifices the completeness of a complicated human confession,
and provides instead all the ease, the gay regularity, the contemporary
satire. His rhetoric is decreed by the sophistication.

Tillotson sees this as the first step on the way towards *Moral Essay*, ii,
Of the Characters of Women. If he is right, then he places Pope in a
very revealing perspective.

Why did Pope choose to translate the *House of Fame*? It is the least
satisfactory of all Chaucer's early poems if only because it is incomplete.
The subject was, certainly, a popular one. Addison and Swift had both
been concerned with it and the debate itself was a popular Renaissance
topic. However, I think the choice represents a particularly personal
preference on Pope's part. From his earliest years he was obsessed with
fame. Not only did the subject appeal to him, but because of the alle-
gorical nature of the original, he could preface the poem with a literary
debate and so carefully parade his reading, as indeed he could when
it came to filling the temple with rather dull portraits of great men,
portraits taken from the illustrations of these figures prefixed to the
translations of the classics where he found them. Even Tillotson is
bound to admit that much of the learning that these figures illustrate
more or less spurious.

The Temple of Fame is less a translation than an imitation. Pope
omits the first book of Chaucer's poem, and is very free with the two
succeeding ones. Even contemporary critics were quick to seize on this
which at least illustrates how wide appreciation of Chaucer was –
and the poem has received much adverse criticism ever since. Dryden
however, dealing with imitation in the abstract, comes nearest to expos-
ing Pope fully:

To state it fairly; imitation of an author is the most advantageous way
for a translator to show himself, but the greatest wrong which can be
done to the memory and reputation of the dead . . .

The *Temple of Fame* is clearly designed to show off Pope to his greatest
advantage. How far it does so may be judged by the reader for himself.

The language is thin and the versification weak. The ideas show little or no originality and the choice of figures in the poem was decided entirely by contemporary taste. The conclusion, which is Pope's own, is banal and priggish:

> But if the Purchase cost so dear a Price,
> As soothing Folly, or exalting Vice:
> Oh! if the Muse must flatter lawless Sway,
> And follow still where Fortune leads the way;
> Or if no Basis bear my rising Name,
> But the fall'n Ruins of Another's Fame:
> Then teach me, Heaven! to scorn the guilty Bays;
> Drive from my Breast that wretched Lust of Praise;
> Unblemish'd let me live, or die unknown,
> Oh grant an honest Fame, or grant me none!

As we have already seen, Pope had translated some portions of Homer when he was a boy. However, at the close of his dedication to *Examen*, Dryden had issued a general challenge to any modern poet to translate him in full. He himself had nominated Congreve. Of Chapman he said that he was guilty of 'harsh Numbers, improper English, and a monstrous Length of Verse'. By early 1714 Pope was occupied with this 'grand undertaking'.

The story of Pope's Homer is, *par excellence*, the story of a man making a modest private fortune out of his writing. The translation of Homer was a calculated best-seller. As such it succeeded. As a Catholic Pope was ineligible for public office. To live as he desired, in other words in imitation of such eighteenth-century arbiters of taste as Lord Burlington, private patronage would be insufficient. In addition, new laws had been passed increasing the rate of taxation levied on Catholic families. However, most important of all, was Pope's need of money to finance the way of life he was establishing for himself at Twickenham. His landscaped gardens, tunnel and shell-grotto were necessary to the life-style that he considered obligatory, and it was the *Iliad* and the *Odyssey* that were to pay for them. Pope worked his friends very hard to gain the maximum number of subscriptions. In the end he collected over ten thousand. Caryll and Swift were particularly valuable supports. If Swift could, for the while, persuade his political friends to support a new and valuable ally, Caryll, 'soliciting with all his might' as he described it, canvassed the gentry. The whole design was very carefully planned, for both Pope and his publisher were, we know, shrewd business men with a good eye for selling the poet in the best possible way. If Pope was later to decry the learning of the gentry he knew perfectly well what sort of book would appeal to them. The public announcement, made in October 1713, that Pope was about to begin on this work has been lost. What does survive is an advertisement in the third edition of *The Rape of the Lock*:

> This work shall be printed in six Volumes in Quarto, on the finest Paper, and on a Letter new Cast on purpose; with Ornaments and initial Letters engraven on Copper. Each Volume containing four Books of the Iliad; with Notes to each Book.

In other words what Lintott and Pope were advertising was a sumptuous library edition – a desirable and modish status-symbol. Judiciously, Pope did not begin work until a sufficient number of subscriptions had been collected. The price was a guinea a volume.

The prospect of translating was a daunting one, yet Pope had made an emotional investment in it since, should it come off, the work would 'keep me a poet (in spite of something I lately thought a resolution to the contrary) for some years longer'. It was not only the act of translation itself which was so time-consuming and exhausting, there was also the necessity of preserving face as a Homeric scholar. Among other commentators 'Dacier's three Volumes, Barnes's two, Valerie's three, Cuperus half in Greek, Leo Allatius three parts in Greek, Scaliger, Macrobius, & (worse than 'em all) Aulus Gellius' had to be digested. These books were very expensive, and the advertisement states that advance subscriptions were necessary for buying them. How deep Pope's scholarship went we will see later. If at times the thought of it daunted him, at others he was cheered:

> I must confess that the Greek fortification does not appear so formidable as it did, upon a nearer approach; and I am almost apt to flatter myself, that Homer secretly seems inclined to correspond with me, in letting me into a good part of his designs. There are, indeed, a sort of underli(n)g auxilars to the difficulty of the work, called commentators and criticks, who would frighten many people by their number and bulk. These lie entrenched in the ditches, and are secure only in the dirt they have heaped about 'em with great pains in the collecting it. But I think we have found a method of coming at the main works by a more speedy and gallant way than by mining under ground; that is, by using the poetical engines, wings, and flying thither over their heads.

What was Pope's actual technique for translating? He was later to tell Spence that he had wanted to get through his first drafts 'fast'. Lying in bed in the morning, he would try and manage 'thirty or fourty verses before I got up', after that he 'piddled with it the rest of the morning'.

It appears that at this rate he got through about fifty lines a day. His most productive period was during the summer, in the autumn and winter he selected, arranged, and prepared for the press.

The first volume of the *Iliad* came out on 6 June 1716, almost three months late. Two days earlier Pope had heard that a translation of Book 1 by Thomas Tickell would be published almost simultaneously by Tonson. He knew that such a translation existed. Addison had told him that Tickell had written his version while at Oxford. What Pope had not realized was that it would come out so soon; further, Pope did not know, and it is likely that Addison did, that Tickell had contracted to translate the whole of the *Iliad*. I shall deal with Pope's friendships later, nevertheless it must be said here that however Pope idealized friendship, the case of Addison shows how violently he could turn. The friendship between the two men had been cooling for some time. Swift, the Tory, used the Homer venture as a means of drawing Pope away from Addison and his Whig circle. Addison was sixteen years older than Pope and pursuing a political career, while, behind his back, Pope had jeered at the older writer's *Cato*. Now he turned on him with the full force of his savagery. 'We have it seems, a great Turk in poetry,' he wrote, 'who can never bear a brother on the throne; and has his mutes too, a set of nodders, winkers, and whisperers, whose business is to strangle all other offsprings of wit in their birth. The new translator of Homer is the humblest slave he has . . .' He was to recall these phrases when he produced his attack on Addison (under the name Atticus) in *An Epistle from Mr. Pope to Dr. Arbuthnot*.

The translation of the *Iliad* was well received, but before discussing it in detail I want to say something of the *Odyssey* and its publication so that both poems can be considered together.

The *Odyssey* has rarely been regarded as a success. Pope was undoubtedly tired of translation when he took it on and, as is well known, he only worked on half of the books himself. A letter from Gay to Swift gives one explanation of why Pope took on the job in the first place

> Pope has just now embark'd himself in another great undertaking as an Author; for of late he has talked only as a Gardener. He has engag'd to translate the Odyssey in three years, I believe rather out of a prospect of Gain than inclination, for I am persuaded he bore his part in the loss of the South Sea.

It is now uncertain as to whether Pope 'bore his part' when the South Sea Bubble burst. However, that the translation of the *Odyssey* was taken on for gain there can be no doubt. It shows little imaginative power, and if imagination was to be the means by which he saw himself winning the struggle over the *Iliad*, the farming out of books wholesale to Fenton and Broome, two poor scholars and minor poets, proved a much easier method when it came to the *Odyssey*.

Pope's treatment of Fenton and Broome was shabby in the extreme. Competent, if not particularly inspired men, they produced drafts for Pope which are often as adequate as his own. He was very careful to keep both of them just where he wanted them, in other words as far in the background as possible. This he did by alternately swearing them to secrecy and writing fulsome letters to them. In December 1723 he wrote to Broome:

> The haste I am in must excuse my short letter, but I would not omit writing the very same day I received yours to give you full assurance how truely and unalterably I am, dear sir, your most affectionate faithful friend and servant.

Four years later, Pope was to pillory Broome in the *Dunciad*:

> Hibernian Politicks, O Swift, thy doom,
> And Pope's, translating three whole years with Broome.

The note to this last line reads:

> He concludes his Irony with a stroke upon himself: For whoever imagine this a sarcasm on the other ingenious person is greatly mistaken. The opinion our author had of him is sufficiently shown by his joining him in the undertaking of the *Odyssey*: in which Mr. *Broome* having engaged without any previous agreement, discharged his part so much to Mr. *Pope*'s satisfaction, that he gratified him with the full sum of *Five hundred pounds*, and a present of all those books for which his own interest could procure him Subscribers, to the value of *One hundred more*.

This is dubious praise, if it is praise at all, as in fact Pope and Broome had quarrelled. Broome had rightly suspected that Pope had no intention of giving him his due share of praise as a translator and at the close of 1725 had written that Pope 'is a Caesar in poetry and will bear no equal'. There was a considerable delay in Pope's handing over of the 'Five hundred pounds', partly because Broome was frightened of asking too often for it. Gratitude is a difficult and mature emotion, and Pope found it easier to attack his collaborator in *Peri Bathos*. Broome's own description of Pope is a good one: 'He has used me ill, he is ungrateful . . I often resemble him to a hedgehog; he wraps himself up in his down, lies snug and warm, and sets his bristles out against mankind.'

What Pope's annotation to this line in the *Dunciad* does not mention is that he got Broome to sign a declaration in a note at the close of the *Odyssey* saying that he had been responsible for only the sixth, eleventh and eighteenth books. He had in fact translated eight of the twenty-four. Fenton had translated four and was persuaded to admit to two alone. Thus at least half of the *Odyssey* was translated by other hands, and there is some evidence that Pope got some Oxford men to translate part of the remaining twelve books. Pope received something like five thousand pounds for this venture, his collaborators earned, between them, a mere seven hundred. In his satires on Curll, Pope had described the hacks whom that publisher kept sleeping three in a bed. Is Pope's conduct towards Fenton and Broome so very different? One of the *Twickenham* editors writes:

> This is the most disreputable episode in a career not free from disreputable episodes, and though it may be explained, it cannot be excused.

Let us look at these translations of Homer in more detail. As we have seen, Pope was determined to succeed in this project by the strength of his imaginative powers. Imagination was what he regarded as a cardinal quality in Homer. This was an idea that he was at pains to emphasize in his *Preface*:

> Homer is universally allowed to have had the greatest Invention of any Writer whatever. . . . Nor is it a Wonder if he has ever been acknowledg'd the greatest of Poets, who most excell'd in That which is the very Foundation of Poetry. It is the Invention that in different degrees distinguishes all great Genius's: The utmost stretch of human Study, Learning, and Industry, which masters every thing besides, can never attain to this. It furnishes Art with all her Materials, and without it Judgement itself can at best but *steal wisely*: For Art is only like a prudent Steward that lives on managing the Riches of Nature. Whatever Praises may be given to Works of Judgement there is not even a single Beauty in them to which the Invention must not contribute.

Pope goes on to elaborate this idea by saying that imagination can transfigure everything it touches and that far from being the enemy to judgement it is an ally, and an ally that must be given priority. If this is what Pope sees as the most important aspect of Homer's poetry, then a criticism of his translation must be concerned with the extent to which he was able to do justice to it. However, the idea of imagination is not as simple as this might imply. One more important consideration must be added. In Pope's view, Homer presents both a historic and an eternal world. He has both an archaeological and a timeless moral interest. To do justice to the historical aspect Pope got Parnell to write a detailed essay on the Homeric period, while Broome provided a great quantity of the material for the historical notes on the *Odyssey*. Pope himself contributed a note on Homer's battles and Achilles' shield as well as an *Index of Arts and Sciences* and a *Poetical Index*.

I want first to deal with Pope's scholarship and then go on to investigate what changes he made to the text to bring out the abiding moral interest in Homer. Finally, I want to see how these two combine with other elements to produce a translation worthy of Homer's imaginative powers.

The first question that we must ask ourselves is how deep and real Pope's scholarship was. Samuel Johnson's answer is as fair as any and I will quote him at length :

At an age like his (for was not more than twenty-five), with an irregular education and a course of life of which much seems to have passed in conversation, it is not very likely that he overflowed with Greek. But when he felt himself deficient, he sought assistance; and what man of learning would refuse to help him? Minute enquiries into the force of words are less necessary in translating Homer than other poets, because his positions are general and his representations natural, with very little dependance on local or temporary customs, on those changeable scenes of artificial life which, by mingling original with accidental notions, and crowding the mind with images which time effaces, produce ambiguity in diction and obscurity in books. To this open display of unadulterated nature it must be ascribed that Homer has fewer passages of doubtful meaning than any other poet in the learned or in modern languages. I have read of a man, who being, by his ignorance of Greek, compelled to gratify his curiosity with the Latin printed on the opposite page, declared that from the rude simplicity of the lines literally rendered, he formed nobler ideas of the Homeric majesty than from the laboured elegance of polished versions.

Those literal translations were always at hand, and from them he could easily obtain his author's sense with sufficient certainty; and among the readers of Homer the number is very small of those who find much in the Greek more than in the Latin, except the music of numbers.

If more help was wanting, he had the poetical translation of Eobanus Hessus, an unwearied writer of Latin verses; he had the French Homers of La Valterie and Dacier, and the English of Chapman, Hobbes and Ogilby. With Chapman, whose work, though now totally neglected, seems to have been popular almost to the end of the last century, he had very frequent consultations, and perhaps never translated any passage till he had read his version, which indeed he has sometimes been suspected of using instead of the original.

Notes were likewise to be provided; for the six volumes would have been very little more than six pamphlets without them. What the mere perusal of the text could suggest, Pope wanted no assistance to collect or methodise; but more was necessary; many pages were to be filled, and learning must supply materials to wit and judgement. Something might be gathered from Dacier; but no man loves to be indebted to his contemporaries, and Dacier was accessible to common readers. Eustathius was therefore necessarily consulted. To read Eustathius, of whose work there was then no Latin version, I suspect Pope, if he had been willing, not to have been able.

This amounts to a polite but thorough and systematic destruction of any claim to true scholarship that Pope might have made.[1] It has all the more weight because it was written by a man who knew the more or less contemporary scene and who was a professional admirer of Pope and even of his *Odyssey*. There were adequate if uninspired translations available and commentaries to hand; what Johnson is implying is that the scholarship of Pope's Homer, except where it is dependent on intuition, could have been achieved by a clever conflation of secondary material.

Pope's contemporaries were quick to point out the mistakes he made. Some attacks are predominantly satirical, like Gildon's in *The New Rehearsal*. Dennis damages his case by misquoting Pope, but both Cooke and Gilbert Wakefield, who were far more considerable scholars than Pope, point out real faults. In the third book of the *Iliad* for example, Pope translates the Greek word for an old woman (ypni) as a proper noun: Graea.

The changes that Pope made to the ethical structure of the Homeric poems are considerable. He confines the Zeus of the original rather more strictly than Homer does, largely so that he can make him approximate to the conception of the deity in the *Essay on Man*. An example of this is a translation of a passage in the first book of the *Iliad* :

> Then thus the God: Oh restless Fate of Pride,
> That strives to learn what Heav'n resolves to hide;
> Vain is the Search, presumptuous and abhorr'd,
> Anxious to thee, and odious to thy Lord.
> Let this suffice; th'immutable Decree
> No Force can shake; What *is*, that *ought* to be.

[1] Maynard Mack, editor of the Twickenham Homer (1967), endorses Johnson's view. 'Johnson's estimate,' he concludes, 'including its concessions and tolerances, stands.'

Here is the more or less literal translation offered in the *Twickenham* edition:

> Then Zeus the cloud-gatherer replied to her: 'Possessed one, you are always imagining, and I cannot escape you; yet you shall not have the power to accomplish anything, but you shall be even further from my heart; and that shall be worse for you. If this is as you say, then it must be dear to me.

It is clear that Pope has imposed something largely alien on the original and this is true of both translations, especially the *Odyssey*, where the hero is made to fit the philosophical concepts of the *Essay on Man* so closely that it has been found possible to follow Odysseus's progression from epistle to epistle as he journeys from one island to another. Odysseus is also given a spurious romanticism which utterly destroys the effect of the original; as this passage from the fifth book illustrates:

> Him pensive on the lonely beach she found,
> With streaming eyes in briny torrents drown'd,
> And inly pining for his native shore;
> For now the soft Enchantress pleas'd no more:
> For now, reluctant, and constrain'd by charms,
> Absent he lay in her desiring arms,
> In slumber wore the heavy night away,
> On rocks and shores consum'd the tedious day;
> There sat all desolate, and sigh'd alone,
> With echoing sorrows made the mountains groan,
> And roll'd his eyes o'er all the restless main,
> Till dimm'd with rising grief, they stream'd again.

Here is a prose version of the same passage:

> Him she found sitting on the shore, and his eyes were never dry of tears, and his sweet life was ebbing away, as he longed mournfully for his return, for the nymph was no longer pleasing in his sight. By night indeed he would sleep by her side perforce in the hollow caves, unwilling beside the willing nymph, but by day he would sit on the rocks and the sands, racking his soul with tears and groans and griefs, and he would look over the unresting sea, shedding tears.

The original Greek is a moving picture of sexual drudgery. Odysseus cannot escape from the nymph Calypso and we are made to feel both the isolation and the human smallness of the hero. He sits on the beach crying, before him is the sea whose constant movement seems to underline the sterility of his miserable state. The scene suggests loneliness.

Pope destroys this by a melodramatic romanticism. He over-exploits the pathetic fallacy, and the little, moving act of crying becomes 'streaming eyes in briny torrents drown'd'. The line 'Absent he lay in her desiring arms' is elegant, but it only conveys the feeling that Odysseus' mind is on Ithaca, it tells us nothing about the real state of his relations with Calypso.

Another obviously un-Homeric and tedious aspect of the translation is the constant allusion to other great works of European literature. This has been widely praised of course. It is considered a good thing that Homer comes to us with bits and pieces of most later epics tacked on, usually in somebody else's translation. The idea is that this impresses upon us how central Homer is to the European literary tradition. Here is an example from the ninth book of the *Odyssey* that contains three echoes of the meeting of Caliban and Stephano:

> More ! give me more, he cry'd: the boon be thine,
> Whoe'er thou art that bear'st *celestial wine* !
> Declare thy name; *not mortal is this juice,*
> Such as th'unblest *Cyclopean* climes produce,
> (Tho' sure our vine the largest cluster yields,
> And Jove's scorn'd thunder serves to drench our fields)
> But this *descended from the b(l)est abodes,*
> A rill of Nectar, streaming from the Gods.

I have ignored Pope's italics and italicized instead those phrases that relate to *The Tempest*. The Shakespearean words are : 'That's a brave god, and bears celestial liquor'; 'the liquor is not earthly'; 'Hast thou not dropp'd from Heaven?' The comparison thus drawn between Polyphemus and Caliban is an interesting one, though strictly limited in application. The effect of such passages is not to make us think either of Homer or, in any real way, of the European literary tradition that stems from him. The result is that our concentration is broken. We lose the drama of the original and gain none of that of the allusion; we are left instead with a confusing memory of books. Personally, I find the technique as annoying as having an unidentified quotation on the brain.

Fenton and Broome, and particularly Fenton, have been widely criticized for having no imagination. This, one might comment in passing, did not deter Pope from employing them. However, they were modest men and avoided the sheer vulgarity that Pope occasionally achieves. Here is his rewriting of lines 71–73 of the first book of the *Odyssey*:

Successless all her soft caresses prove,
To banish from his breast his Country's love.
To see the smoke from his lov'd palace rise
While the dear isle in distant prospect lyes,
With what contentment could he close his eyes?

Here is Fenton's draft:

Yet all her blandishments too pow'rless prove,
To banish from his breast his Country's love.
Might the dear Isle in distant prospect rise,
That view vouchsaf'd, let instant death surprize
With (ever-during) shade his blissful eyes.

Fenton's version is adequate though rather pedestrian verse. It is possible to think of it as speech, even if it does not really become Athene. Pope's first line on the other hand is barbarous, despite the fact that its six 's' sounds have been praised for their 'sibilant femininity'. Furthermore, he twists the construction of the passage in such a way that the question at the close is uncomfortable and unexpected. It certainly bears no relation to the rhythms of normal speech and as a result the earnestness of the original, or even Fenton's version, is lost.

According to one story, though it may be apocryphal, the celebrated Dr Bentley, a well-known classical scholar and exposer of forgeries, declared: 'It's a very pretty poem, Mr Pope, but you mustn't call it Homer'. Bentley was an honest wit and true scholar and if this remark, which has set the tone for much later criticism, is not his, then the *Letter to Mr Pope* of 1735 certainly is.

You are grown very angry, it seems, of Dr. Bentley of late. Is it because he said (*to your face*, I have been told) that your Homer was *miserable stuff*? That it might be called, Homer *modernised*, or something to that effect; but that there were very little or no *vestiges* at all of the *old Grecian*. Dr Bentley said right. Hundreds have said the same thing *behind your Back*. For Homer *translated*, *first* in English, *secondly* in rhyme, *thirdly* not from the Original, but *fourthly*, from a French Translation, and that in *Prose*, by a *woman* too, how the devil should it be *Homer*? As for the *Greek* Language, everybody that *knows* it and has compared must *know* too that you *know* nothing of it. I myself am satisfied, but don't expect to make anybody else believe so, that you can barely construe *Latin*. . . . You have not that compass of human Learning, always thought necessary to a true Poet. . . . Let me advise you as a Friend (for Friend I am, and adore your very Foot-steps as a polite writer) don't hurt yourself by your own Writings; have it always before your eyes, That no Man is demolished but by himself.

The sting of this attack derives from the schoolmasterly tone which, in its turn, comes from sufficient scholarship to see through to the secondary sources with complete clarity. It is interesting not only as an indictment of Pope's scholarship but also as a witness to the fact that not only Bentley but 'hundreds' were dissatisfied with the modernizing of the ethical content. The Twickenham editors have seen the *Odyssey* especially as Pope's attempt 'to legislate ordered values to every aspect of his threatened society . . . a political act'. Clearly, those who read the work wanted their Homer and were not fooled by anything less.

Arnold's criticism of the translation is well known. He says that Homer's eye was fixed on his object, Pope's only on his style, that the heroic couplet was wholly unsuitable as a medium, which is right, and that Pope's chief merit is speed. Arnold's is the last major criticism of a translation, which nowadays is little read, though I have heard dons urge it on undergraduates as superior to modern prose versions. In what ways it is superior it is difficult to see; inaccurate and often insensitive, it is much better replaced by something less pretentious.

Allied to Pope's work as a translator is his work as an editor, and especially as the editor of Shakespeare. His edition, which appeared in six quarto volumes in 1725, was the second attempt at a scholarly re-printing of the text. Pope himself worked only on the plays, the poems and a history of the stage appeared in a seventh volume for which Dr George Sewell was responsible.

Pope's Shakespeare can in no way be regarded as either successful or scholarly. The second edition, which appeared in 1728, lists some twenty-nine quartos which he knew, but it seems that his basic text is substantially that of Rowe; in other words it was based on the Fourth Folio. However, the emendations that he made, purely on the basis of personal taste, were many and now seem rather absurd. The reason he felt able to take so many liberties stems from his conception of Shakespeare himself as it is revealed in Pope's *Preface*. Bonamy Dobrée has called this work 'impeccable' though it is difficult to see why, for although Pope's praise of Shakespeare is obvious, his list of criticisms is conventional and condescending. 'As he has certainly written better,' Pope exclaims, 'so he has perhaps written worse, than any other.' Shakespeare is excused however because of the conditions under which he wrote. He had to appeal to 'the meaner sort of people' and was obliged to conform to the taste of actors. Nevertheless, despite Shakespeare's ignorance of the rules of the ancients and 'the two disadvantages which I have mentioned (to be obliged to please the lowest sort of people, and to keep the worst of company), if the consideration be extended as far as it reasonably may, will appear sufficient to mislead and depress the greatest genius upon earth'.

As far as the actual technique of editing is concerned, Pope's procedure was to mark out the scenes 'so distinctly that every removal of place is specified' while whatever he did not like was 'degraded to the bottom of the page'. He then tightened up the rhythm and punctuation of whatever was left. Naturally the edition was widely censured. Welsted saw through it and Johnson commented that after its failure 'Pope became an enemy to editors, collators, commentators, and verbal criticks; and hoped to persuade the world, that he miscarried in this undertaking only by having a mind too great for such minute employments'.

The chief editor who incurred Pope's hatred was Theobald. Theobald was a sincere scholar of considerable ability. Pope recognized this sufficiently to make a considerable number of alterations – far more than he admitted to – in response to Theobald's criticisms when the second edition appeared. In 1726 Theobald published *SHAKESPEARE RESTORED: or, a Specimen of the Many Errors as well committed as unemended, by Mr. Pope in his late edition of this poet. Designed not only to correct the said edition, but to restore the true reading of Shakespeare in all editions ever yet published*. The book was thus an honest and worthy attempt to preserve Shakespeare in something like his proper image, though perhaps Theobald allowed for greater emendation than we would. It was written for Shakespeare's sake and not as a personal attack on Pope. The title makes this clear, but in the book itself Theobald is at pains to point out that he admires Pope as an original writer:

> I have so great an Esteem for MR. POPE, and so high an Opinion of his Genius and Excellencies, that I beg to be excused from the least intention of derogating from his Merits, in this attempt to restore the true Reading of SHAKESPEARE. Tho' I confess a Veneration, almost rising to Idolatry for the Writings of this inimitable Poet, I would be very loathe even to do *him* Justice at the Expense of *that other* Gentleman's Character.

Theobald's belief was that Shakespeare should be edited in the same spirit of 'literal criticism' – that is amending corrupt words – as had animated Bentley in his classical editing. Shakespeare was sufficient of a classic and sufficiently corrupt textually for this procedure to be warranted. He then quietly demonstrates that many of Pope's readings are absurd, for example 'onyx' instead of 'union' in *Hamlet* (V.v).

Similarly he dismissed Pope's conjecture that the 'table of green fields' is an interpolated stage direction and conjectures 'talked of green fields' instead. His book amounts to a quietly devastating attack. Pope himself, obviously deeply embarrassed, made Theobald the hero of the first *Dunciad*. Thus the first prince of the dunces was a true man of letters who, despite some trivial literary and theatrical compositions, had a real and proven care for literary values. In his relations with Pope, Theobald was, in the words of the Twickenham editor of the *Dunciad*, 'always a dignified opponent'.

6 Epistles to Several Persons

A complicated story surrounds the publication of Pope's so-called *Moral Essays,* a group of four poems which I, following Bateson and the *Twickenham* edition, prefer to call the *Epistles to Several Persons.* In chronological order these are the Epistles to Burlington, Bathurst, Cobham, and a Lady.

The confusion over the title, as well as the text of these works, derives from Pope's choice of Warburton as the editor of the 'Great Edition' of his poems that he was planning at the end of his life. This projected edition, of which only the *Dunciad,* the *Essay on Criticism* and the *Essay on Man* appeared before Pope died, was to contain the definitive texts of all the works and extensive commentaries on each of them by Warburton. Pope died half-way through the work on the *Epistles* and Warburton was left to make radical and confusing alterations. Both men had invested considerable faith in this group of poems, and Pope had written to his editor that 'I know it is there I shall be seen most to advantage'.

Pope had enormous respect for Warburton's editorial skill; this is shown not only by his trusting so important an assignment to him, but also in many references he made to him in letters and conversation. Warburton, however, was not a great editor and Pope was later to find it necessary to curb his activities. Warburton possessed some of Pope's own worst faults. He was exceptionally free with the text he received. *To Bathurst* for example became, in his hands, a dialogue between Pope and his dedicatee. This change was effected by the simple device of placing the initial of the speaker before those passages Warburton assigned to Bathurst and the considerably longer ones he ascribed to Pope. Pope himself considered it necessary to attach a special clause to his will specifically forbidding Warburton to make any verbal changes. This did not stop him from adding fulsome and often inaccurate notes to the poems. Some of these inaccuracies however were approved by Pope himself. Again, the *Epistles to Several Persons* reveal a considerable deviousness on Pope's part.

The change that Warburton made from the present title to *Moral Essays* marks a considerable change in the supposed intention of the poems. Pope himself had called them 'epistles' and reserved the word 'essay' for the *Essay on Criticism* and the *Essay on Man*. The word 'essay' implied something serious and philosophical. It was designed to throw the weight of a reader's interest on to the didactic elements in a work. Considering the copy-book maxims that underlie the *Epistles,* this was an unfortunate move. The true Horatian Epistle conveyed a lighter idea. It was a vehicle for more conversational satire and criticism. It was a more personal form. The unfortunate Ambrose Philips had given some idea of what was expected from the form in *The Spectator* (no. 618) and Pope follows him, and Horace, fairly closely. 'A good fund of strong Masculine sense' was called for and this was to be aided by 'a thorough knowledge of Mankind' and an 'insight into the Business and the prevailing Humours of the Age'. As to the actual tone of expression, Philips required 'refined raillery, and a lively turn of wit, with an easy and concise manner of expression'. Naturally it was required that the diction should be 'correct', and it was widely considered that in this respect Pope failed in *To Burlington*.

Both *To Burlington* and *To Bathurst* are concerned, at least ostensibly, with money. It was a subject that interested Pope deeply. 'He seems,' wrote Dr Johnson, 'to be of an opinion not very uncommon in the world, that to want money is to want everything.' This interest is clear not only from Pope's conduct and these two epistles, but from the *Essay on Man*. Spence told Warburton that Pope had planned a number of epistles on avarice, prodigality, and the moderate use of riches. In fact Pope's ideas on money are far from profound, let alone original, and, as I shall show, much of what he says in these two poems is Tory propaganda against the mercantile activities of the Whigs. However, the statement of the obvious was something that Pope prided himself on in certain cases. He described his *Epistles* to Swift as consisting 'more of morality than wit' and that they were growing graver 'which you will call duller'. He made a direct, public comparison between himself and Swift in the Advertisement prefixed to their joint imitation of Horace's sixth satire in the second book, a work that yet again is concerned with money:

> His manner, and that of Dr. *Swift* are so entirely different, that they can admit of no Invidious Comparison. The Design of the one being to sharpen the Satire, and open the Sense of the Poet; of the other to render his native *Ease* and *Familiarity* yet more easy and familiar.

This sounds like special pleading. He admits to Swift's superior imaginative power, which was obvious enough, but the two comparisons seen

to imply that as a writer of 'grave *Epistles,* bringing Vice to light', his
task is the more serious, the more urgent.

We must ask first what Pope's conception of virtue is in respect to
money. Essentially it is to avoid *'falling into one of two extremes, avarice
or profusion'.* The pursuit of money becomes, rather naïvely, the opposite of the pursuit of virtue. We find this passage in the Epistle to
Bolingbroke:[1]

> Here, Wisdom calls: 'Seek Virtue first! be bold!
> 'As Gold to Silver, Virtue is to Gold.'
> There London's voice: 'Get Money, Money still!
> 'And then let Virtue follow, if she will.'

It is clear from this that wisdom is considered to be opposition to the
own, and of course all the three dedicatees that Pope names for his
Epistles are members of the landed aristocracy. Bateson comments well
on this: 'Virtue, on this interpretation, is a class-concept, the system of
values of the "landed-interest", the "Country Party". Vice is therefore
the social philosophy of the urban capitalists, the rising middle-classes
who, with their champions in Parliament and at Court, were already a
potential threat to the supremacy of the squire-archy.' What really lies
behind the conception of virtue in the third and fourth *Epistles* is a sort
of romantic snobbery, an ingratiating projection of Pope himself. His
own wish, in his paraphrase of Horace, was:

> ... that I had clear
> For life, six hundred pounds a year,
> A handsome House to lodge a Friend,
> A River at my Garden's end,
> A Terras-walk, and half a Rood
> Of Land, set out to plant a Wood.

Most of this he had got for himself. He designed his own life as an
imitation of his aristocratic friends'. A taste for architecture and land-
scape-gardening was something they had in common. It was with such
matters that Pope elaborated the central ethical idea of the *Epistles,*
which is very close to that in the *Essay on Man.* The relationship
between the *Epistles* and the *Essay on Man* will be discussed later.
Suffice it to say here that the concept to be illustrated is that of the
'balance of things' – in other words how, in the *Epistle to Burlington,*
'prodigality scatters abroad money that may turn out to be useful in

[1] Epistles of Horace, Book I. 1.

other hands', while, in the *Epistle to Bathurst,* 'Avarice lays up money that in other hands would be hurtful'.

This takes us to the heart of the problem as to why the *Epistles to Several Persons* fail as satire. How is it possible to be anything other than mildly angry when one accepts the doctrine that 'Whatever IS, is RIGHT' when one holds that even vice labours on the side of good? In the *Epistle to Burlington* the 'Timon's villa' passage is a well-known – in Pope's own day a notorious – piece of satire. It is certainly very impressive. What is usually forgotten however is the mere four lines that follow it, four lines that make up a verse paragraph. They are, of course, designed to emphasize the philosophical aspects of the poem:

> Yet hence the Poor are cloath'd, the Hungry fed;
> Health to himself, and to his Infants bread
> The Lab'rer bears: What his hard Heart denies,
> His charitable Vanity supplies.

If one follows the strict sense of the poem, and is not deflected by the energy of the satirical excitement, then it will be seen that Pope is not complaining of very much. Timon might be vain and wasteful, but at least he serves the common good. Pope says as much himself. All he can really complain about is Timon's bad taste, which is not a fatal fault and his hospitality, which he need not accept. Pope, in fact, was an exceptionally difficult guest. Servants left because of his excessive demands on them, and it appears that his hosts were often not even compensated with adequate conversation.

However, let us examine the *Epistle to Burlington* in more detail Pope begins by criticizing 'the Prodigal' thus:

> Not for himself he sees, or hears, or eats;
> Artists must chuse his Pictures, Music, Meats:
> He buys for Topham, Drawings and Designs,
> For Pembroke Statues, dirty Gods, and Coins;
> Rare monkish Manuscripts for Hearne alone,
> And Books for Mead, and Butterflies for Sloane.
> Think we all these are for himself? no more
> Than his fine Wife, alas! or finer Whore.

This is, simply, ludicrous. What is wrong with buying gifts for collector surely it is an admirable use of wealth? Besides, Topham was a schola who left a valuable collection to Eton, while Hearne was the mo esteemed medievalist of his day, a pioneer editor and a considerab scholar. Surely such a man should be provided with manuscripts, would Pope have preferred him to bankrupt himself by buying the

out of his own limited means as Stow had done? It is a contradiction
in terms for a supporter of literary standards to resent purchases for
other men's libraries, while the vast collection of Sir Hans Sloane
formed the nucleus of the British Museum. Pope is thus satirizing a
number of eminent and commendable scholars. Herne (sic) retorted in
his own terse way: 'This Alexander Pope, tho' he be an English poet,
yet he is but an indifferent scholar, mean at Latin & can hardly read
Greek. He is a very ill-natured man, and covetous and excessively
proud.'

Pope next offers a treatise on landscape gardening which is interesting
enough, though out of proportion, proportion being the very virtue he
is praising. As Bateson says: 'instead of being an "ethic epistle" on the
vice of prodigality, *To Burlington* turned out to be something of a
hotch-potch, one third philosophy, one third gardening, and one third
architectural compliment'. The architectural compliment, of course, is
addressed to Burlington himself:

> You too proceed! make falling Arts your care,
> Erect new wonders, and the old repair,
> Jones and Palladio to themselves restore,
> And be whate'er Vitruvius was before:
> Till Kings call forth th' Idea's of your mind,
> Proud to accomplish what such hands design'd. . . .

In fact, since 1716, Burlington had been employing first Gibbs, then
Campbell, then Bridgeman and William Kent, on his houses in Picca-
dilly and Chiswick. He possessed a vast private fortune which he was
willing to spend. His outlay in one year alone was eighteen thousand
pounds. Naturally he fell into debt, and was obliged to sell his Irish
estates. It is not my intention to criticize him. He had superb taste and
exerted a considerable and important influence. The point I wish to
make is that he does not really form an adequate opposite to Timon –
indeed as far as expenditure is concerned he was rather like him –
and to show in this way the lack of true sincerity in Pope's approach
and the way in which he insinuated himself into friendships with the
great.

On its publication, the *Epistle to Burlington* was a considerable
succès de scandale. The reason for this was that the 'Timon's Villa'
passage was immediately taken to refer to Cannons, the new house of
the Duke of Chandos at Edgeware. It is now clear, especially after the
brilliant research of Sherburn, that the passage does not refer directly
to Chandos, though it does allude to him. Chandos however recognized

himself in it: 'I am not so ignorant of my own weakness, as not to be sensible of its Justness [i.e. that of the "Timon" passage] in some particulars.' It is undoubtedly true that Timon is a composite character and that many of the references in the passage are to such buildings as Blenheim. It may be that Pope played with the dangerous possibility that the Timon passage would receive the immediate interpretation that it did; after all it was so quickly made that the idea must have crossed his mind, but it is also true that he went to some trouble to clear himself. Chandos certainly fully forgave him, despite Johnson's assertion to the contrary. Nevertheless, Pope did not publish his *Master Key to Popery*, which would have more or less cleared him, though he probably wrote two anonymous letters to the newspapers of which the first was 'incorrectly printed'. In addition, there is the public letter prefixed to the third edition. While it is undoubtedly true that the 'Timon' episode put Pope very much in front of the public, it is also true that as a result of it he changed his method of attack, and the future *Epistles* show him increasingly using proper names.

However, to show how little interested Pope was in seriously promoting taste in his time it is only necessary to recount how he intrigued to deprive Hogarth of a royal commission. Early in 1732 Hogarth published his print called variously *Taste, The Man of Taste* and *Burlington Gate*. It is a damningly accurate satire against Pope's poem. It shows Pope spattering Chandos's coach with whitewash. The Duke's achievement of arms can be seen in the corner of the picture. Hogarth's note, which Bateson suggests parodies Pope's disclaimers to the newspaper reads: 'not a Duke's Coach as appears by ye Crescent at one Corner'. The other three corners, of course, are shown surmounted by coronets, and Burlington and Kent are shown climbing on the gate itself. Pope intrigued at court through William Kent. Hogarth lost a promised commission for two portraits and was naturally upset at the loss. Who knows what the pictures might have added to English painting?

The *Epistle to Bathurst* is the longest of the four *Epistles* and it was the one that caused Pope the most trouble in composition. He wrote to Swift that he 'never took more care in my life of any poem' and he reported much the same to Spence. These remarks are unfortunate since the work contains much that is thinnest of Pope's mature writing. The ideas are often simplistic to the point of being embarrassing, and there is much sentimental rhetoric and banality. Many of the ideas on economics to be found there are taken from Mandeville, a writer whom Pope professed to despise.

The argument of the *Epistle to Bathurst* concerns the use of riches and, more directly, avarice. Pope had concluded the letter prefixed to the third edition of *To Burlington* thus:

> Even from the Conduct shewn on this occasion, I have learnt there are some who wou'd rather be *wicked* than ridiculous; and therefore it may be safer to attack *Vices* than *Follies*. I will leave my Betters in the quiet Possession of their *Idols*, their *Groves*, and their *High-Places*; and change my Subject from their *Pride* to their *Meanness*, from their *Vanities* to their *Miseries*: And as the only certain way to avoid Misconstruction, to lessen the Offence, and not to multiply ill-natured Applications, I may probably in my next make use of *Real* Names and not Fictitious Ones.

This paragraph reveals a number of mixed motives. To 'lessen the Offence' of a satire seems, as Bateson comments, to betray one of the main functions of satirical poetry. In addition, is it not a contradiction in terms to assume that he will 'lessen the Offence' if he uses '*Real* names'? The person who had been offended in the first epistle published was Chandos, though under the name Timon; surely someone who had been actually named in person would be far more upset. This desire to name individual people may be taken in conjunction with what he wrote to Arbuthnot, that 'General Satire in Times of General Vice has no force', and that 'tis only by hunting One or two from the Herd that any Examples can be made'. Surely this incurs the risk of reducing satire to the level of gossip and personal vitriol? Besides, if the real intention of satire is the improvement of morals, is it not better to create a composite satiric portrait which is generally applicable and raises general disquiet? In this way the reader's attention is focused on the vice satirized and not on the individual destroyed. What Pope was trying to do was to have his cake and eat it: to attack individuals while masquerading as a high-minded moralist. He was vitally interested in the sales of his satires, and he well knew that these depended to a large extent on their scandalous content. In fact, of course, the naming of names in the *Epistle to Bathurst* is not as simple as this. Thirty-one characters are introduced into the work, but only sixteen appear under their own names. These men are the Dukes of Buckingham and Wharton, who were dead, aristocrats such as Sir William Colepepper and Joseph Gage who were notoriously disreputable, and various members of the middle classes. Any aristocrats who might have done Pope harm are given Latin tags, similar or imaginary names. In other words Pope avoided the responsibilities he had set himself.

It must also be said that of two of the victims named – the Duke of

Buckingham and Sir John Cutler – the accounts that Pope gives are wholly inaccurate. However, both men were safely dead. The account of Buckingham's death is based on gossip, though it must be admitted that Pope works it up into something powerful, even if it is a lie:

> In the worst inn's worst room, with mat half-hung,
> The floors of plaister, and the walls of dung,
> On once a flock-bed, but repair'd with straw,
> With tape-dy'd curtains, never meant to draw,
> The George and Garter dangling from that bed
> Where tawdry yellow strove with dirty red,
> Great Villiers lies – alas! how chang'd from him,
> That life of pleasure, and that soul of whim!

'As it fell to my share,' wrote John Gibson, 'to know as much of the last moments of the Duke of Buckingham as any there about him, so at your instance I shall readily give answer to satisfy any that he died in the best house in Kirkby Moorside, which neither is nor ever was an ale house.' The account of the miser, Sir John Cutler, is similarly inaccurate.

The poem opens with an account of the 'Ballance of things' which, as I have said, is central to the *Epistles* and which receives its fullest exposition in the *Essay on Man*. Savage told Spence that Bolingbroke had sent Pope two long letters on this subject, but if Pope's ideas derive from the peer, they also owe considerably to Mandeville's *Fable of the Bees,* a pragmatic and somewhat cynical book. Pope, we know, professed to despise Mandeville, but his thought here reveals something rather more than 'at least a superficial sympathy' which Bateson finds. Pope writes:

> ... careful Heav'n supply'd two sorts of Men,
> To squander these, and those to hide agen.

Mandeville has: 'Was it not for Avarice, Spendthrifts would soon want Materials ... Was it not for Prodigality, nothing could make us amends for the Rapine and Extortion of Avarice in Power. When a Covetous Statesman is gone . . . it ought to fill every good Member of Society with Joy to behold the uncommon Profuseness of his Son.'

A little later Pope gives us a *non sequitur* as ridiculous as it is ignorant of economic reality. The comparison he draws however reveals an underlying viciousness which tells us far more about Pope than about money or morality:

> And if we count among the Needs of life
> Another's Toil, why not another's Wife?

'Meat, Fire and Cloaths,' he later defines as the only necessities. Taken in conjunction with the couplet I have just quoted, this means either that every man must keep his own farm or that he has the right to possess his butcher's and his outfitter's wives. The laws of financial interdependence, which Pope ignores, are primary to any conception of economics or cultural development. Pope then offers an account of the uses and dangers of money which is commonplace in the extreme :

> Useful, I grant, it serves what life requires,
> But dreadful too, the dark Assassin hires:
> Trade it may help, Society extend;
> But lures the Pyrate, and corrupts the Friend:
> It raises Armies in a Nation's aid
> But Bribes a Senate, and the Land's betray'd.

These comparisons never rise above the level of platitude, but setting this aside, the verbs are weak and banal: money 'hires' an assassin, will 'help' trade, 'extend' society, 'lure' a pirate, 'corrupt' a friend, 'raise' an army or 'bribe' a senate and so on. Not one of these verbs fulfils anything other than a grammatical function. Pope also rather naïvely attacks paper credit. This was anti-Whig propaganda. He shows himself fascinated by its power to corrupt but quite ignorant of its economic significance:

> A single leaf shall waft an Army o'er,
> Or ship off Senates to a distant Shore;
> A leaf, like Sibyl's, scatter to and fro
> Our fates and fortunes, as the winds shall blow:
> Pregnant with thousands flits the Scrap unseen,
> And silent sells a King, or buys a Queen.

There then follows a lengthy and episodic attack on the avaricious and the prodigal, most of which, except for such attacks as those on *Sappho,* who is Lady Mary, appear to have been worked up for the occasion. As Bateson says: 'Almost all of his information, for example, about the two great financial scandals of 1732 – the misappropriations by the Commissioners for the sale of the Earl of Derwentwater's estates and by the Directors of the Charitable Corporation for the Relief of the Industrious Poor – seems to have been derived from the newspapers.' The epistle closes with the moralistic little tale of *Sir Balaam*. This is a lively piece of light verse which recalls and may have inspired Byron. However, it is symptomatic of the weak construction of the poem that it is tacked on to the end after the line:

> But you are tir'd – I'll tell a tale. Agreed.

Bathurst himself declared this to be 'insupportably insipid and flat'.

The *Epistle to Cobham* is concerned with 'the knowledge and characters of men' and naturally it is closely allied to the *Essay on Man*; indeed, both the parts of a projected *magnum opus* that Pope never completed. The Advertisement prefixed to Warburton's edition of the *Epistles* offers the most comprehensive exposition of this 'system of Ethics in the Horatian way' that Pope had been planning since 1729. It was to consist of four books, each divided into a number of epistles. The present *Essay on Man* comprised the first book. It is then stated that:

> The FOURTH and last Book pursues the subject of the *Fourth* Epistle of the *First*, and treats of *Ethics*, or practical Morality; and would have consisted of many members; of which the following Four Epistles were detached portions: the *two first*, on the *Characters of Men and Women* being the *introductory* part of this concluding Book.

There is little original thought in the *Epistle to Cobham*. Most of Pope's ideas, particularly those in the first half of the work, and the theory of the 'Ruling Passion', derive from Montaigne. Indeed, the first hundred lines or so are more or less entirely dependent for their thought on Montaigne's 'Of the Inconstancy of our Actions', though Prior contributed something towards the phrasing. This and other sources were commonly available books, though Pope seems to have convinced himself, or tried to convince Spence, that the 'New Hypothesis' of the ruling passion was really his own. As for the examples at the close of the poem, Bateson comments: 'The anecdotes with which he illustrates the ruling passion strong in death at the end of his Epistle are among the oldest stories in the world.' The theory of the poem thus amounts to a sequence of more or less familiar commonplaces, and at one point at least the facts with which they are illustrated are not logically the most appropriate.

Apart from certain passages of invective, the *Epistle to Cobham* makes dull reading. This derives partly from the monotonous regularity of the couplets. A dozen or so lines of encapsulated 'wisdom' leave the mind deadened. The thought is bald and its natural medium is prose. One can illustrate this by comparing a couplet of Pope to its original, in La Rochefoucauld. Here is Pope:

> Not therefore humble he who seeks retreat,
> Pride guides his steps, and bids him shun the great ...

Here is La Rochefoucauld:

> L'humilité n'est souvent qu'une feinte soumission dont on se sert pour soumettre les autres; c'est un artifice de l'orgueil qui s'abaisse pour s'élever.

Both Pope and La Rochefoucauld expand their ideas through a partial repetition. In the French, 'L'humilité' and 'L'orgueil' are contrasted in such a way as leads to a detailed comparison suggesting first the psychological state that confuses humility and pride, and secondly, and as acutely, a precision of response and an awareness that much more has been observed and experienced by the writer. There is a sort of plenitude even in its cynicism, because La Rochefoucauld permits us to see the chemistry of his thought, the actual manner in which he combines the elements of his deduction. Our moral awareness is greater for contact, however generalized, with a personality. Pope, on the other hand, only gives us words. His antithesis is predominantly verbal. He is playing with an idea, not an experience. The construction and rhythm of the La Rochefoucauld passage draw out our capacity to respond, the couplet merely presents us with a 'fact' that leaves the imagination dormant. However, the central paradox is that whereas La Rochefoucauld's maxim nourishes our own intuition, it does so by the utmost precision of language, while the more rigid demands of Pope's couplet – something external to the thought and not dependent on it – requires an unpleasantly tortuous use of language. The first line is crudely inverted and the second follows on awkwardly while the 'pride-guides' clash is unfortunate.

Such analysis is important if we are really to come to grips with the reason for the failure of the *Epistle to Cobham*. As a medium, in Pope's hands at least, the couplet is rapid and perfunctory. It encapsulates, rather than realizes, and the poem passes on. The verse paragraphs are breathless and smug; the reader is hurried along, subjected by the device of antithesis to the illusion of true analysis. Antithetic form is presented as a substitute for thought. It is as if there were no need to qualify anything further, no need to rest, and, above all, no need to have any critical or intuitive response to what is evidently fact – fact and no more. Here is the whole paragraph from which the previous illustration was taken:

> Not always actions show the man: we find
> Who does a kindness, is not therefore kind;
> Perhaps prosperity becalm'd his breast,
> Perhaps the Wind just shifted from the east:

Not therefore humble he who seeks retreat,
Pride guides his steps, and bids him shun the great:
Who combats bravely is not therefore brave,
He dreads a death-bed like the meanest slave:
Who reasons wisely is not therefore wise,
His pride in Reas'ning, not in Acting lies.

In the last analysis the *Epistle to Cobham* fails because it is creatively interested neither in ideas, nor, really, in man. Its true centre is Alexander Pope. The inherent arrogance of the means of expression, its speed and the semblance of logic are nothing more than a display of Pope's rhetorical ability – an ability that rapidly collapses when we judge it from any standpoint other than that of the enthusiasm it evokes. Who really wants to know, or did not know already, that 'Not always Actions show the man'? This is not a case of 'What oft was *Thought, but ne'er so well Exprest*' since the a-sounds in the phrase are execrable and Hamlet learned the lesson from Claudius's character rather more eloquently. It is simply the commonplace masquerading as insight.

Bateson writes that 'as a peg for hanging anecdotes on no doubt Pope's hypothesis [of the ruling passion] was adequate, but as the basis of an ethical system it would seem to be altogether too naïve.' One of the longest of these anecdotes is that concerning Wharton and it shows clearly how Pope was increasingly filling his work with personal spite. Lady Mary Wortley Montagu was a friend of the Duke of Wharton and she 'told Lady Pomfret that when she became acquainted with the Duke . . . Mr Pope grew jealous, and that occasioned the breach between them.' There are, as we shall see, many stories concerning the break-up of the relation between Pope and Lady Mary. The savage portrait of Wharton is clearly put in as much for revenge as to illustrate the ruling passion, which Pope claimed was in Wharton's case 'Lust of Praise'. However, other anecdotes, as Cobham pointed out, do not really fit the argument. Gluttony, for example, which Pope satirizes at the end, is an appetite 'that from nature we indulge as well for her ends as for our pleasure' and Cobham continues that 'a passion or habit that has not a natural foundation' would have served better as an example of the ruling passion. Cobham himself, of course, is praised at the close as the aristocrat whose ruling passion is patriotism:

And you! brave *Cobham*, to the latest breath
Shall feel your ruling passion strong in death:
Such in those moments as in all the past,
'Oh, save my Country, Heav'n!' shall be your last.

Pope had previously applied almost identical lines to Atterbury, lines that he had stolen from Atterbury's last letter to him.

Before discussing the *Epistle to a Lady* which is concerned with 'the characters of women', let us look at the *Epistle to Miss Blount, on her leaving the Town, after the Coronation* since this shows Pope in a delicately satirical vein and forms an illuminating contrast to the later work.

The *Epistle to Miss Blount* – Teresa seems to have been the sister in question, but Pope was always equivocal about this – is a charmingly observed love poem. It is the warmest and, apart from the suppressed ending, the least sinister of Pope's works. Teresa had been sent back to Mapledurham just after the coronation of George I. Pope describes the boredom of country life:

> She went, to plain-work, and to purling brooks,
> Old-fashion'd halls, dull aunts, and croaking rooks,
> She went from Op'ra, park, assembly, play,
> To morning walks, and pray'rs three hours a day;
> To pass her time 'twixt reading and Bohea,
> To muse and spill her solitary Tea,
> Or o'er cold coffee trifle with the spoon,
> Count the slow clock, and dine exact at noon;
> Divert her eyes with pictures in the fire,
> Hum half a tune, tell stories to the squire;
> Up to her godly garret after seven,
> There starve and pray, for that's the way to heav'n.

Then Pope describes the squire who is pursuing her. Such writing has humanity. It lacks the sordid details that were to become a feature of his later work, and reveals a side of Pope which did not live; geniality was soon to be supplanted by spite and rancour:

> Some Squire, perhaps, you take delight to rack;
> Whose game is Whist, whose treat a toast in sack,
> Who visits with a gun, presents you birds,
> Then gives a smacking buss, and cries – No words!
> Or with his hound comes hollowing from the stable,
> Makes love with nods, and knees beneath a table;
> Whose laughs are hearty, tho' his jests are coarse,
> And loves you best of all things – but his horse.

Lastly we get Pope's wistfully ironic self-portrait as he is left in London:

> So when your slave, at some dear, idle time,
> (Not plagu'd with headache, or the want of rhime)
> Stands in the streets, abstracted from the crew,
> And while he seems to study, thinks of you:

> Just when his fancy paints your sprightly eyes,
> Or sees the blush of soft *Parthenia* rise,
> Gay pats my shoulder, and you vanish quite;
> Streets, chairs, and coxcombs rush upon my sight;
> Vext to be still in town, I knit my brow,
> Look sow'r, and hum a tune – as you may now.

The *Epistle to a Lady* lacks this gay and realistic delicacy. There is much that is no more than personal malice, a form of macabre revenge. Mackail accurately defined what Pope had progressed to when he declared in his Leslie Stephen lecture of 1919 that 'his cynicism with regard to women is really sentimentality gone tainted; some would say, gone putrid.' Thus in this work we find (on the one hand) passages that are no more than personal abuse, on the other hand passages of heavy-handed condescension which are awkwardly suspended between satire and didacticism:

> In Men, we various Ruling Passions find,
> In Women, two almost divide the kind;
> Those, only fix'd, they first or last obey,
> The Love of Pleasure, and the Love of Sway.
> That, Nature gives; and where the lesson taught
> Is still to please, can Pleasure seem a fault?
> Experience, this; by Man's oppression curst,
> They seek the second not to lose the first.
> Men, some to Bus'ness, some to Pleasure take;
> But ev'ry Woman is at heart a Rake:
> Men, some to Quiet, some to public Strife;
> But ev'ry Lady would be Queen for life.

An excellent example of 'sentimentality . . . gone putrid' is the picture of Lady Mary Wortley Montagu that now emerges in this poem and in some of the *Imitations of Horace*. The exact cause of their quarrel is difficult to ascertain. Probably, as in the breakdown of many long-standing relationships that involve a little more than friendship, a series of incidents led to a slow estrangement. Lady Mary appears to have laughed at Pope; Pope seems to have been jealous of such friends of hers as Wharton. Whatever it was that finally divided them, she seems to have shown little interest in Pope after her return from Turkey. She certainly did not justify the image of her that Pope had been creating in his letters to her. Indifference on her side was met with savage retaliation on his. The woman who had charmed him into friendship was a whore, an avaricious and pox-ridden woman of disreputable personal

habits. She becomes the *Sappho* of many cruel lines, lines inserted into
several poems on the flimsiest pretext :

> Rufa, whose eye quick-glancing o'er the Park,
> Attracts each light gay meteor of a Spark,
> Agrees as ill with Rufa studying Locke,
> As Sappho's diamonds with her dirty smock,
> Or Sappho at her toilet's greasy task,
> With Sappho fragrant at an ev'ning Mask:
> So morning Insects that in muck begun,
> Shine, buzz, and fly-blow in the setting-sun.

Increasing coprophilia is a distinctive mark of Pope's later satire, and
we can observe it here. It is as if he literally needed to throw muck at
his victims. However, the lines on Sappho in the *Epistle to a Lady* were
not the first in which Pope had attacked Lady Mary under that name.
In *The First Satire of the Second Book of Horace, Imitated,* he had
written this:

> From furious *Sappho* scarce a milder Fate,
> P - x'd by her Love, or libell'd by her Hate.

She is ridiculed in the *Epistle to Arbuthnot,* the imitation of the second
satire of Donne, and the *Epilogue to the Satires.* Of course she fought
back, as I shall show, but exactly how Pope's victims could suffer
from being ridiculed under assumed names is revealed in a letter
of Lady Mary's to Arbuthnot, a letter she asked the Doctor to show
Pope :

> 'I have perused the last lampoon [*Epistle to Arbuthnot*] of your ingenious
> friend, and am not surprised you do not find me out under the name
> of Sappho, because there is nothing in our characters and circumstances
> to make a parallel; but as the town (except you, who know better)
> generally suppose Pope means me, whenever he mentions that name, I
> cannot help taking notice of the horrible malice he bears against the
> lady signified by that name.'

Attacking in this way fascinated Pope. He wrote and prevaricated about
it endlessly. He said to Warburton in an undated letter that 'I have just
run over ye Second Epistle fro Bowyer. I wish you c^d add a Note at y^e
End of it, to observe ye authors Tenderness in using no *living Examples*
or *Real Names*'. This had to be altered when the final revision appeared
since a portrait of Mrs Howard, carefully disguised under the name
Cloe, had been added. We have seen the effect of the Timon passage
and the facts, rather than the theories, of Pope's use of names in the

other *Epistles.* It is a fact, and one that Pope cannot have been ignorant of, that while assumed names preserved his *persona* as the public moralist, the gossip of the town, trying to find prototypes for his characters, made half-correct identifications which served to discomfort the victims personally. Aristocrats he attacked obliquely, little men by name. There is a good example of this in the *Epistle to Arbuthnot*:

> Yet soft by Nature, more a Dupe than Wit,
> *Sappho* can tell you how this Man was bit:
> This dreaded Sat'rist *Dennis* will confess
> Foe to his Pride, but Friend to his Distress:
> So humble, he has knock'd at *Tibbald's* door,
> Has drunk with *Cibber,* nay has rhym'd with *Moor.*

That this was a particularly effective technique is proved by the powerful Duchess of Marlborough's attempt to suppress the *Epistle to a Lady* since she feared that she was ridiculed, as indeed to a small measure she was, in the portrait of Atossa. She was, also, guarding the reputation of her husband. The 1744 edition was suppressed.

The *Epistle to a Lady* also throws interesting light on Pope's deviousness in the matter of plagiarism. James Moor-Smythe had quoted the first version of these lines in his comedy *The Rival Modes*:

> See how the World its Veterans rewards!
> A Youth of frolicks, an old Age of Cards,
> Fair to no purpose, artful to no end,
> Young without Lovers, old without a friend,
> A Fop their Passion, but their Prize a Sot,
> Alive, ridiculous, and dead, forgot!

He printed them in italics to show that they were quoted, as were two other lines of Pope's; however, as Bateson says, Pope 'chose to look upon the insertion of his lines as a plagiarism and a quarrel developed'.

The *Epistle to Arbuthnot* is Pope's self-portrait. Superficially it appears controlled and civilized and Leslie Stephen has called it 'his most perfect work'. Pope himself described it thus:

> This Paper is a Sort of Bill of Complaint, begun many years since, and drawn up by snatches, as the several Occasions offer'd. I had no thought of publishing it till it pleas'd some Persons of Rank and Fortune (the Authors of *Verses to the Imitator of Horace*, and of an *Epistle to a Doctor of Divinity from a Nobleman at Hampton Court,*) to attack in a very extraordinary manner, not only my Writings (of which being publick the Publick judge) but my *Person, Morals,* and *Family,* whereof to those who know me not, a truer Information may be requisite.

Pope continues by saying that if he has anything pleasing to write it will be 'the *Truth* and the *Sentiment*', while if he offends 'it will be only . . . those I am least sorry to offend, the *Vicious* or *The Ungenerous*'. He cannot lose. He ends by once again elaborating the theory behind his use of assumed names in his satires. As I have already shown, his use of this technique in the *Epistle to Arbuthnot* follows his usual practice of naming only those who could not harm him significantly – along with the Sporuses and Sapphos come the Cibbers and the Dennisses. Pope's actual statement of this contains one phrase that is crucial to any real discussion of the poem:

> Many will know their own Pictures in it, there being not a Circumstance but what is true; but I have, for the most part spar'd their Names, and they may escape being laugh'd at, if they please.

'Not A Circumstance but what is true' – in the poem itself Pope supplements this statement with the lines:

> That not in Fancy's Maze he wander'd long,
> But stoop'd to Truth, and moraliz'd his song.

Pope is saying that it is by the truth of what he has written that his name will be cleared. Let us examine this claim in a little more detail. However, before we do so, and thereby fulfil what Pope asks of us, it is necessary to clear away the elaborate defence and intricate special pleading that such modern critics as Maynard Mack have erected. Mack demands that instead of listening to Pope the man, as the poet asks us to, we respect the *persona* instead. In other words, the truth that Pope insists upon is irrelevant compared to the poem as an artefact. Here it is worthwhile to repeat some remarks quoted in an earlier chapter: 'Inquiries into the biographical and historical origins, or into the effects on audiences and readers,' Mack declares, 'can and should be supplemented, we are beginning to insist, by a third kind of inquiry treating the work with some strictness as a rhetorical construction: as a "thing made", which, though it reaches backward to an author and forward to an audience, has its artistic identity in between – in the realm of artifice and artefact.' Extending the argument to Pope's satires, Mack writes that 'we overlook what is most essential if we overlook the distinction between the historical Alexander Pope and the dramatic Alexander Pope who speaks them'. Mack insists on the existence of 'the Muse', and seems to claim that, by continually invoking her, Pope disclaims responsibility for his utterances. In fact Pope rarely if ever calls on the Muse. When he comes to deal with the *Epistle to Arbuthnot* itself Mack attacks those who find Pope insincere or vain, on the ground that the poem is a piece of self-portrayal in the image of the classical satirist and his necessary ethos. This is indeed true. But what Pope claimed in addition is that the truth supports him. That this is not borne out by an examination of the facts is irrelevant to such critics as Mack. He claims that the poem is only tangentially related to both history and audience, that it is related to nothing except itself. In other words what is satirized is no more important than the effect of the inherent morality of the poem on the audience. Like Milton's Satan the poem is *sui generis*. It only exists to be praised.

The *Epistle to Arbuthnot* opens with a vigorous and exhibitionistic description of Pope being besieged by other poets wanting their work corrected and their careers advanced. It 'resembles', to use Butt's word, the first of Edward Young's *Two Epistles to Mr. Pope, Concerning The Authors of the Age*. Young describes himself as being pestered in this way and then goes on to elaborate the different reasons for writing that such men have in terms very similar to Pope's. The most graphic couplet in Pope's lines:

> Is there, who lock'd from Ink and Paper, scrawls
> With desp'rate Charcoal round his darken'd walls?

is taken straight from Boileau. Pope then depicts his gentlemanly behaviour as he dispenses Horace's advice that a poet should keep his poems nine years before publishing them. However:

> Glad of a quarrel, strait I clap the door,
> Sir, let me see your works and you no more.

Pope then begins a new paragraph with two execrable lines which are followed by a 'resonance' from Addison who some lines later he will savagely attack:

> You think this cruel? take it for a rule,
> No creature smarts so little as a Fool.
> Let Peals of Laughter, *Codrus*! round thee break,
> Thou unconcern'd canst hear the mighty Crack.

The 'break – Crack' rhyme is awful. It is Addison's and Pope quoted it in the twelfth chapter of *Peri Bathous* to show that 'Sometimes a single *Word* (crack) will vulgarize a poetical idea.'

In the following lines, alluding to the retired Horatian ideal which he is later to expound, Pope blames both his friends and his enemies for involving him in the frenzy of the literary world which, as we have seen, he did so much to promote. However, for the moment, borrowing from Ovid and from Boileau again, he asks why he began to write in the first place, and then why he published:

> ... *Granville* the polite,
> And knowing *Walsh*, would tell me I could write;
> Well-natur'd *Garth* inflam'd with early praise
> And *Congreve* lov'd, and *Swift* endur'd my Lays;
> The Courtly *Talbot, Somers, Sheffield* read,
> Ev'n mitered *Rochester* would nod the head,
> And *St. John*'s self (great *Dryden*'s friends before)
> With open arms receiv'd one poet more.
> Happy my Studies, when by these approv'd!
> Happier their Author, when by these belov'd!
> From these the world will judge of Men and Books,
> Not from the *Burnets, Oldmixons*, and *Cooks*.

This deplorable piece of name-dropping is as significant for its omissions as for its inclusions. Pope had dedicated *Windsor Forest* to Granville, who was a mediocre poet, but an aristocrat, whom Wycherley had introduced to Pope. Wycherley himself is not mentioned, despite the fact that Pope, at the beginning of his career, was keen to court the playwright's favour. Here is a passage from a letter he wrote to him:

> It was certainly a great satisfaction to me to see and converse with a man, whom in his writings I had so long known with pleasure. But it was a high addition to it, to hear you, at our very first meeting, doing justice to your dead friend Mr. Dryden. I was not so happy as to know him; *Virgilium tantum vidi*—Had I been born early enough, I must have known and lov'd him: for I have been assur'd, not only by yourself, but by Mr. Congreve and Sir William Trumbull, that his personal qualities were as aimiable as his poetical....

Pope had dedicated his third pastoral, *Autumn*, to Wycherley, though now he did not choose to remember him. Similarly, Pope had dedicated *Spring* to the Sir William Trumbull he mentions in this letter. Sir William was an oldish man with a deep and sincere love of poetry whom Pope, as a boy, had ridden with frequently in Windsor Forest. He gained much from him, though he did not trouble to remember it now. Exactly how much Pope owed to Garth, I have detailed in my discussion of *The Rape of the Lock*. Pope then lists three politicians. The self-congratulatory note to some first editions of these lines reads:

These are the persons to whose account the Author charges the publication of his first pieces: Persons with whom he was conversant (and he
adds belov'd) at 16 or 17 years of age; an early period for such acquain-
tance! The catalogue might be yet more illustrious, had he not confined
it to that time when he writ the *Pastorals* and *Windsor Forest*, on which
he passes a sort of Censure in the lines following,

> *While pure Description held the place of Sense, &c*
>
>   P.

The lines are thus a sort of half truth, which the note in no way excuses,
but those on Dennis that follow shortly afterwards are a misrepresentation and show how far Pope was prepared to rake up the past – inaccurately – in order to dwell on old feuds.

> Yet then did *Dennis* rave in furious fret;
> I never answer'd, I was not in debt.

Despite protestations that Dennis was beneath his notice, he satirized
him in the *Essay on Criticism* under the name of the hero of his failed
tragedy and printed anonymous and obscene lampoons against him.
Dennis had offered to make peace. Pope agreed and then quarrelled
again. This attack is then followed by one on Bentley and Theobald who
are ridiculed for the humble task of textual editing at which Pope was so
bad and for which they had censured him. It is probably Philips who
is attacked as 'The Bard whom pilfer'd Pastorals renown' – an impossible grammatical construction? – but one only has to look at the
Twickenham edition and a biography of Pope to see how accurately
these lines apply to himself. Thus in the first half of the poem we have
falsification by deliberate omission which is inaccurately covered up in
a footnote; total misrepresentation of the truth with regard to Dennis,
a ridiculous satire on two able scholars who are mocked for their
ability and to whose criticism Pope submitted, despite the implication
one naturally derives from his line: 'If wrong, I smil'd; if right, I kiss'd
the rod.'; and a criticism of plagiarism that is most applicable to himself. Of the many plagiarized lines in the first half of the *Epistle*
Arbuthnot, a number come from Addison whom he then satirizes in
lines 193–214.

   The portrait of *Atticus* is another example of Pope's bringing of
quarrels into this poem. Addison had been dead for fourteen years when
the *Epistle to Arbuthnot* appeared, though the portrait had been
existence in a rough form since the days of the *Iliad* quarrel. However
this had been made up three years before Addison died and Pope had
written his complimentary *To Mr. Addison, Occasioned by his Dialogue*

on MEDALS in which he suggests that Addison is worthy of having a medal struck to his fame. Thus Pope had agreed to end the quarrel and Addison was dead. Why then publish? In this instance Pope cannot have been urged to it by any of his aristocratic friends. It had been printed anonymously three and a half years after Addison's death, but that is all. There is, however, a revealing note printed in some of the 1735 editions which reappears in Warburton's edition of 1751 :

> It was a great Falsehood which some of the Libels reported, that this Character was written after the Gentleman's [Addison's] death, which we see refuted in the Testimonies prefix'd to the Dunciad. But the occasion of writing it was such, as he would not make publick in regard to his memory; and all that could further be done was to omit the Name, in the Editions of his Works.

In other words Pope had agreed to publish it as a piece of general satire. It was too good to omit from this anthology of hatred. If it is general satire, however, is it not out of place in a work which it is declared was 'drawn up by snatches, as the several occasions offered'? What place has the portrait in the poem if it is not a specific attack? The answer is, of course, that it *is* a specific attack and was taken as such by Pope's contemporaries, hence the note. The couplet that precedes the portrait reads:

> How did they fume, and stamp, and roar, and chafe?
> And swear, not *Addison* himself was safe.

while Addison's review of the *Essay on Criticism* had used the image of the great Turk that Pope now employs (a commonplace that Pope had used in his own letters to describe Addison), while in addition, as the most obvious hint of all, there is a reference to Addison's *Cato*, a reference that is neatly adapted from Lansdowne's poem praising the poet-politician, *Verses sent to the Author in his Retirement*. After this dubious passage come lines so obviously untrue that they only need the most rudimentary knowledge of Pope's career to be disproved:

> I ne'r with Wits or Witlings past my days,
> To spread about the Itch of Verse and Praise;
> Nor like a puppy daggled thro the Town,
> To fetch and carry Sing-song up and down . . .

After a satirical portrait of a bad patron – *Bufo* is generally reckoned to be a combination of Bubb Dodington and the Earl of Halifax - Pope then proceeds to sketch out his own image as the honest man of letters living harmlessly in a Horatian retirement.

Oh let me live my own! and die so too!
('To live and die is all I have to do:')
Maintain a Poet's Dignity and Ease,
And see what friends, and read what books I please.
Above a Patron, tho' I condescend
Sometimes to call a Minister my Friend:
I was not born for Courts or great Affairs,
I pay my Debts, believe, and say my Pray'rs,
Can sleep without a poem in my head,
Nor know, if Dennis be alive or dead.

. . .

    Curst be the Verse, how well soe'er it flow,
That tends to make one worthy Man my foe,
Give Virtue scandal, Innocence a fear,
Or from the soft-ey'd Virgin steal a tear!

The portrait of *Sporus* which follows this section is probably the masterpiece of Pope's invective. Leavis has praised its 'destructive vivacity', and Byron's admiration of it is famous:

> Taking passage for passage, I will undertake to cite more lines teeming with *imagination* from Pope than from any *two* living poets, be they who they may. To take an instance at random. From a species of composition not very favourable to imagination – Satire: set down the character of Sporus, with all the wonderful play of fancy which is scattered over it, and place by its side an equal number of verses, from any two existing poets, of the same power and the same variety – where will you find them?

Sporus, as is well known, represents Lord Hervey. For the reason why his portrait is included we must refer once more to Pope's quarrel with Lady Mary. As I have said, the relation between them had been cooling ever since Lady Mary had returned from Turkey, but in June 172? an anonymous lampoon called *A Popp upon Pope* appeared which Pope assumed had been written by Lady Mary. He also accused her of being involved in various other pieces directed against him. Pope' immediate revenge was the couplet in the first *Imitation* which I have quoted. Lady Mary then enlisted Lord Hervey's aid and together they composed *Verses addressed to the Imitator of Horace*. Hervey also brought out *An Epistle to a Doctor of Divinity from a Nobleman a Hampton Court*, writing soon afterwards to a friend that 'Pope is in most violent fury and j'en suis ravi'.

Pope paints his picture with strong outlines that guarantee the maximum effect. Hervey is shown as a failed poet, as an ambitious, gossipin transvestite, and, above all, as a personification of impotence. The range of imagery is exceptionally wide, Pope bringing in everything from the diet of ass's milk that he himself was enduring, and which had already been applied to Hervey in the anonymous lampoon *The Lord H – – r – – y's first speech in the House of Lords*, through the Satan of *Paradise Lost*, through to a reference to wasps which is taken from Hervey's own satire against Pope. Naturally, as the Queen's confidant, Hervey does not appear under his own name, but he was at once recognized. The reason why the identification was so immediate is quite simple. As Robert Halsband, Hervey's latest biographer, has written: 'every stroke that Pope used in his Sporus-image had already been exploited by previous satirists.' Hervey's position alone, setting aside his personal characteristics, which were of course grossly inflated by the satirists, made him the natural butt of satire and lampoon, and Halsband comments that 'the profusion and virulence of all these satires, in manuscript and in print, seem astonishing.' Thus the *Sporus* portrait, which has long been held to show Pope at his best, also shows him at his most typical. He has taken everything from other writers and refashioned it with the energy of his own hatred. He has sifted what is the best out of predominantly Grub Street journalism and built up his portrait that way. He carefully follows it with a self-portrait designed to show his own integrity in a hurtful world:

> Not Fortune's Worshipper, nor Fashion's Fool,
> Not Lucre's Madman, nor Ambition's Tool,
> Not proud, nor servile, be one Poet's praise,
> That, if he pleas'd, he pleas'd by manly ways;
> That Flatt'ry, ev'n to Kings, he held a shame,
> And thought a Lye in Verse or Prose the same:
> That not in Fancy's Maze he wander'd long,
> But stoop'd to Truth, and moraliz'd his song:
> That not for Fame, but Virtue's better end,
> He stood the furious Foe, the timid Friend,
> The damning Critic, half-approving Wit,
> The Coxcomb hit, or fearing to be hit;
> Laugh'd at the loss of Friends he never had,
> The dull, the proud, the wicked, and the mad;
> The distant Threats of Vengeance on his head,
> The Blow unfelt, the Tear he never shed:
> The Tale reviv'd, the Lye so oft o'erthrown;
> Th'imputed Trash, and Dulness not his own;
> The Morals blacken'd when the Writings scape;
> The libel'd Person, and the pictur'd Shape;

> Abuse on all he lov'd, or lov'd him, spread,
> A Friend in Exile, or a Father, dead;
> The Whisper that to Greatness still too near,
> Perhaps yet vibrates on his SOVEREIGN'S Ear –
> Welcome for thee, fair Virtue ! all the past:
> For thee, fair Virtue ! welcome ev'n the *last* !

Even if this were true, as it is not, it would still be unbearably self-satisfied, but as it is, the greater part of the details can be proved to be falsehoods. It is unpleasant, but necessary, to illustrate this. The *Epistles to Several Persons* show all too clearly how interested Pope was in money, while his addresses to the great in these works, carrying little or no poetic conviction, demonstrate his concern with rank, even if we accept Mack's conception of the satiric *persona*. Pope was proud, horribly proud; much of what he says about Addison is applicable to himself, while Fenton and Broome, among numerous other contemporaries, decry Pope's haughtiness in their letters. What exactly he meant when he says that he 'thought a Lye in Verse or Prose the same' is difficult to ascertain. Pope lied and prevaricated constantly, as I have shown. I do not believe that he was more interested in virtue than fame. From the beginning of his career he was obsessed with fame. His manoeuvres kept him constantly in the public eye, despite his professed love of retirement, and Johnson declared that the *Dunciad* was written first to advertise Pope and only secondly to castigate dullness, a judgement that is harsh but perceptive. If we consider the *Epistle to Arbuthnot* chiefly as an artefact, which Pope declared he did not, then the lies make up an elegant *persona*, but if we consider the truth, which is what Pope asks us to look at, then the picture is wholly untenable. The *Epistle to Arbuthnot* clearly shows Pope trying to make the facts fit the *persona* and failing lamentably. Would one suppose, from the obviously sincere filial sentiments at the end that Pope was the author of this:

> See good Sir *George* of ragged Livery stript,
> By worthier Footmen pist upon and whipt !
> Plunder'd by thieves, or Lawyers which is worse,
> One bleeds in Person, and one bleeds in Purse;
> This meets a Blanket, and that meets a Cudgel –
> And all applaud the Justice – All, but *Budgel*.

These lines appear in *Sober Advice from Horace*, a poem that Pope published anonymously in 1734 for a fee of sixty guineas. It is an unpleasant, suspiciously energetic poem about the more sordid aspects of sex in society. Its strength lies not so much in its scandal, as in the complete conviction with which it appears to be written. The diction on the whole is natural, the observation acute, and the proliferation of ideas organic. It is a convincing picture of desperate and shallow lust and it is one of Pope's most psychologically coherent works. Technically too it bears the marks of inspiration, the rhymes are less predictable than usual, less soporific, and the hurried tone is at one with the subject:

> A Lady's Face is all you see undress'd;
> (For none but Lady M – – – shows the Rest)
> But if to Charms more latent you pretend,
> What Lines encompass, and what Works defend !
> Dangers on Dangers ! obstacles by dozens !
> Spies, Guardians, Guests, old Women, Aunts and Cozens !
> Could you directly to her Person go,
> Stays will obstruct above, and Hoops below,
> And if the Dame says yes, the Dress says no.
> Not thus at N – – dh – – m's; your judicious Eye
> May measure there the Breast, the Hip, the Thigh !
> And will you run to Perils, Sword and Law,
> All for a Thing you ne're so much as *saw*?

'Lady M – – – –' is of course Lady Mary Wortley Montagu, while Cozens was a well-known corset-maker whose name Pope utilizes for a clever *double entendre*. The italicized abbreviation refers to Mother Needham who kept a well-known London brothel. Pope's attitude to brothels and whoring is typical of his general moral prevarication since we find the all-male company tone of this passage juxtaposed against numerous criticisms of whoring.

The authorship of *Sober Advice from Horace* was soon correctly guessed and Pope repudiated the work. The excuses that he made naturally confirmed his image of the unfairly attacked moralist and they constitute one of the most extraordinary and transparent examples of Pope's compulsive lying in the whole of his career. For example, he wrote a letter to the Earl of Oxford and commended himself in a postscript to Oxford's nephew Viscount Dupplin. 'I hope,' he wrote, 'he will defend me from the imputation which all the town I hear lay upon me, of having writ that impudent satire.' Viscount Dupplin was the 'prating Balbus' who had been roundly censured for gossiping about Pope's poetry in the *Epistle to Arbuthnot*. In other words Pope was perfectly aware that a vice that he censured was, in the right circumstances, a most useful weapon on his side. In the light of the note attached to the *Epistle to Arbuthnot* and Pope's satirical *persona*

pictured in the poem, this action is most revealing. To Caryll he wrote
in self-justification: 'There is a piece of poetry from Horace come out,
which I warn you not to take for mine, though some people are willing
to fix it on me: in truth I should think it a very indecent sermon, after
the Essay on Man.' To Pope's admirers such incidents are of course
embarrassing. John Butt for example sees the letter to Caryll as an
example of 'genteel equivocation', but in the following sentence refers
to the publication of the piece under the title *The Second Satire of the
First Book, Imitated in the Manner of Mr Pope* as a 'deceit'. Pope,
of course, had dedicated the first printing of the poem to himself, including in the dedicatory letter a snide reference to Bentley whose
Latin text he had used :

> *SIR,*
> I have so great a Trust in your Indulgence towards me, as to believe
> you cannot but Patronize this Imitation, so much in your own Manner,
> and whose Birth I may truly say is owing to you. In that Confidence, I
> would not suppress the Criticisms made upon it by the *Reverend
> Doctor*, the rather, since he has promised to *mend the Faults* in the next
> Edition, with the same Goodness he has practised to *Milton*. I hope you
> will believe that while I express my Regard for you, it is only out of
> Modesty I conceal my Name; since, tho' perhaps, I may not profress
> myself your Admirer so much as some others, I cannot but be, with as
> much inward Respect, Good-will, and Zeal as any Man,
> > *DEAR SIR,*
> > *YOUR MOST AFFECTIONATE*
> > *AND*
> > *FAITHFUL SERVANT.*

The whole thing is an extraordinary performance. Pope must have
known of the possibility at least of his authorship being guessed at,
while this letter assists this obvious construction. Why then publish
at all? If he needed to write the poem he could have hidden it away
in a drawer. Many poets have left collections of strange erotica? one
only needs to think of Tennyson or Swinburne. It is as if Pope, now fully
proficient in the literary game – a game for which he had offered so
many of the precedents – was trapped in the mirror-maze of his own
vanity. The most coherent construction one can put on his actions is
that by publishing in this crypto-anonymous way he could insult his
enemies and afterwards, when authorship had been detected, fall back
on protestations of being ill-used which would justify what he had said
about himself in the *Epistle to Arbuthnot*. He included the poem, with
its spurious title, in the 1738, 1740 and 1743 editions of his works, and,

as Butt perceptively comments, 'perhaps to aid the deceit, Parnell's versification of Donne's *Third Satire* was printed in these editions immediately after *Sober Advice*'.

In his *First Satire of the Second Book of Horace, Imitated*, Pope describes himself as 'To VIRTUE ONLY and HER FRIENDS, A FRIEND', which is the sort of bald, defensive statement that is common in Pope's writing at this period. In the Advertisement prefixed to the poem we get a more detailed description of his satirical position, one however that depends on an inadequately qualified play on the words 'Satyrist' and 'Libeller', two words that Pope clearly found awkwardly similar:

> *And indeed there is not in the world a greater Error, than that which Fools are so apt to fall into, and Knaves with good reason to Encourage, the mistaking of a* Satyrist *for a* Libeller; *whereas to a* true Satyrist *nothing is so odious as a* Libeller, *for the same reason as to a man* truly Virtuous *nothing is so hateful as a* Hypocrite.

The discussion is taken up yet again in the *Epilogue to the Satires: Dialogue Two*, a work somewhat similar to the *Epistle to Arbuthnot*, but lacking the restraint that that poem shows. The second epilogue is cast in the form of a dialogue though the second protagonist is never really given a chance and only serves as an object to be spoken to. When he does raise a legitimate point the answers are often interesting. Pope portrays himself as the archetypal satirist, lashing vice from a pure love of virtue, as the last guardian and proclaimer of virtue in an utterly degenerate age. The arrogance of many of these lines may be sincere, but in expression they owe much to Boileau. Pope is asked why he names names, and, on the theoretical level, dodges the question. He is then asked why he does not praise virtue more often. Pope attacks himself with a good question, but again his answer is unsatisfactory. In the course of the dialogue he mentions about thirty names of virtuous friends, but half-way through come the lines in which he suggests that merely to be a friend of his or to escape his censure is an adequate reward for virtue:

> Find you the Virtue, and I'll find the Verse
> But random Praise – the Task can ne'er be done,
> Each Mother asks it for her Booby Son,
> Each Widow asks it for the Best of Men,
> For him she weeps, and him she weds again.
> Praise cannot stoop, like Satire, to the Ground;
> The Number may be hang'd, but not be crown'd.

> Enough for half the Greatest of these days
> To 'scape my Censure, not expect my Praise:
> Are they not rich? what more can they pretend?
> Dare they to hope a Poet for their Friend?

The works I have been discussing in this chapter are not, poetically, among Pope's most successful. There are many patches that are uninteresting. The best portraits are probably those of Atticus, Sporus, the Duke of Buckingham, and this, the portrait of Avidien and his wife from Horace's second satire in the second book – the characters are Lady Mary Wortley Montagu and her husband:

> *Avidien* and his Wife (no matter which,
> For him you'll call the dog, and her a bitch)
> Sell their presented Partridges, and Fruits,
> And humbly live on rabbits and on roots:
> One half-pint bottle serves them both to dine,
> And is at once their vinegar and wine.
> But on some lucky day (as when they found
> A lost Bank-bill, or heard their Son was drown'd)
> At such a feast old vinegar to spare,
> Is what two souls so gen'rous cannot bear;
> Oyl, tho' it stink, they drop by drop impart,
> But sowse the Cabbidge with a bounteous heart.

All these characters are to some extent self-portraits. Pope was avaricious, though his hosts accused him of gluttony, a vice that he satirizes both in this poem and in the *Epistle to Cobham*. *Sporus* too contains elements of self-portraiture, for although most of the images are borrowed, they are curiously applicable to Pope. Moreover, the exceptional energy of the piece argues something rather more than simple hatred; as Johnson said dryly: 'no man thinks much of that which he despises.' As a picture of sexual imbalance and a compensating verbal violence, especially towards the great, Sporus appears much like a picture of Pope himself, an image of his own self-disgust. Likewise the picture of Addison who can 'Bear, like the *Turk*, no brother near the throne', is strongly reminiscent of the image of himself that Pope was constructing at this time. To quote Johnson once again: 'Men do not suspect faults which they do not commit.' Undoubtedly, however, the power and energy of such passages as those on Sporus, Atticus, and Avidien and his wife derive mainly from the personal spite, malice and hatred which inspire them. It is as if Pope were aware of the killing power of satire in his age, a power almost diabolical, as if drawn from witchcraft. In this context it may be noted that Buckingham said of Dryden's portrait of him as Zimri in *Absalom and Achitophel* that, just as a witch's image has power to waste away a living person, so Dryden's 'ill-made resemblance wastes my fame'. It need hardly be pointed out, however, that Dryden's satirical portraits, on which Pope's are ostensibly modelled, are motivated less by personal animosity than by political conviction.

7 An Essay on Man

The *Essay on Man* and the *Epistles to Several Persons*, as I have already illustrated, are closely connected. They are part of an unfinished *magnum opus*. The *Essay on Man* itself, published separately, was designed as an attempt to give an explicit moral framework within which to write satire. In Pope's words:

> Having proposed to write some pieces on Human Life and Manners, such as (to use my Lord Bacon's expression) *come home to Men's Business and Bosoms*, I thought it more satisfactory to begin with considering *Man* in the abstract, his *Nature* and his *State*; since, to prove any moral duty, to enforce any moral precept, to examine the perfection or imperfection of any creature whatsoever, it is necessary to know first what *condition* and *relation* it is placed in, and what is the proper *end* and *purpose* of its *being*.

This sounds fair and reasonable. In fact 'The Design', as Pope calls his introduction, is an important part of the dishonesty that surrounds the publication of the work; and indeed, the history of the *Essay on Man* makes a revealing story.

In December 1731 Pope had published his *Epistle to Burlington*, which had achieved a certain notoriety but a significant amount of critical censure. It was considered by many of the 'Dunces' for example, to reveal an inadequate sense of decorum. Pope was also deeply involved in what was to him the difficult debate between legitimate satire and straightforward libel. He was beginning to fully discover, in his own words, that 'the life of a wit is a warfare upon earth'. He had published the first version of the *Dunciad* early in 1728. Early in 1733, after a year somewhat out of the public eye, he published the *Epistle to Bathurst* and the first of his *Imitations of Horace* under his own name. Between February and May the first three epistles of the *Essay on Man* appeared anonymously and with the introduction I have quoted. Thus Pope had not only 'purposed' as he wrote, 'some pieces on Human Life and Manners', but he had already written and published at least two of them. He was determined that, at least for the while, the two projects were to be kept as distinct as possible. Although the *Essay on Man* was ostensibly a philosophical framework for satirical writing, Pope, by his actions, made sure that the two never met. It was a ploy, of course, and as such it worked. While the controversies over the *Epistles to Several Persons* and the *Imitations of Horace* raged he could never hope for any praise for a philosophical work published in his own name. But by publishing it anonymously, that is by playing the literary game, he could have his cake and eat it. While his victims suffered and retaliated against attacks which we have seen were often illfounded or purely personal, Pope could also enjoy the praise that was being lavished on the *Essay*. Welsted, for example, wrote that:

> I must own, after the reception which the vilest and most immoral ribaldry hath lately met with, I was surprised to see what I had long despaired, a performance deserving the name of a poet. Such, Sir, is your work. It is, indeed, above all commendation, and ought to have been published in an age and country more worthy of it.

This is quoted in that extraordinary example of Pope's conduct of literary affairs, the *Testimonies of Authors* prefixed to the *Dunciad*. Clearly, Pope was excessively anxious to derive the maximum from publishing anonymously. Having privately enjoyed the esteem of 'dunces' – obviously unaware that 'fools' approval stings' – he could then use it against them to ridicule them further in public. Eminent divines, he reported, had been forced to deny authorship, and he appears to have told Warburton that the *Essay* was variously ascribed to Young, Desaguliers, Bolingbroke, and Paget. It all pleased him enormously. As he wrote to Jonathan Richardson, comparing the reception of the *Essay* to that of the *Epistle to Burlington*, 'I am as much overpaid this way now as I was injured that way before'. What might have caused Pope some disappointment was that almost nobody attributed the *Essay* to him. Maynard Mack has traced the first public attribution of the poem to Pope to an epigram in the *Universal Spectator*, 23 June 1733, but Pope himself did not acknowledge authorship until the *Essay* was included in the second volume of his *Works* in 1735. A public which, as we have seen, was quick and eager to expose hidden literary personalities, failed by and large to discover Pope. They could detect his hand in *Sober Advice from Horace*, but could not deduce the authorship of the *Essay* from their reading of the *Epistles*, from the style of the work or from its content. As we have seen, they preferred to think it had been composed by Young, Bolingbroke, or one of the divines of the period. Indeed, if we accept the *persona* of the anonymous philosopher that Pope adopted, it is hard to reconcile the poem with the facts we know about his others.

Where Pope was criticized, both before and after his formal acknow-ledgement of the *Essay*, was in his choice of dedicatee. For example in the *Corn-Cutter's Journal* of 31 December 1734 there is a poem entitled *To Mr. P – pe, upon his addressing his Poem to the Pattern of exem-plary Piety, Chastity, and Virtue, the Lord V – – – t B – – – – e.* Bolingbroke was a mercurial, sensual man whose favourite philoso-pher was Aristippus the hedonist. Pope was to address to him his *First Epistle of the First Book of Horace, Imitated* and to picture him, with borrowed sentiments, as the honoured ideal of the philosophic man who is above wealth and place.

Bolingbroke had recently returned from exile in France. His political heyday was over and the time was now gone when he could boast that 'in one day he was the happiest man alive, got drunk, harangued the Queen, and at night was put to bed to a beautiful young lady, and was tucked up by two of the prettiest young peers in England . . .' He had returned to England through manipulation – his second wife had been bribing the King's mistress – and he had intended to govern. Power was to him the highest of pleasures, and having failed in his Jacobite plottings on the continent and been forced to spend a number of years building and gardening (and, incidentally, receiving Voltaire) he was determined to resume his position. He was pardoned, he returned, but he was not allowed to resume his place in the House of Lords. Instead he acquired a small estate in Middlesex, not many miles from Pope's house at Twickenham, and proceeded to rusticate it and to write letters. One of his correspondents was Pope. 'Sure I am,' he wrote to him, 'that you must not look on your translations of Homer as the great work of your life. You owe a great deal more to yourself, to your country, to the present age, and to posterity. Prelude with translations if you please, but after translating what was writ three thousand years ago, remem-ber that it is incumbent upon you that you write, because you are able to write, what will deserve to be translated three thousand years hence into languages as yet perhaps unformed.'

Bolingbroke himself was a poor versifier. He recognized this, and in a letter to Swift he expresses relief at Pope's keeping quiet about this. He was however also a philosopher. The degree to which he influenced the thought in the *Essay on Man* is now difficult to ascertain. Warton relates that Lord Bathurst had seen the whole scheme for the *Essay* in Bolingbroke's handwriting. This appears to have been a series of pro-positions which Pope was to versify and illustrate. Spence seems to verify this:

He mentioned then, and at several other times, how much (or rather how wholly) he himself was obliged to him [i.e. Bolingbroke] for the thoughts and reasonings in his moral work; and once in particular said, that beside their frequent talking over that subject together, he had received, I think seven or eight sheets from Lord Bolingbroke, in relation to it, as I apprehend by way of letter; both to direct the plan in general, and to supply the matter for the particular epistles.

These seven or eight sheets are no longer extant, but Bolingbroke himself, again in a letter to Swift, talks of 'the noble work which, at my instigation, he has begun'. There are however, as Maynard Mack points out, significant differences between the *Essay on Man* and Bolingbroke's *Fragments or Minutes of Essays* which was published later and seems to owe something, in expression at least, to Pope. What is fairly central to Bolingbroke's thought – that the purely sensory origins of human knowledge give no indications of a supra-human order – is rejected by Pope; whereas the ideas which Pope incorporates are all commonplace. As Mack says: 'The *Essay* contains nothing not derivable from other sources.' The differences between the two men being significant then, and the content of Pope's work being wholly unoriginal, is it not possible that Bolingbroke was the mentor to a Pope almost totally unschooled in philosophic thought, that the points on which he advised Pope were fairly fundamental? Pope clearly wished to be associated with Bolingbroke the philosopher, however opposed their ideas really were, and so, accepting the differences and Pope's vaunted dependence, is it not likely that Bolingbroke's name added status to the *Essay*, particularly in Tory circles?

All this tends to show that Pope's philosophical ability was not finely developed. It is clear that he did not really understand the differences between himself and his mentor. This was clear to Bolingbroke himself. He never minutely dissects Pope, but he frequently hints that Pope is unwilling, or unable, to follow his arguments to their logical conclusions. In August 1731 he wrote to Swift:

He pleads the cause of God (I use Seneca's expression) against the famous charge which atheists in all ages have brought – the supposed unequal dispensations of Providence – a charge which I cannot heartily forgive your divines for admitting. You admit it indeed for an extreme good purpose, and you build on this admission the necessity of a future estate of rewards and punishments. But if you should find, that this future estate will not account, in opposition to the atheist, for God's justice in the present state, which would you give up? Would it not have been better to defend God's justice in this world, against these daring men, by irrefragable reasons, and to have rested the proof of the other point on revelation? I do not like concessions made against demonstration, repair or supply them how you will. The epistles I have mentioned will compose a first book; the plan of the second is settled. You will not understand by what I have said, that Pope will go so deep into the argument, or carry it so far as I have hinted.

Similarly, he found that Pope's caution, or prevarication, over whole-heartedly accepting either Christian doctrines or deism, protected his handling of philosophy 'against any direct charge of heterodoxy'. Warburton reports that Bolingbroke said flatly that Pope did not 'understand' the implications of his thought, while in the Advertisement to his own philosophical work he wrote that many of his friends (i.e. Pope's) would find 'their own opinions and prejudices . . . frequently contradicted'. Clearly, although Bolingbroke admired Pope as a poet, he could not treat him as an equal in philosophy. It seems that he did not find Pope either sufficiently critically self-aware or, in the final analysis, intellectually honest. Pope, as I have indicated, refused in the poem to openly embrace or reject full Christian doctrines; and as I shall show, when the attacks against the *Essay on Man* achieved some intellectual status, he was more than pleased to accept the spurious interpretations of his friends and argue that the safest position was what he had meant all the time despite previous assertions to the contrary.

'Surely a man of no very comprehensive search may venture to say that he has heard all this before,' wrote Dr Johnson of the *Essay on Man*, and indeed the work is little more than a compendium of received ideas. It was useful as such, of course, and the poem was translated into languages as diverse as Welsh and Turkish. I do not intend to criticize the philosophy in detail, but rather I want to examine the relationship of the thought to poetry, to see in other words whether and in what ways the *Essay on Man* is a valid poetic statement.

In the discussion of the *Epistles to Several Persons* I tried to show how the couplet, in Pope's hands at least, was a rapid means of encapsulating knowledge and imparting the appearance of thought by the use of antithesis. The danger, I suggested, was its inherent smugness. It appears cogent and forthright, and makes critical thought difficult. It is essentially a medium of assent to either satire or constructive thought. In many ways it functions like a mnemonic – it makes things easy to memorize. This is not the same as making them memorable. A fair example of this is the closing couplet of the first epistle:

> And, spite of Pride, in erring Reason's spite,
> One truth is clear, 'Whatever IS, is RIGHT.'

Taken in long stretches, the effect of such writing, though mesmeric, is deadening. It also makes Pope's position curiously arrogant. Bewildered by proper nouns that are rarely given the touch of detail that makes them alive, and which are juxtaposed in rapid antithesis as the couplets run on, we slowly become aware of the fact that Pope is talking down to Man. The conversational tone of the poem has been frequently re-marked upon and as often praised. The *Essay on Man*, it is usually observed, obeys the decorum of Augustan polite conversation. If we examine this in the light of the whole paragraph from which I took my previous illustration it will be seen that this is quite simply not true. Gone, if it ever existed, is the sentiment *homo sum; humani nihil a me alienum puto*, and in its place is the voice of 'Big Brother' using the second rather than the third person plural, manipulating words at a furious rate, and making sure that Man knows his position rather than suggesting that we are all in the human predicament together:

> Cease then, nor Order Imperfection name:
> Our proper bliss depends on what we blame.
> Know thy own point: This kind, this due degree
> Of blindness, weakness, Heav'n bestows on thee.
> Submit – In this, or any other sphere,
> Secure to be as blest as thou canst bear:
> Safe in the hand of one disposing Pow'r,
> Or in the natal, or the mortal hour.
> All Nature is but Art, unknown to thee;
> All Chance, Direction, which thou canst not see;
> All Discord, Harmony, not understood;
> All partial Evil, universal Good:
> And, spite of Pride, in erring Reason's spite,
> One truth is clear, 'Whatever IS, is RIGHT.'

What one might expect from the *Essay on Man* is humanity, and it is precisely here that it fails. There is something rather jejune about trying to define the human condition in under a thousand couplets, but setting this not unimportant consideration aside, let us examine the work's more poetic and linguistic failings. What is lacking is a respect for pain, mystery and love. This results in part from the unfettered use of generali-ations, from the kaleidoscopic perspectives, and from the fact that the real core of the work is no more than rhetoric. This satire on human effort for example, despite its pretensions, really says nothing at all:

> Go, wond'rous creature! mount where Science guides,
> Go, measure earth, weigh air, and state the tides;

> Instruct the planets in what orbs to run,
> Correct old Time, and regulate the Sun;
> Go, soar with Plato to th'empyreal sphere,
> To the first good, first perfect, and first fair;
> Or tread the mazy round his follow'rs trod,
> And quitting sense call imitating God;
> As Eastern priests in giddy circles run,
> And turn their heads to imitate the Sun.
> Go, teach Eternal Wisdom how to rule –
> Then drop into thyself, and be a fool!

There is no feeling that life is noble, human effort worth while, or that life is valuable. Great perspectives are built up simply to diminish man. Aspects of experience are no more than nouns, no more than facts:

> Love, Hope, and Joy, fair pleasure's smiling train,
> Hate, Fear, and Grief, the family of pain;
> These mix'd with art, and to due bounds confin'd,
> Make and maintain the balance of the mind. . . .

The chief reason for the failure of humanity in the *Essay on Man* is Pope's implied position in it. Long stretches of the poem – and the cumulative effect is most important – give the impression that Pope is observing a species to whom he is unable to talk. The poem cannot be objective because of its implied dramatic situation. The *persona* of the observing satirist fails to make the poem human because of the implied superiority of the writer, who thus appears guilty of what he regards as the cardinal sin of pride. Allied to this, indeed inherent in it, are the spurious imaginative qualities of the poem. Imaginative response is kept at a clinical distance. Maynard Mack, borrowing from Josephine Miles' study *The Vocabulary of Poetry*, cites a list of adjectives which are supposed to illustrate the 'sensory qualities' of the *Essay*; this, he says is 'an element in the poem that modern readers are likely to forget' Why modern readers are more likely to forget it than any others I can not understand; perhaps it is because the list of words contains so man *gradus* epithets: giddy, vast, ardent, fiery, dull, watery, nectarous, balmy livid, cloudless and so on. None of these words really strikes home. As result we get samples of purely verbal afflatus such as this:

> He, who thro' vast immensity can pierce,
> See worlds on worlds compose one universe,
> Observe how system into system runs,
> What other planets circle other suns,
> What vary'd being peoples ev'ry star,
> May tell why Heav'n has made us what we are.

> But of this frame the bearings, and the ties,
> The strong connections, nice dependencies,
> Gradations just, has thy pervading soul
> Look'd thro'? or can a part contain the whole?

Maynard Mack compares this passage from the first epistle to four lines from Dryden's *Religio Laici*:

> In this wild maze their vain endeavours end:
> How can the less the greater comprehend?
> Or finite reason reach infinity?
> For what could fathom God were more than He.

'It is clear,' Mack writes, 'that Dryden uses [the proposition] as an axiom whose appeal is to the intellect while Pope translates it into a crescendo of images of cosmic grandeur and intricacy, shrinking the proud soul that is not, like God's, pervasive but would nevertheless pervade.' I am not sure that the implied superiority of Pope to Dryden here is wholly demonstrated. As the idea is primarily an intellectual one, I think Dryden conveys it more clearly. The question at the end of the Pope is syntactically awkward, and because Pope contracts the two aspects of the question into one, it is not easy to see what he means. However, there is an important difference in tone. The Dryden passage is simple, slow, and Miltonic; it reads like a humble and sincere soliloquy; the Pope, on the other hand, is essentially rhetorical, it is a climax of verbal indignation based more on sarcasm than on the troubled modesty of Dryden. Dryden succeeds because of his obvious conviction, Pope fails because he tries to impose grandeur on his subject rather than draw it out from it. For him, the subject itself was unpoetical:

> What is now published, is only to be considered as a *general Map* of man, marking out no more than the *greater parts*, their *extent*, their *limits*, and their *connection*, but leaving the particular to be more fully delineated in the charts which are to follow. Consequently, these Epistles in their progress (if I have health and leisure to make any progress) will be less dry, and more susceptible to poetical ornament. I am here only opening the *fountains*, and clearing the passage. To deduce the *rivers*, to follow them in their course, and to observe their effects, may be a task more agreeable.

This is the concluding paragraph of The Design prefixed to the *Essay*. In the piece as a whole Pope virtually admits that his attempt to make his maxims concise and memorable has resulted in a loss of poetry. It is my conviction that in trying to replace this by rhetoric he has produced a work of which the effect is, in the final analysis, trivializing.

However, let us examine the first epistle of the *Essay* in more detail. The subject is 'the nature and state of Man, with respect to the UNIVERSE'. The peroration alludes twice to *Paradise Lost*, the final line being: 'But vindicate the ways of God to Man.' This, I think, is spurious. In what is, significantly, purely verbal matter, it allies the poem to a work of much greater imaginative strength and humanity. It raises false expectations which operate to the detriment of Pope. There are similarities between the two poems, but let me quote Mack again:

> Pope's is distinctly a poem of middle flight, as its opening lines assure us . . . Furthermore, though his theme is analogous to Milton's, Pope cannot and does not probe it to Milton's depth, one reason being that he has no characters involved in dramatic action.

The poem then proceeds to place man in his universal setting which is, of course, the first necessary step in the discussion. Having proved that all is right with the world, it is then possible to extend the argument and show first how mankind's other relations fit this scheme – relationships both to himself and to society – and then state that the only happiness is inward and based on virtue.

The satirist as philosopher who tries to attack intellectual pride is sometimes ensnared by his own vocabulary, and the results are often crass. The implied position is so assuredly that of a man superior to the object he is addressing that any possible humanity in the poem dissolves. Such apostrophes as the following are embarrassingly crude:

> Presumptuous Man! the reason wouldst thou find,
> Why form'd so weak, so little, and so blind!
> First, if thou canst, the harder reason guess,
> Why form'd no weaker, blinder, and no less!

The passage in Romans ix, 20 from which Pope derives this is similar in formulation, but more sincere and less jejune: 'Nay but, O Man who art thou that repliest against God? Shall the thing formed say to him that formed it, Why hast thou made me thus?'

Let us continue this verbal analysis by examining a paragraph of the first epistle with the help of the Twickenham Edition. It will be seen that not only is the philosophy derivative, but so are most of the more poetic touches:

> The bliss of Man (could Pride that blessing find)
> Is not to act or think beyond mankind;
> No pow'rs of body or of soul to share,
> But what his nature and his state can bear.

> Why has not Man a microscopic eye?
> For this plain reason, Man is not a Fly.
> Say what the use, were finer optics giv'n,
> T'inspect a mite, not comprehend the heav'n?
> Or touch, if tremblingly alive all o'er,
> To smart and agonise at ev'ry pore?
> Or quick effluvia darting thro' the brain,
> Die of a rose in aromatic pain?
> If nature thunder'd in his op'ning ears,
> And stunn'd him with the music of the spheres,
> How would we wish that Heav'n had left him still,
> The whispering Zephyr, and the purling rill?
> Who finds not Providence all good and wise,
> Alike in what it gives, and what denies?
>
> (189–206)

The first four lines owe much to Montaigne and Aquinas, while the debate about man's sensory powers was a commonplace of the time discussed by Bentley, Locke, and Pope's friend Cheselden. The point about feeling being diffused through the whole body derives of course from *Samson Agonistes* where the hero asks why sight was:

> . . . not, as feeling, through all parts diffused,
> That she (the soul) might look at will through every pore?

the line: 'Die of a rose in aromatic pain' has been widely praised. It comes, in fact, from *The Spleen* by the Countess of Winchelsea:

> Now the jonquil o'ercomes the feeble Brain,
> We faint beneath the Aromatick pain.

This conceit itself may owe something to Pliny, but does not the word 'Jonquil' rather than the more obvious 'rose' give to the Countess's version a sensuous reality which is lacking in the Pope? The passage closes with an allusion to the belief that angels and not mortals can hear the music of the spheres. The sources of this are many, but how dry and factual Pope's account is compared to Shakespeare's in the last act of *The Merchant of Venice*.

The second epistle is concerned with '*the Nature and State of* Man, *with respect to* Himself, *as an Individual.*' and begins with the famous couplet:

> Know then thyself, presume not God to scan;
> The proper study of Mankind is Man.

which Pattison called 'the oldest dictum of philosophy or logic on record'. It is in this epistle that the doctrine of the ruling passion receives its most thorough treatment in Pope:

> Pleasures are ever in our hands or eyes,
> And when in act they cease, in prospect rise;
> Present to grasp, and future still to find,
> The whole employ of body and of mind.
> All spread their charms, but charm not all alike;
> On diff'rent senses, diff'rent objects strike;
> Hence different Passions more or less inflame,
> As strong or weak, the organs of the frame;
> And hence one master Passion in the breast,
> Like Aaron's serpent, swallows up the rest.
> As Man, perhaps, the moment of his breath,
> Receives the lurking principal of death;
> The young disease, that must subdue at length,
> Grows with his growth, and strengthens with his strength:
> So, cast and mingled with his very frame,
> The Mind's disease, its ruling Passion came;
> Each vital humour which should feed the whole,
> Soon flows to this, in body and in soul.
> Whatever warms the heart, or fills the head,
> As the mind opens, and its functions spread,
> Imagination plies her dang'rous art,
> And pours it all upon the peccant part.
>   (123–144)

As I have already pointed out, there is nothing original in Pope's idea of the ruling passion, despite his suggestions to the contrary, since it dates back to Theophrastus and was developed by Montaigne. In the *Essay* Pope sees it as that which gives man his direction. Without it he would be hopelessly adrift on a sea of conflicting passions. Given this direction, it is up to man to make the most of it in the development of his moral nature. In addition, by differentiating man, it allows the manifold activities of the world to prosper. It also allows us an insight into the doctrine of the 'balance of things' which, as I showed in my discussion of the *Epistles to Several Persons*, is a central doctrine in Pope's thought, often leading him to some degree of confusion. We are shown in the first epistle that when the ruling passion grows out of proportion it becomes a vice, and Pope cites the Borgias. However, since man's calculations cannot affect God's will, such men are part of the divine plan whereby 'ALL subsists by elemental strife'. Having elaborated his ideas on man in his own right in the second epistle, and concentrated on his essential smallness, Pope then develops his view of man as a social animal. He insists that society is natural to man and that the 'state of nature' is essentially peaceable, despite his assertions in the first epistle. We find here the tension of opposed forces resulting in harmony through self and social love. The 'elemental strife' has become watered down. The fourth epistle praises the pre-eminence of virtue, and in so doing vindicates Providence for the unequal distribution of advantages:

> Condition, circumstance is not the thing
> Bliss is the same in subject or in king. . . .

The epistle ends with a picture of Bolingbroke as the ideal man and a neat little summary of the most important precepts:

> Come then, my Friend, my Genius, come along,
> Oh master of the poet, and the song!
> And while the Muse now stoops, or now ascends,
> To Man's low passions, or their glorious ends,
> Teach me, like thee, in various natures wise,
> To fall with dignity, with temper rise;
> Form'd by thy converse, happily to steer
> From grave to gay, from lively to severe;
> Correct with spirit, eloquent with ease,
> Intent to reason, or polite to please.
> Oh! while along the stream of Time thy name
> Expanded flies, and gathers all its fame,
> Say, shall my little bark attendant sail,
> Pursue the triumph, and partake the gale?
> When statesmen, heroes, kings, in dust repose,
> Whose sons shall blush their fathers were their foes,
> Shall then this verse to future age pretend
> Thou wert my guide, philosopher, and friend?
> That urg'd by thee, I turn'd the tuneful art
> From sounds to things, from fancy to the heart;
> For Wit's false mirror held up Nature's light;
> Shew'd erring Pride, WHATEVER IS, IS RIGHT:
> That REASON, PASSION, answer one great aim;
> That true SELF-LOVE and SOCIAL are the same;
> That VIRTUE only makes our Bliss below;
> And all our Knowledge is, OURSELVES TO KNOW.
> (373–398)

As we have seen, the *Essay on Man* was initially accorded considerable critical acclaim. It was only after it had been translated, and particularly after a rather inaccurate translation into French had been made, that a different note was sounded. From this time on the critical history of the *Essay on Man* follows the characteristic tendency of Pope's works to be both praised and dismissed.

Several translations into French were made, some in verse, some in prose. Du Resnel's translation into verse was more of an imitation than a translation. He deleted much, although his final version is seven hundred lines longer than the original. It was this version that was attacked by the eminent Swiss theologian J. P. de Crousaz. Much of what he attacks is not Pope at all but the interpolations of his translator. However, his *Commentaire sur la traduction en vers . . . de l'Essai . . . sur l'homme* is important in so far as its translation into English under the auspices of Curll marks the beginning of systematic English attacks on the *Essay*. Curll's action, of course, was largely motivated by revenge. He declared that Crousaz's work was a satirical attack and that Pope was bound to reply to it. In addition, he declared his intention of pursuing 'M. Crousaz in his Attacks on Mr. Pope regularly'. Curll's translation was followed by another rendition of Crousaz's previous attack on an earlier translation of the *Essay*, and early in March 1739 an announcement was made that Ayre was to publish his *Truth. A counterpart to Mr. Pope's Essay on Man. Epistle the First.* This was followed by a second epistle published in June. These attacks were of some significance, especially those of Crousaz who was a respected if pedantic theologian. Pope gratefully accepted the refutation of his opinions that Warburton had been publishing in a series of sycophantic letters which were finally collected under the title *A Vindication of Mr. Pope's Essay on Man* in 1739.

Warburton's defence is an interesting and important aspect of Pope's conduct of literary and philosophical affairs. It is, first of all, very inaccurate. As Mack says: 'It strains passages in the poem toward a literally pietistic interpretation that they will not bear, and claims for it a ratiocinative rigour that is impossible in poetry and probably undesirable.' Over the more difficult questions, such as the basis of sin in the principle of plenitude, Warburton covers Pope not by defending his arguments, but by asserting that the same arguments had been often used before.

At first Pope dismissed Warburton's defence. The younger Richardson, whose records of his and his father's conversations with Pope about the *Essay* allow us a number of important insights, states categorically that Pope initially had no intention of interpreting his poem along Warburton's lines. However, when 'the general alarm of [the work's] fatalism, and deistical tendency' broke out, he was pleased to cling to it. For example, in 1742 Louis Racine published a poem in which he attacked the *Essay on Man* as being a collection of heresies. Louis Racine's preface to his poem is distinguished by a quiet generosity that it is difficult to imagine on the part of Pope, and which testifies to the importance of the *Essay* abroad. He attacks the heretical opinions: 'qui sont devenus si communs parmi nous depuis la lecture de son *Essai sur l'homme*, dont les principes n'étant pas assez développés pour nous, sont cause que plusieurs personnes croient y trouver un système qui n'est peut-être pas celui de l'auteur.' His attack is similar to Bolingbroke's in so far as he criticizes Pope for not developing his arguments adequately. Pope eventually struck up a correspondence with Louis Racine and sent him a copy of Warburton's defence with which to explain himself.

In fact it appears obvious that when the *Essay* was publicly attacked for its philosophical content, Pope found himself in far deeper water than he cared to be. Deism was a dangerous thing to be accused of since, as a blanket term, it covered anything from minor differences from accepted Christian doctrine to a coherent conception of natural religion. The conversations of Bolingbroke would certainly have inclined Pope towards the latter, but as we have seen, Bolingbroke himself complained that Pope had prevaricated adequately for his poem to be interpreted in both ways. In other words he complained that Pope did not come clean. He also claimed that Pope did not 'understand' the full implications of his thought. This seems to be supported by Richardson, who apparently discussed the fatalism and deistic tendencies in the poem with Pope: 'we talked with him (my father and I) frequently at Twickenham, without his appearing to understand it otherwise, or ever thinking to alter those passages, which we suggested as what might seem the most exceptional.' This statement has been variously interpreted. Warton, for example, thought that in these passages Pope was being deliberately heterodox and this was a common opinion. Mack excuses Pope on the ground that Pope's letters to Caryll show him wanting to be as orthodox as possible. This, of course, is no real defence, since Pope's letters to Caryll are so unreliable that they are factually all but worthless. For example, he strenuously denied composing both the prose attacks on Curll and the *Sober Advice from Horace*. Caryll, indeed, appears to have been an example of the retired Horatian ideal that Pope so continually praised when adopting his

satirist's *persona*, and Pope's letters to him are full of the need to impress that he is in the same position. Mack says that Pope may have
been evasive, 'solemnly refusing to combat interpretations of the parts
which he did not see how any careful reader of the *Essay* in its entirety
could make'. This sort of quasi-mystical silence is most unlikely. The
men who attacked the *Essay* were highly intelligent and able to raise
legitimate objections. If they could not understand, it was not, as Mack
implies, because they were careless readers. Likewise, an enigmatic
silence goes contrary to the aims of being memorable and concise that
Pope sets out in his 'Design'. Here the accent is all on Augustan clarity;
after this a refusal to be precise is hardly consistent. In fact Mack's
statement in his succeeding paragraph comes nearer to the truth.
Though it is far from being an excuse, it is a typical example of Pope's
prevarication:

> On the whole, the most eligible conclusion appears to be that in 1733
> Pope may have wished to have it both ways: that he had sympathies
> with the liberal theology which was stirring the great religious contro-
> versy of his time, and sympathies with an older view; that he wanted
> to be enlightened and tell the truth as he conceived it, without wanting
> to be un-Christian or start a fight.

Such sitting on the fence is moral cowardice. To write a poem about
man and refuse to find a real position between two camps is pretentious
and philosophically worthless.

In his attempt to provide 'a fair and candid criticism on the character
and merits of our last great poet, Mr. Pope', Warton justifies the wholly
didactic poem by a curious *non sequitur*:

> If it be a true observation, that for a poet to write happily and well,
> he must have seen and felt what he describes, and must draw from
> living models alone, . . . it will then follow, that those species of poetry
> bid fairest to succeed at present, which treat of things, not men; which
> deliver doctrines, not display events.

Dr Johnson, however, refusing to accept the divorce between theory
and experience, realized clearly that the *Essay* is based on platitudes
and written with a rhetoric that irredeemably trivializes the subject.
Indeed there is no better description than his of the impression that
the poem makes while it is being read and then when it is being
analysed :

> Never was penury of knowledge and vulgarity of sentiment so happily
> disguised. The reader feels his mind full, though he learns nothing.

Of course the *Essay on Man* was attacked by the Romantic critics, and not simply for its dry didacticism. Hazlitt pithily declared, as noted earlier, that the philosophy of the poem proved 'just as well that what ever is, is *wrong*, as that whatever is, is *right*'; and Charles Lloyd conducted a reasoned argument against the philosophy of the *Essay*. Byron, taking his criticism of Pope into the field of his own hatred of the Lake-poets, declared that the *Essay on Man* was ten times more poetical than the *Excursion*. Dennis too admired it for its poetry, though he had to admit that the lines to Bolingbroke at the close are 'as beautiful as they are false'.

This two-sided approach to the *Essay on Man* has not been a distinguishing feature of modern criticism, which tends rather to praise the work, Wilson Knight, for example, rhapsodizes thus: 'With what imperturbable and untroubled ease, comparable to that of Shakespeare's "cloud-capp'd towers", the couplets roll out their mighty images'. Goethe, Blake and Nietzsche are invoked as well as Shakespeare in an attempt to install the poem in the European pantheon.

For Brower, 'the *Essay on Man* marks [Pope's] arrival at maturity as a poet who combined moral seriousness with satiric wit'. I hope I have adequately illustrated that this is not true, for the statement puts a very high value on the *Essay* which is manifestly inappropriate. The morality may or may not be serious; this is unimportant in view of the condescending tone which, allied to a satiric *persona*, completely dehumanizes the poem and accounts for the poverty and vulgarity that Johnson noted. Indeed, Brower consistently refuses to recognize the significance of the rhetoric in the poem and is one of those critics who praise it for its 'illusion' of 'well-bred good talk' and 'conversational tone'. As I have shown, with the possible exception of the opening, this is simply not true. Brower then continues by giving implicit praise to the confusion between Christian and natural religion which, as we have seen, galled so many of Pope's contemporaries:

> While the *Essay on Man* does in a way 'magnify Christian doctrine', it is Christian without any clear reference to Christ or to revelation. The worldly audience implied, the quality and tone of the talk hardly make it possible for Pope to speak in terms that bring us close to the Gospels or the mysteries of the Christian faith.

This claim is absurd. What can be Christian about a poem that has no reference to Christ, the Gospels, 'the mysteries of the Christian faith' and, above all, revelation? What Brower is really saying is that the poem is crippled by the conventions in which it was written and that these

excuse Pope's refusal to commit himself. No doubt — but we are discussing what has been called great poetry. For Root, the *Essay* is
'packed with poetry', while for Dobrée, who admires the conclusion and
finds the opening of the second epistle 'as glorious a piece of "philosophic" poetry as ever was penned', the *Essay on Man* is one of Pope's
numerous major works by which he is not to be judged.

8 The Letters

The reader who has followed me so far will have seen that one of the chief themes stressed in this book is the chicanery, dishonesty, and frequent downright cruelty by which Pope manipulated his career so as to keep himself constantly in the public eye – a necessity which he realized from the start – and to appear both as a man of moral integrity and as one more sinned against than sinning. His efforts to publish his letters, and in particular his dealings with Swift and his friends, are the most distressing examples of this.

At the outset, I must acknowledge my indebtedness to Professor Sherburn whose immense labours resulted in the definitive edition of the *Letters* – something that Pope himself, despite his protestations scrupulously avoided – and a monument of modern scholarship. However, I am bound to dissent from Sherburn over a number of points he makes in his *Introduction*. In an early letter to Caryll, Pope wrote that 'a letter should be a natural image of the mind of the writer'. How true this is when we hold all of Pope's correspondence in our own minds! We shall find, along with letters of genuine concern over people in distress and offers of help and advice to connoisseurs, examples of deviousness, Pope's sophisticated devices for bullying, and his recurrent lying.

Again, writing about his letters to Caryll, Pope declared:

> I will review them, and return whatever can do no hurt to either of us, or our memories, or to any other man's particular character; but so much, as would serve to bear testimony of my own love for good men, or theirs for me, I would not but keep on all accounts, and shall think this the very article more to my reputation than all my works put together.

His letters, then, were of great importance to Pope and his 'reputation' – a word that he used ambiguously in so far as it related both to the immediate moment and, in his own mind, to posterity. Caryll being an unimportant country squire, Pope ascribed to Wycherley and Addison some of the letters originally addressed to him. The publisher Curll was made to appear the culprit by a device of immense complexity and intrigue on the part of Pope himself which I will attempt to elucidate

later. However, when Pope finally allowed an authorized edition of
his letters to appear, he emerged as a man of moral rectitude exchang-
ing the noblest *sententiae* with the noblest minds, and, as often as
possible, the noblest born. As Sherburn says: '. . . the letters became in
a sense part of his works, capable of polish, revision, amalgamation,
even, though very seldom, of factual falsification.' Yet the amount of
factual falsification is considerable – what a man omits is as important
as what he includes, and Pope omitted a great deal. Victorian editors
discovered much of this, as Sherburn admits, but he declares that
'. . . Pope is a fascinating problem, and if the letters here presented
are read without Victorian prejudice, the picture of his mind will be
different in some respects from that which in many quarters has been
current, and much nearer the truth.' To use 'Victorian' as a blanket
term of condemnation is convenient but misleading. It begs the question. Sherburn himself is an heir to the great tradition of scholarship
consolidated by nineteenth-century textual editors. What he implies is
that the Victorians postulated a moralistic outlook, with overtones of
self-righteousness and hypocrisy, which would not have applied in Pope's
time. I doubt this. Pope himself persistently adopted a high moral
tone, claiming the right to be judged by standards not unlike those of
the Victorians at a later time. However this may be, we can only present
the facts and let them speak for themselves; but I hope too that we can
put aside the equally deceptive modern cant about the 'masks of satire'
– a critical formula that Pope does not seem to have been familiar with,
except vaguely through his reading of Boileau, as I tried to show when
discussing the *Epistle to Arbuthnot*. Let us look at Pope himself and at
his complete letters as 'a natural image of the mind of the writer'.

I have already offered a number of examples of factual inexactitude
in Pope's correspondence – for example the letter to Caryll in which
he asks how the poet who wrote moral essays and epistles *could* write
what he calls that 'obscene thing' the *Sober Advice from Horace*. Being
by then adept in the art of lying, he sent Caryll the poem and told him
'I want you not to take it for mine'. However, rather than repeat such
instances as this, I think it will be more interesting if we tell the intricate story of Pope's publication of his correspondence and quote some
of those letters that abetted his plans and some of those people who got
caught.

In February 1730 Swift wrote to Pope:

I find you have been a writer of Letters almost from your infancy, and
by your own confession had schemes even then of Epistolatory fame

Montaigne says that if he could have excelled in any kind of writing, it would have been in Letters; but I doubt they would not have been natural, for it is plain that all Pliny's Letters were written with a view of publishing, and I accuse Voiture himself of the same crime, although he be an Author I am fond of. They cease to be Letters when they become a jeu d'esprit.

In fact the 'schemes' started out none too well for Pope. In 1726 Edmund Curll published the letters Pope had written to Henry Cromwell, having obtained them from Cromwell's discarded mistress. The book was probably a disappointment to Curll since it roused little interest. Pope, of course, did not let the opportunity slip and began immediately to write round to all his friends and ask for the return of any letters from him that they might have. He could not allow such similes as that which he coined about one Major-General Tidcome to interfere with his own reputation, and when he came to edit the letter himself he cut out the passage in which he declared that Tidcombe's 'beastly, laughable Life is . . . not unlike a Fart, at once nasty & diverting'.

By 1733 Pope had made the firm decision that his letters were to be published. Only one thing stood in the way – a gentleman did not publish his letters in his lifetime. Pope decided to turn this to his advantage. Curll, by now an old enemy of Pope's, declared that he wanted to publish a biography of the poet and advertised for information. On 11 October 1733 the following letter was delivered to Curll:

Mr. Curll, Understanding you propose to write the *Life of Mr. Pope,* this is only to inform you, I can send you divers Memoirs which may be serviceable, if your Design be to do him neither Injustice nor show him Favour. . . . You may please to direct an Answer in the *Daily Advertiser* this Day-sennight in these Terms – *E.C. hath received a Letter, and will comply with P. T.*

Yours.

However Curll did not respond to this cloak-and-dagger approach, and on 15 November Pope tried again:

Sir, – I troubled you with a Line sometime since, concerning your Design of the *Life of Mr. Pope,* to which I desir'd your answer in the *Daily Advertiser* of *Thursday* the 10th Instant *October.* . . . *A Propos* to his Life, there have lately fall'n into my Hands a large Collection of his *Letters,* from the former Part of his Days to the Year 1727, which being more considerable than any yet seen, and opening very many Scenes new to the World, will alone make a Perfect and the most authentick *Life* and *Memoirs* of him that could be. . . . print the Advertisement I sent you, and you shall instantly hear from or see me. Adieu, *P. T.*

Curll did nothing until the start of the following year when he began to negotiate with Pope in person, sending him these letters from *P.T.* As Sherburn says: 'Pope loudly scorned the overture; but P.T. (doubtless, as Curll later said, 'Trickster Pope' himself) again went into action, and after long, sly, and even melodramatic intrigues, on 12 May 1735 mysterious agents began delivering at the shop of Curll octavo volumes of Pope's printed letters, in various states of completeness. Pope's intrigue through P.T. had worked: he himself seemed perfectly concealed, and now his loud, hypocritical outcries of injury, as well as the pre-publication advertisements announcing and denouncing the edition, aroused such interest that the letters were the literary event of the year. Several printings were called for.'

Pope, of course, declared that he would have to bring out an authorized edition of the letters. There also appeared the 'Pope-inspired' *Narrative of the Method by which Mr. Pope's Private Letters were procured and published by Edmund Curll*. Meanwhile, Pope used this opportunity he had himself created to ingratiate himself with his aristocratic friends. He wrote to the Earl of Orrery about the *Letters* in terms which must have afforded him a great deal of strange amusement:

> I am greatly obliged by your Lordships Generosity in promising to contradict malicious Reports in my regard. I embrace 'em with all transport, while they procure me such Defenders as show I cannot be What Envy reports, for they are such as never could befriend an Ill man. I am not quite at the bottom of that Business, but very near it, & find a person whom I cannot think quite dishonest, has contributed to that suspicion by Exceeding a Commission which was given him, rather by my Friends than by myself. And what is the greatest mystery of all, is, that if he proves absolutely guilty, I must be merciful to him & screen him, or never know the Whole of it. This often happens when one is obliged to guard against Rogues, & many a Minister I dare say is wronged this very way in the opinion of half mankind.

'An interestingly disingenuous paragraph about the publication of the *Letters*', comments Sherburn. He does not mention that Pope the moralist had published the first version of the *Dunciad*.

However, despite disputes over copyright which Curll was taking to Chancery, Pope had now solicited the friendship of the wealthy Ralph Allen who persuaded Pope to publish an authorized version of his letters in both folio and quarto by subscription. Octavo editions, clearly supervised by Pope, were also issued. Pope chose to disown them. How far he was prepared to go in editing the letters can best be illustrated by

the following extract from Sherburn's note to a letter allegedly from
Pope to Arbuthnot: 'This obviously spurious letter is fabricated from
two letters to Caryll dated 23 Nov. 1725 and 25 Dec. 1725. It appears
in all Pope's editions (except the 'afternoon' issue of 12 May 1735); but
in the editions of 1735 it was printed as to Robert Digby and dated
'Sept 10, 1724'. In the editions of 1737–42 it is addressed to Dr.
Arbuthnot and the impossible year is dropped.'

Pope's next venture in publishing his letters was the so-called Pope-
Swift correspondence. It is a long and intricate story of bullying and
deceit. We have seen already that Swift did not approve of the publication of private letters and in 1735, after Pope had clearly been asking
for the return of his own to Swift in case they should fall into the wrong
hands, we find Swift answering with touching modesty:

> I answer'd your letter relating to Curll, &c. I believe my letters have
> escap'd being publish'd, because I writ nothing but Nature and Friend-
> ship, and particular incidents which could make no figure in writing.

Swift goes on to say that he is old and ill and that he has ordered his
executors to destroy Pope's letters to him. However, Pope and Lord
Orrery continued to press Swift to relinquish the letters. In April 1736
Swift was forced to reply:

> As to what you say of your Letters, since you have many years of life
> more than I, my resolution is to direct my Executors to send you all
> your letters, well sealed and pacqueted, along with some legacies men-
> tioned in my Will, and leave them entirely in your disposal: those things
> are all tied up, endors'd, and locked in a cabinet, and I have not one
> servant who can properly be said to write or read. No mortal shall copy
> them, but you shall surely have them when I am no more.

It is true that Swift wanted the friendship between himself and Pope
be recorded by more than the dedication to the *Dunciad* – he wanted
an epistle. Yet surely this letter is not peevish. Is it not rather the plea
an exasperated man who believed that private letters *were* private
and who is at last allowing an intimate relationship to be exposed after
his death? Surely Swift was holding back the letters out of dignified
self-respect rather than petulance.

However, Swift was not to be left in peace. Towards the end of 1736
Curll produced a pamphlet called *New Letters of Mr. Alexander Pope*
containing a letter from Pope to Swift which Curll claimed in his
advertising came from 'original manuscripts transmitted from Ireland'.
This gave Pope the perfect opportunity to force the issue. Pope worked
Orrery doubly hard and Swift gave in, adding the highly significant

comment that he 'found nothing in any of them to be left out'. In other words they were harmless, merely private letters. As Sherburn says though: 'If Swift returned anything like sixty letters (i.e. the figure mentioned by Swift) from Pope to himself, Pope suppressed at least half of them.' He also excluded Swift's criticism of his poetry, for example the Dean's remark that the *Essay on Man* 'is too philosophical' for me'.

When Pope had finished editing the volume (suppressing in the process all his pleas to be sent the letters, so as to give the impression that they were still in Ireland) he secretly printed a small octavo edition and sent it by devious and complicated means to Swift. Swift at once set about correction, adding a long, moving and very important letter from January 1721 describing his enforced exile and telling 'what my Political principles were in the time of her late glorious Majesty . . .' Pope pretended to be horrified, protested against publication, and affected to wonder why Swift had initiated publishing the letters at all. However, Pope meanwhile made sure that his own London edition – which had been awaiting publication while Swift was preparing his version – came out just before the Dublin edition, thereby laying claim to authenticity. It is a disgraceful story, crowned by this letter from Pope to Allen:

> My vexation about Dr Swift's proceeding has fretted, & employed me a great deal, in writing to Ireland, & trying all the means possible to *retard* it; for it is put past preventing, by his having (without asking my Consent or so much as letting me see the book) printed most of it. . . . But as to your own apprehension that any Suspicion may arise of my own being any way consenting or concerned in it, I have the pleasure to tell you, the whole thing is so Circumstanced, & so plain, that it can never be the Case. . . . The excessive Earnestness the Dean has been in for publishing them, makes me hope they are castigated in some degree or he must be totally deprived of his understanding.

Opportunist cynicism, not even stopping short at the gratuitous defamation of a dying man, a man of probity, who had befriended and encouraged him at the outset of his own career – such cynicism breathtaking, especially from one who proclaimed himself the connoisseur of friendship. Even Pope's most complaisant admirers have found it hard to excuse this episode.

Pope's letters have, of course, received the adulation of the critics. John Butt finds 'moral truisms which shine almost as brightly in his letters as in his poetry' and declares that Pope has 'unwittingly erected a monument of English civilization in the eighteenth century'. Tillotson believed that 'no other English poet (or letter-writer) puts and answers the question how to live with such sensitive and noble concern. The tone of this poetry (and this prose) must convince the reader that he is in the presence of one whose sense of virtue is as alert as the trembling, vivid eye one notes in his portraits.' He declares that 'Pope's letters seem more concerned with friendship than with any other subject. Pope was indeed concerned with friendship – he had to be – he is also capable of great delicacy. There could be no finer example of the eighteenth-century 'cult of friendship' than this letter to the serviceable Broome:

> You please me not a little in seeming pleased with my letter, for I dare say you are what you seem. Nothing is more agreeable than the mutual reconnaissance of two well-meaning men, after they find that only ill-meaning men have endeavoured to set them at variance. I assure you, if you are as sincere as you express yourself, and as I believe, being so myself, you shall be convinced of every good office that shall be in my future power, that I am in earnest on my part by every testimony I can give you.

The 'good office' of the future was the imminent publication of *Peri Bathous* with its quotations viciously turned against Broome. Hypocrisy could go little further.

9 The Dunciad

In the *Prolegomena* to *The Dunciad Variorum* we read that 'A *Satyre* upon *Dulness,* is a thing, that hath been *used* and *allowed* in All Ages'. Pope took great pains to ensure that his particular satire would achieve the maximum attention of his age, and in 1727 he composed his *Peri Bathous, or The Art of Sinking in Poetry* to prepare his audience. Sherburn states that *The Art of Sinking* was 'under way in 1714', and it is clear that it was a result of the formation of the Scriblerus Club a year or two before. Swift had been the leading spirit of this, and the idea had germinated at the time when he was beginning to be disillusioned with politics and the hope of positive political progress. The direction of his thought – and consequently that of his disciples who, of course, included Pope – was towards negative and destructive satire. Attacks on pedantry and stupidity were of particular importance, and Pope may have been the author of an anonymous essay in the *Guardian* in August 1712 which sketched out intentions of attacking these vices. Swift attributed the idea of Scriblerus himself to Pope, and in Spence's words, the function of the club was to publish 'the memoirs of Scriblerus . . .to ridicule all the false tastes in learning, under the character of a man of capacity enough: that had dipped into every art and science but injudiciously in each.' In connection with this aim, Pope had been collecting extracts from the solemn nonsense of Blackmore – a frequent target for wits – who had been offensive to both Swift and Arbuthnot but who did not become entangled with Pope until 1717. *The Art of Sinking* begins with some heavy-handed irony about the necessity of studying bad poetry and uses many quotations from Blackmore's works.

Pope began *The Art of Sinking* with Arbuthnot as a collaborator. The picture of Arbuthnot that emerges from Lester M. Beattie's biography shows a basically tolerant and carefree man, despite his being out of office and plagued with gloomy presentiments towards the end of his life. It is clear that he enjoyed working on *The Art of Sinking* in its early stages but that he eventually dissociated himself from it. 'It is easy to see why the interest of Arbuthnot fell off,' writes Beattie. 'The original plan had been innocently humorous. The flights of nonsense were to be used in the Scriblerus spirit. As time went on, more bits were collected. . . The whole thing became Pope's property. The talents of Martinus were not suited to the immediate purpose.' This purpose was, of course, the furtherance of the *Dunciad*. When questioned about the authorship of *The Art of Sinking* Pope was, as usual, evasive. He sought to excuse both himself and Arbuthnot in letters to Broome, but writing to Aaron Hill in 1738 he tried to excuse himself at the expense of Arbuthnot who had died some three years earlier. Both Hill and Broome had been sneered at in the work. The criticism of Broome is particularly interesting since he is described as one of the 'Parrots . . . they that repeat another's words, in such a hoarse, odd voice, as makes them seem their own'. Nevertheless, Pope had used this 'hoarse odd voice' for his translation of Homer, and with sufficient confidence to assume that it would be mistaken for his own.

However, *The Art of Sinking* need not concern us much. Despite declarations that it is unduly neglected, it is at bottom a tedious, heavily ironic attack on the ordinary run-of-the-mill poetry of the day, which could have been written about the minor verse of any age. Its moments of cleverness and its ruthless ridicule of the 74-year-old Blackmore, its repeated attacks on Broome, and its general contempt for all poets of the day (and the previous day) are tasteless and offensive. But it is well-aimed at its true purpose – that of stirring up the Grub Streets 'hornet's nest' as Pope called it and so provoking the reaction which, in the eyes of Pope, Swift, and the world, would justify the *Dunciad*. It is really not very funny, being nothing but an elaborate and extended *sottisier*. A familiar idea had been cunningly revivified by abusing personalities. After its publication, the literary world would be ready for the first *Dunciad*.

In the Preface to his excellent Twickenham edition of the *Dunciad*, James Sutherland remarks that 'The reader whom Pope had in view was one who possessed the intellectual background of a well-read amateur of letters in the early eighteenth century'. This is one side of what we may call the '*Dunciad* problem' – Pope's concern for the status of letters. Later, Sutherland remarks that the notes and commentary supplement 'the picture of the self-righteous poet that one meets so often in the Letters, and it makes clearer than ever the care that he took to preserve and to extend his literary reputation . . . Pope's enemies were to be humbled, but – equally important – Pope himself was to be aggrandized . . . [his] primary concern is not to write mock epic, but to make use of that form to ridicule his enemies. The dunces come first, the *Dunciad* second.' This is the other side of the '*Dunciad* problem' – the fact that the work is a consummate act of revenge and personal spite. Among the questions we must ask are whether all of the dunces are really dull, and secondly, how comprehensive is the selection and on what grounds were some writers included and others left out. Let us first look at Pope's concern for letters.

The 1729 edition of *The Dunciad Variorum* contains *A Letter to the Publisher* which purports to have been written by Cleland. It is fairly clear that Pope himself wrote this letter and got Cleland to sign it. Sutherland supports this, and we must remember that Pope was to use the device again when, in December 1731, he published an elaborate defence of his satirical methods under the guise of a letter from Cleland to Gay. It was, in fact, the first letter that Pope published. The *Letter to the Publisher* sets Pope up as a sort of English Boileau:

> I cannot help remarking the resemblance betwixt Him [i.e. Boileau] and our Author in Qualities, Fame and Fortune; in the distinction shewn to them by their Superiors, in the general Esteem of their Equals, and in their extended reputation amongst Foreigners . . . But the resemblance holds in nothing more, than in their being equally abus'd by the ignorant pretenders to Poetry of their times; of which not the least memory will remain but in their own writings, and the notes made upon them.

The letter continues with more self-glorification and self-justification including a statement which, written under a pseudonym, is particularly interesting. Pope, the sentence runs:

> . . . can almost singly challenge this honour, not to have written a line of any man, which thro' Guilt, thro' Shame, or thro' Fear, thro' variety of Fortune, or change of Interests, he was ever willing to own.

The letter concludes:

> . . . what a pleasure it must be to every reader of humanity, to see all along, that our Author, in his very laughter, is not indulging his own Ill nature, but only punishing that of others.

Pope's 'own' defence – *Martinus Scriblerus, of the Poem* – is designed to be both intellectual and patriotic. I shall quote from it and include where appropriate the references to the poem itself that Pope makes in the footnotes so that we may have his argument clearly before us:

> We shall next declare the occasion and the cause which moved our Poet to this particular work. He lived in those days, when (after providence had permitted the Invention of Printing as a scourge for the Sins of the learned) Paper also became so cheap, and printers so numerous, that a deluge of authors cover'd the land: Whereby not only the peace

of the honest unwriting subject was daily molested, but unmerciful demands were made of his applause, yea of his money, by such as would
forthwith publish slanders unpunish'd, the authors being anonymous;
nay the immediate publishers thereof lay sculking under the wings of
an Act of Parliament, assuredly intended for better purposes.

Now our author living in those times, did conceive it an endeavour well
worthy of an honest satyrist, to dissuade the dull and punish the malicious,
the only way that was left. In that public spirited view he laid the plan
of this Poem, as the greatest service he was capable (without much hurt
of being slain) to render his dear country. First, taking things from their
original, he considereth the Causes creative of such authors, namely
Dulness and *Poverty*; the one born with them, the other contracted,
by neglect of their proper talent thro' self conceit of their greater abilities.
This truth he wrapped'd in an *Allegory* (as the constitution of Epic poesy
requires) and feigns, that one of these Goddesses had taken up her abode
with the other, and that they jointly inspir'd all such writers and such
works. He proceedeth to shew the *qualities* they bestow on these authors,
and the *effects* they produce:

> Fierce champion Fortitude, that knows no fears
> Of hisses, blows, or want, or loss of ears:
> Calm Temperance, whose blessings those partake
> Who hunger, and who thirst, for scribbling sake:
> Prudence, whose glass presents th'approaching jayl:
> Poetic Justice, with her lifted scale;
> Where in nice balance, truth with gold she weighs,
> And solid pudding against empty praise.

Then the materials or stock with which they furnish them:

> How Hints, like spawn, scarce quick in embryo lie,
> How new-born Nonsense first is taught to cry,
> Maggot half-form'd, in rhyme exactly meet,
> And learn to crawl upon poetic feet.
> Here one poor Word a hundred clenches makes,
> And ductile dulness new meanders takes;
> There motley Images her fancy strike,
> Figures ill-pair'd, and Similies unlike.
> She sees a Mob of Metaphors advance,
> Pleas'd with the Madness of the mazy dance:
> How Tragedy and Comedy embrace;
> How Farce and Epic get a jumbled race;
> How Time itself stands still at her command,
> Realms shift their place, and Ocean turns to land.
> Here gay Description Ægypt glads with showers;

> Or gives to Zembla fruits, to Barca flowers;
> Glitt'ring with ice here hoary hills are seen,
> There painted vallies of eternal green,
> On cold December fragrant chaplets blow,
> And heavy harvests nod beneath the snow.

and (above all) that *self-opinion* which causeth it to seem to themselves vastly greater than it is, and is the prime motive of their setting up in this sad and sorry merchandize. The great power of these Goddesses acting in alliance (whereof the one is the mother of industry, so is the other of plodding) was to be exemplified in some *one, great* and *remarkable action.* And none cou'd be more so than that which our poet hath chosen, the introduction of the lowest diversions of the rabble in *Smithfield* to be the entertainment of the court and town; or in other words, the action of the Dunciad is the Removal of the Imperial seat of Dulness from the City to the polite world; as that of the Æneid is the Removal of the empire of *Troy* to *Latium.* But as *Homer* singeth only of the *Wrath* of *Achilles,* yet includes in his poem the whole history of the *Trojan* war, in like manner our author hath drawn into this single action the whole history of Dulness and her children. To this end she is represented at the very opening of the poem, taking a view of her forces, which are distinguish'd into these three kinds, Party writers, dull poets, and wild criticks:

> Much she revolves their arts, their ancient praise,
> And sure succession down from Heywood's days.
> She saw with joy the line immortal run,
> Each sire imprest and glaring at his son;
> So watchful Bruin forms with plastic care
> Each growing lump, and brings it to a Bear.
> She saw old Pryn in restless Daniel shine,
> And Eusden eke out Blackmore's endless line;
> She saw slow Philips creep like Tate's poor page,
> And all the Mighty Mad in Dennis rage.

Thus Pope, under the guise of being 'public spirited' and guided by love for 'his dear country', set out to criticize the situation whereby anonymous pamphleteers could slander with impunity. As we have seen, he himself issued time after time anonymous pamphlets of the most vicious nature. If he did not need to profit from them financially, then he at least made considerable personal capital out of them. In other words he practised the very abuse he attacked. Self-knowledge is the key to wisdom in the *Essay on Man*; bearing this in mind, what are we to make of this hypocrisy?

Pope declares that the origins of this 'deluge of authors' are '*Dulness*',

'*Poverty*' and '*self-opinion*'. 'Dulness' is defined in the 1742 edition of the *Dunciad* as:

> . . . not to be taken contractedly for mere Stupidity, but in the enlarged sense of the word, for all Slowness of Apprehension, Shortness of Sight, or imperfect Sense of things. It includes (as we shall see by the Poet's own words) Labour, Industry, and some degree of Activity and Boldness: a ruling principle not inert, but turning topsy-turvy the Understanding, and introducing Anarchy or Confused state of Mind.

In the eighteenth century a quick understanding – or wit – was valued particularly highly, so there is nothing new in Pope's argument here except its extension which claims that Dulness makes the 'understanding' 'topsy-turvy' and introduces 'Anarchy or Confused state of Mind'. Surely this is not so. What is dull stands self-condemned and another's stupidity rarely makes a clever man a fool.

As for poverty being a spur to literary production, we must not allow ourselves to forget that Pope made himself a considerable private income from his translations of the *Iliad* and the *Odyssey* and so could presumably enter the ranks of those with private incomes who, not needing to write for money, made up the would-be closed shop of authors. As to the self-esteem of writers – this was a subject on which Pope was an authority.

In his interesting book *Pope's Dunciad: A Study of its Meaning*, Aubrey L. Williams notes the parallel that Pope draws between the progress of the Dunces from the city to 'the polite world' and the progress of the Trojans to Latium, and derives from it the socio-literary idea of the invasion of the court by the mercantile morality and values of the city; this becomes, in Pope's hands, a metaphorical presentation of the general breakdown of order and culture which he foresees. Williams believes that Pope visualized in artistic trifling and dilettantism a general symbol of national decay. He says: 'The debased literature of the dunces and the patronage of such literature by the nobility became the token for more profound failings.' This theme, however, is hidden in the poem itself by a more obvious directing energy. It is at this point that the two aspects of what I call the 'Dunciad problem' clash. The moral thesis (the idea of Pope's high-minded concern for letters) can only be seen as the chief reason for writing the poem if it outweighs the power of the personal spite lavished on the individual portraits and if those portraits themselves are really of true 'Dunces'. In other words, we, as critics, must allow what is most poetically powerful in the poem to determine the poem's real meaning. At the same time

we must be fully aware of the situation as it truly was rather than as
Pope alone presents it.

Let us take the idea of the true 'Dunces' first. Most serious writers of
Pope's age were concerned with what they considered to be the imminent decline of Britain through bad moral and aesthetic standards.
Williams cites Oldmixon as an example. Oldmixon however is presented
as one of the Dunces:

> But now for Authors nobler palms remain:
> Room for my Lord! three Jockeys in his train;
> Six huntsmen with a shout precede his chair;
> He grins, and looks broad nonsense with a stare.
> His honour'd meaning, Dulness thus exprest;
> 'He wins this Patron who can tickle best.'
> ....
> .... Oldmixon the Poet's healing balm
> Strives to extract from his soft, giving palm;
> Unlucky Oldmixon! thy lordly master
> The more thou ticklest, gripes his fist the faster.
> (*Variorum*, II, 183–8, 199–202)

Oldmixon is made a laughing-stock as much for not gaining patronage
(something at which Pope was singularly adept) as for being a party
hack. However, two things are of particular interest. First, the footnote
(199):

Mr. *John Oldmixon* (next to Mr. *Dennis* the most ancient Critick of our
Nation) not so happy as laborious in Poetry, and therefore perhaps [note
the uncertainty] characteris'd by the *Tatler*, No. 62. by the name of
Omicron the *unborn Poet. Curl,* Key to the D. p. 13. [Pope was always
ready to make use of his enemies] An unjust censurer of Mr *Addison,*
[One recalls the story of the inclusion of the portrait of *Atticus* in the
Epistle to Arbuthnot] whom in his imitation of *Bouhours* (call'd the
Arts of Logic and Rhetoric) he misrepresents in plain matter of fact.
In p. 45. he cites the *Spectator* as abusing Dr. *Swift* by name, where
there is not the least hint of it: And in p. 304. is so injurious as to suggest,
that Mr. *Addison* himself writ that *Tatler* No. 43. which says of his *own
Simile,* that "tis as great as ever enter'd into the mind of man.' This
person wrote numbers of books which are not come to our knowledge.
'Dramatick works, and a volume of Poetry, consisting of heroic Epistles,
&c. some whereof are very well done,' saith that great Judge Mr. *Jacob.
Lives of Poets, Vol. 2. p. 303.*

I remember a *Pastoral* of his on the *Battle of Blenheim*; a Critical
History of *England*; Essay on Criticism, in prose; The Arts of Logic
and Rhetoric, in which he frequently reflects on our Author. We find

in the *Flying-Post* of *Apr. 13. 1728*. Some very flat verses of his against him and Dr. *Sw*——, and Mr. *Curl* tells us in the *Curliad,* that he wrote the ballad called the *Catholic Poet* against the Version of *Homer,* before it appear'd to the public.

But the Top of his Character was as a Perverter of History, in that scandalous one of the *Stuarts* in folio, and his Critical History of England, 2 vols. 8°. Being employ'd by Bishop Kennet in publishing the Historians in his Collection, he falsified Daniel's Chronicle in numberless places. Yet this very man, in the Preface to the first of these, advanc'd a *particular Fact* to charge three Eminent Persons of falsifying the Lord Clarendon's History; which Fact has been disprov'd by the Bishop of Rochester, then the only survivor of them, and the particular part produc'd since, after almost ninety years, in that noble Author's own Hand. He was all his life a virulent Party-writer for hire, and received his reward in a small place which he yet enjoys.

The first paragraph of this note makes it clear that Oldmixon is included partly because he had the temerity to attack Pope's friends, while the second makes it abundantly clear that he was included because he attacked Pope himself – a point to which I shall return. However, the final paragraph, in which Pope, of all people, attacks a man for his editorial failings, is a piece of sheer hypocrisy. Yet what sticks in the mind is the poetic image of the patron becoming more tight-fisted the more Oldmixon tries to gain money from him. It is Oldmixon made ridiculous that we remember, not of course the Oldmixon of the note, the last sentence of which rather contradicts the picture presented in the poem. Oldmixon *did* get patronage, but he wrote for money and was poor: that was his chief crime.

The second quotation of interest is that which appears in the *Testimonies of Authors Concerning our Poet and his Works;* an extraordinary collection, the very presence of which proves beyond doubt the personal motivation of the *Dunciad*:

Mr. Oldmixon.
    I dare not say anything of the Essay on Criticism in verse; but if any more curious reader has discovered in it something *new* which is not in Dryden's prefaces, dedications, and his essay on dramatic poetry, not to mention the French critics, I should be very glad to have the benefit of the discovery.

This is a straightforward indictment, the more damning for being true, which shows once again both the scorn in which wholesale plagiarism was held and the interest that the eighteenth century undeniably had in new critical ideas.

I have dealt with Oldmixon at some length, not because he is of particular importance, but rather because his case exemplifies perfectly that of so many of the 'Dunces' – Pope's attack on him is inaccurately stated, uncalled for, and motivated by neurotic personal spite.

I now turn to Theobald, the 'hero' of the first *Dunciad*. It is a point worth making at the outset, that a work which has been so lavishly praised for its construction and called the poem in which the perfect artist found his perfect medium could change its central figure from one version to the next according to how seriously he had offended the author.

I must ask the reader to bear with me if I reiterate some of the facts mentioned in the discussion of Pope's edition of Shakespeare. In editing Shakespeare, Pope's technique was to mark out the scenes as clearly as possible, tighten up the punctuation and rhythm, and then, if anything was left that he did not like, it was 'degraded to the bottom of the page'. The edition that emerged from this procedure has always been widely censured, and the result was, in Johnson's words, already quoted, that 'Pope became an enemy to editors, collators, commentators, and verbal criticks; and hoped to persuade the world, that he miscarried in this undertaking only by having a mind too great for such minute employments.'

Theobald's *SHAKESPEARE RESTORED: or, a Specimen of the Many Errors committed as unemended, by Mr. Pope in his late edition of this poet. Designed not only to correct the said edition, but to restore the true reading of Shakespeare in all editions ever yet published,* was issued in 1726. Its long title makes its intention quite clear. The book was not a personal attack on Pope, it was a work of scholarship prepared for readers of Shakespeare. Theobald worked along the same lines as Bentley had done in his editions of the classics – in other words he emended what he found corrupt in the spirit of 'literal criticism'. In so doing he demonstrated that many of Pope's readings were manifestly absurd, for example the reading of 'onyx' for 'union' in *Hamlet*, V.v. Mistakes of this nature must have infuriated Theobald's scholarly mind, but he is usually temperate when he points them out. Only occasionally is he a little heavy-handed as when he indulges in sarcasm and implies that Pope's printer could not have sent him certain sheets to revise, so gross and obvious are the errors undetected. The book is silently devastating, but that, as I have said, was not its chief aim. Indeed, Theobald went out of his way to praise Pope as an original writer. This passage is both fulsome and polite:

> I have so great an Esteem for MR. POPE, and so high an Opinion of his Genius and Excellencies, that I beg to be excused from the least Intention of derogating from his Merits, in this Attempt to restore the True Reading of SHAKESPEARE. Tho' I confess a Veneration, almost rising to Idolatry for the Writings of this Inimitable Poet, I would be very loath even to do *him* Justice at the Expense of *that other* Gentleman's Character.

If there is a trace of irony here, it is mild and not uncalled for. Pope, of course, was furious, and Theobald, a man of real learning and a profound lover of literature, was to be made the 'hero' of a poem about the oncoming age of cultural darkness. Naturally Pope has been partially excused. Sutherland writes of Theobald's book that 'to one as sensitive as Pope, the publication of this volume must have caused intense annoyance and some acute mental suffering'. Sir Maurice Bowra puts the case more accurately:

> . . . Theobald was in fact a highly gifted pioneer of textual criticism. . . . But Pope dismissed 'Tibbald' with deadly contempt . . . Yet even this is not really the hatred of poetry for scholarship but the hatred of a poet, who has pretentions to being a scholar, for a better scholar than himself. What roused Pope's fury was Theobald's destructive treatment of his own work on Shakespeare, and his motive was more injured vanity than artistic disdain.

In selecting his hero Pope wrote thus:

> A *Person* must be fix'd upon to support this action, who (to agree with the said design) must be such an one as is capable of being all three [i.e. one of the guild of 'Party writers, dull poets, and wild criticks']. This *phantom* in the poet's mind, must have a *name*. He seeks for one who hath been concerned in the *Journals,* written bad *Plays* or *Poems,* and published low *Criticisms*: He finds his name to be *Tibbald,* and he becomes of course the Hero of the poem.

At the very start of the poem, in the ironic footnote appended to the title, Pope writes:

> The *Dunciad, Sic* M.S. It may well be disputed whether this be a right Reading. Ought it not rather to be spelled *Dunceiad,* as the Etymology evidently demands? *Dunce* with an *e,* therefore *Dunceiad* with an *e.* That accurate and punctual Man of Letters, the Restorer of *Shakespeare,* constantly observes the preservation of this very letter *e,* in spelling the Name of his beloved Author, and not like his common careless Editors, with the omission of one, nay sometimes of two *ee's* (as *Shak'spear*) which is utterly unpardonable.

This is mere childishness. Perhaps we should remember that the title of
the poem was originally to be *The Progress of Dulness* until it was
remembered that on the spines of the smaller editions this would
probably appear as *Pope's Dulness*. As it is, Pope ridiculed Theobald's
scholarship, libelled him in the notes, and then criticized him for things
that he had not seen such as his 'cold' translation of Aeschylus. Pope
blames Oldmixon for criticizing his Homer unseen and then writes of
Theobald:

> He had been (to use an expression of our Poet), *about Aeschylus* for ten
> years, and had received Subscriptions for the same, but then went *about*
> other Books. The character of this tragic Poet is Fire and Boldness in
> a high degree; but our Author supposes it to be very much cooled by the
> translation.

Theobald was not a distinguished poet, but then he was certainly
not a party-hack either. However, he *was* an admirable pioneer scholar.
For this love of literature he was pilloried thus:

> ... 'Great Tamer of all human art!
> First in my care, and nearest to my heart:
> Dulness! whose good old cause I yet defend,
> With whom my Muse began with whom shall end!
> O thou, of business the directing soul,
> To human heads like byass to the bowl,
> Which as more pond'rous makes their aim more true,
> Obliquely wadling to the mark in view.
> O ever gracious to perplex'd mankind!
> Who spread a healing mist before the mind,
> And, lest we err by Wit's wild, dancing light,
> Secure us kindly in our native night.
> Ah! still o'er Britan stretch that peaceful wand,
> Which lulls th'Helvetian and Batavian land.
> Where rebel to thy throne if Science rise,
> She does but show her coward face and dies:
> There, thy good Scholiasts with unweary'd pains
> Make Horace flat, and humble Maro's strains;
> Here studious I unlucky moderns save,
> Nor sleeps one error in its father's grave,
> Old puns restore, lost blunders nicely seek,
> And crucify poor Shakespear once a week.
> For thee I dim these eyes, and stuff this head,
> With all such reading as was never read;
> For thee supplying, in the worst of days,
> Notes to dull books, and prologues to dull plays;

For thee explain a thing till all men doubt it,
And write about it, Goddess, write about it;
So spins the silkworm small its tender store,
And labours, till it clouds itself all o'er.
Not that my quill to Critiques was confin'd,
My Verse gave ampler lessons to mankind;
So gravest precepts may successless prove,
But sad examples never fail to move.
....
Had heav'n decreed such works a longer date
Heav'n had decreed to spare the Grubstreet-state.
But see great Settle to the dust descend,
And all thy cause and empire at an end!
Cou'd Troy be sav'd by any single hand,
His gray-goose-weapon must have made her stand.
But what can I? my Flaccus cast aside,
Take up th'Attorney's (once my better) Guide?[1]
Or rob the Roman geese of all their glories,
And save the state by cackling to the Tories?
Yes, to my Country I my pen consign,
Yes, from this moment, mighty Mist! am thine,
And rival, Curtius! of thy fame and zeal,
O'er head and ears plunge for the publick weal.

Theobald did not reply. In a sense he did not need to, for from 1740 onwards Cibber, the new Poet Laureate, was to be the butt of Pope's satire.

Cibber had earned Pope's undying hatred when, in January 1717, he had attacked *Three Hours After Marriage,* a mediocre play by Pope, Gay, and Arbuthnot. Cibber appears to have been a pleasant, easygoing, if somewhat vain, man with no great artistic pretensions but a ready fund of humour. In his autobiography, *An Apology for the Life of Colley Cibber,* he wrote:

... not our great Imitator of *Horace* himself can have more Pleasure in writing his Verses than I have in reading them, tho' I sometimes find myself there (as Shakespear terms it) *dispraisingly* spoken of: if he is a little free with me, I am generally in good Company, he is as blunt with my Betters; so that even here I might laugh in my turn. My Superiors, perhaps, may be mended by him; but, for my part, I own myself incorrigible.

In much of Pope's literary activity, especially during the composition of the *Dunciad,* there is an element of emotional retardation: we have

[1] A reference to the fact that Theobald had started life as a lawyer.

all met the spoilt child who succeeds in getting the attention of which he feels himself deprived by goading his older companions into overt hostility. Repeated attacks by Pope at last wore Cibber's patience down and in 1742 he published *A Letter From Mr. Cibber, To Mr. Pope, Inquiring Into The Motives That Might Induce Him In His Satyrical Works, To Be So Frequently Fond Of Mr. Cibber's Name*. Pope had accused Cibber of having 'his Lord and Whore'. Cibber replied by saying that this was 'the flattest Piece of Satyr that ever fell from the formidable Pen of Mr Pope',

As to the latter Charge, the *Whore*, there indeed, I doubt you will have the better of me; for I must own, *that I believe* I know more of *your* whoring than you do of *mine*; because I don't recollect that ever I made you the least Confidence of *my* Amours, though I have been very near an Eye-Witness of *Yours* – By the way, gentle Reader, don't you think, to say only, *A Man has his Whore,* without some particular Circumstances to aggravate the Vice, is the flattest piece of Satyr that ever fell from the formidable Pen of Mr. *Pope*? because (*defendit numerus*) take the first ten thousand Men you meet, and I believe, you would be no Loser, if you betted ten to one that every single Sinner of them, one with another, had been guilty of the same Frailty. But as Mr. *Pope* has so particularly picked me out of the Number to make an Example of: Why may I not take the same Liberty, and even single him out for another to keep me in Countenance? He must excuse me, then, if in what I am going to relate, I am reduced to make bold a little private Conversation: But as he has shown no Mercy to *Colley,* why should so unprovok'd an Aggressor expect any for himself? And if Truth hurts him, I can't help it. He may remember, then (or if he won't I will) when *Button*'s Coffee-house was in vogue, and so long ago, as when he had not translated above two or three Books of *Homer*; there was a late young Nobleman (as much his *Lord* as mine) who had a good deal of wicked Humour, and who, though he was fond of having Wits in his Company, was not so restrained by his Conscience, but that he lov'd to laugh at any merry Mischief he could do them: This noble Wag, I say, in his usual *Gayeté de Coeur*, with another Gentleman still in being, one Evening slyly seduced the celebrated Mr. *Pope* as a Wit, and myself as a Laugher, to a certain House of Carnal Recreation, near the *Haymarket*; where his Lordship's frolick propos'd was to slip his little *Homer*, as he call'd him, at a Girl of the Game, that he might see what sort of Figure a Man of his Size, Sobriety and Vigour (in Verse) would make, when the frail Fit of Love had got into him; in which he so far succeeded, that the smirking Damsel, who serv'd us with Tea, happen'd to have Charms sufficient to tempt the little-tiny Manhood of Mr. *Pope* into the next room with her: at which you may imagine, his Lordship

was in as much Joy as at what might happen within, as our small
Friend could probably be in Possession of it: But I (forgive me all ye
mortified Mortals whom his fell Satyr has since fallen upon) observing
he had staid as long as without hazard of his Health he might, I
          Prick'd to it by foolish Honesty and Love,
as *Shakespear* says, without Ceremony, threw open the door upon him,
where I found this little hasty Hero, like a terrible *Tom-Tit*, pertly
perching upon the Mount of Love! But such was my Surprize, that I
fairly laid hold of his Heels, and actually drew him down safe and sound
from his Danger. My Lord, who staid tittering without, in hopes the
sweet Mischief he came for would have been compleated, upon my
giving an Account of the Action within, began to curse, and call me an
hundred silly Puppies, for my impertinently spoiling the Sport; to which
with great Gravity I reply'd! pray, my Lord, consider what I have done
was, in regard to the Honour of our Nation! For would you have had so
glorious a Work as that of making *Homer* speak elegant *English,* cut
short by laying up our little Gentleman of a Malady, which his thin
Body might never have been cured of? No, my Lord! *Homer* would
have been too serious a Sacrifice to our Evening Merriment. Now as his
Homer has since been so happily compleated, who can say, that the
World may not have been obliged to the kindly Care of *Colley* that so
great a Work ever came to Perfection?

And now again, gentle Reader, let it be judged, whether the *Lord* and
the *Whore* above-mentioned might not, with equal Justice, have been
apply'd to sober *Sawney* the Satyrist, as to *Colley* the *Criminal*?

Though I confess Recrimination to be but a poor Defence for one's own
Faults; yet when the Guilty are Accusers, it seems but just, to make use
of any Truth that may invalidate their Evidence: I therefore hope,
whatever the serious Reader may think amiss in this Story, will be
excus'd, by my being so hardly driven to tell it.

he younger Richardson records that Pope's features writhed in
nguish when reading Cibber's retaliation. Nevertheless, as Pope de-
ared, 'These things are my diversion'. Pope relished his revenge, and
ssages such as this one from his letters show quite clearly that any high-
inded concern for the state of letters, any endorsement of the similar
mplaints of Marvell and Dryden, were by now subsumed in neurotic
ger:

He will do me more good than a dose of hartshorn [Pope declared to
Warburton] and, as a stink revives one who has been oppressed with
perfumes, his railing will cure me of a dose of flatteries.

another letter to Warburton, Pope declared:

. . . I am told, the Laureate is going to publish a very abusive pamphlet:
that is all I can desire; it is enough if it be *abusive,* & if it be his.

In fact, Cibber was ridiculed in almost identical terms to those used formerly about Theobald and a revealing sense of the inherent weakness of the *Dunciad* can be derived from a comparison between the two versions of the opening of the second book.

When 'Tibbald' was his hero Pope wrote:

> High on a gorgeous seat, that far outshone
> Henley's gilt Tub, or Fleckno's Irish Throne,
> Or that, where on her Curlls, the Public pours
> All-bounteous, fragrant grains, and golden show'rs;
> Great Tibbald sate : The proud Parnassian sneer,
> The conscious simper, and the jealous leer,
> Mix on his look. All eyes direct their rays
> On him, and crowds grow foolish as they gaze.
>
> (*Variorum*, II, 1–8)

When Cibber became the hero, Pope wrote:

> High on a gorgeous seat, that far out-shone
> Henley's gilt tub, or Fleckno's Irish throne,
> Or that where on her curls the Public pours,
> All-bounteous, fragrant Grains and Golden show'rs,
> Great Cibber sate: The proud Parnassian sneer,
> The conscious simper, and the jealous leer,
> Mix on his look: All eyes direct their rays
> On him, and crowds turn Coxcombs as they gaze.
>
> (*Dunciad*, II, 1–8)

The poetic power of the *Dunciad* has been widely praised. Even we set aside Edith Sitwell's fulsome praise, we find that much which th other critics have to say is contradictory or hesitant. Sutherland fc instance declares that 'It has never been sufficiently recognized that i the *Dunciad* one of the greatest artists in English poetry found th perfect material for his art'. Of the personal venom in the poem, I says that 'Pope's callousness . . . is surely that of the sportsman; I concentrates on the pursuit, and thinks little of the victim'. Evading th moral problem, Sutherland retreats into a justification of the *Duncia* as art for art's sake. He says: '. . . the criticism of the nineteenth ar twentieth centuries has been far too much concerned with the mor issues raised by Pope's satire, and too little interested in its pure aesthetic values.' He himself has little to say about these 'aesthet values', and perhaps critics have not been wrong to concern themselv with the moral issues of the poem if to ignore them means to conce trate on the 'aesthetic values' of 'callousness'.

Root's criticism is vitiated by similar *non sequiturs*. 'The *Dunciad* is not only great satire,' he writes, 'but in its kind great poetry. In none of his writings is Pope's mastery of the couplet more complete than here. Line answers line and couplet on couplet, with the sure inevitability of supreme literary craftsmanship.' Already we find that the *Dunciad* is great poetry 'in its kind' and one is reminded of Dr Johnson's use of similarly hesitant phrases. 'The *Dunciad*,' Root continues, 'is great poetry not only in the music of its verse, but in its power to evoke images which carry immediate conviction, if not to the imagination in the higher meanings of that word, at least to the poetic fancy of the reader, images which with nicest accuracy embody the poet's thought.' I have tried to show not only that where these images are effective it is not 'poetic fancy' but rather neurotic hatred that lies behind them, but also that there are passages in the poem, such as this from the third book, which are purely abstract, corresponding to no concrete reality; the versification is faulty and the development of the thought confused:

> 'And see, my son ! the hour is on its way,
> That lifts our Goddess to imperial sway;
> This fav'rite Isle, long sever'd from her reign,
> Dove-like, she gathers to her wings again.
> Now look thro' Fate ! behold the scene she draws !
> What aids, what armies to assert her cause !
> See all her progeny, illustrious sight !
> Behold, and count them, as they rise to light.
> As Berecynthia, while her offspring vye
> In homage to the Mother of the sky,
> Surveys around her, in the blest abode,
> An hundred sons, and ev'ry son a God:
> Not with less glory mighty Dulness crown'd,
> Shall stake thro' Grub-street her triumphant round;
> And her Parnassus glancing o'er at once,
> Behold an hundred sons, and each a Dunce.
> *(Dunciad*, III, 123–38)

This is very confused and essentially mere repetition. The description of Dulness and her children leads to a laboured comparison with Berecynthia and her children who can in turn be compared to Dulness and her children. Such is the construction of the passage, but the ironic comparison fails since it is insufficiently pointed, while the effect of self-generated rhetoric is not helped by such meaningless or near-meaningless phrases as 'This fav'rite Isle . . . Dove-like, she gathers to her wings again' and the expression 'look thro' Fate'. What does 'gather to her wings' mean, how can you gather an island and what has the action to do with doves? Similarly, what does 'look thro' Fate' mean : look through the eyes of fate, see into future times or what?

Root admits that 'from the nature of its substance, [the *Dunciad*] cannot often touch our sensibility or move our sympathy. It offers instead the keen joy of recognition which comes as we watch the flashing play of a disciplined mind, which is also indubitably the mind of a poet'. I am not sure what a poetry is that does not 'touch our sensibility or move our sympathy'. Is it a display of verbal pyrotechnics such as Root seems to admire? Why such a creator has 'indubitably' the mind of a poet I do not understand. A 'disciplined mind' and 'the keen joy of recognition' are phrases equally applicable to the devotees of crossword puzzles. It is quite simply not possible to divorce technique and content in this way but, having attempted to do so, and still wanting to call Pope a poet, Root is forced to adopt such equivocal phrases as 'poetry of a kind'. We can, I think, legitimately ask what kind.

It is however, the peroration that has attracted most attention. Of the fourth book Leavis says: 'I am inclined to think it the most striking manifestation of his genius', while earlier in the century Mackail declared:

> The concluding passage of the new *Dunciad* is poetry before which all criticism has bowed down in admiration. Spence mentions that Pope himself could not repeat it without his voice faltering. 'And well it might', said Johnson when this was told him, 'for they are noble lines'. . . . The admiration can hardly be called excessive, or the praise extravagant.

Let us examine the passage:

> In vain, in vain, – the all-composing Hour
> Resistless falls: The Muse obeys the Pow'r.
> She comes! she comes! the sable Throne behold
> Of *Night* Primaeval, and of *Chaos* old!
> Before her, *Fancy's* guilded clouds decay,
> And all its varying Rain-bows die away.
> *Wit* shoots in vain its momentary fires,
> The meteor drops, and in a flash expires.
> As one by one, at dread Medea's strain,
> The sick'ning stars fade off th'ethereal plain;
> As Argus' eyes by Hermes' wand oppress'd,
> Clos'd one by one to everlasting rest;
> Thus at her felt approach, and secret might,
> *Art* after *Art* goes out, and all is Night.

See skulking *Truth* to her old Cavern fled,
Mountains of Casuistry heap'd o'er her head !
Philosophy, that lean'd on Heav'n before,
Shrinks to her second cause, and is no more.
Physic of *Metaphysic* begs defence,
And *Metaphysic* calls for aid on *Sense* !
See *Mystery* to *Mathematics* fly !
In vain ! they gaze, turn giddy, rave, and die.
Religion blushing veils her sacred fires,
And unawares *Morality* expires.
Nor *public* Flame, nor *private*, dares to shine;
Nor *human* Spark is left, nor Glimpse *divine* !
Lo ! thy dread Empire, *Chaos* ! is restor'd;
Light dies before thy uncreating word:
Thy hand, great Anarch ! lets the curtain fall;
And Universal Darkness buries All.

Certainly this passage contains none of the obsessive cloacal imagery of the earlier books but it is, essentially, untrue. It is a melodramatic gesture of cultural impotence made when eighteenth-century English culture was nearing its prime: Hogarth was at the height of his powers, Fielding had just published *Joseph Andrews,* while *Pamela* and the *Messiah* had also just appeared. But even if we ignore the basic falsity of the social criticism, is the rhetorical grandeur an adequate compensation ? The closing image is an anti-climax:

Thy hand, great Anarch ! lets the curtain fall;
And Universal Darkness buries All.

During nearly two thousand lines of concentrated hatred and philosophic justification we have merely been in a theatre watching a few poor poets strutting and fretting. Perhaps it was not very important after all. How far Pope is from the majesty and seriousness of real poetry, from the passage in *Henry IV,* Part II which he was trying to imitate:

Let Order die . . . . .
And darknesse be the burier of the dead.

What truth does this poem, with its grandiloquent peroration, convey ? We are deceived, as it were, by the grandiloquence of the language into believing that cultural ruin is imminent, through the activities of a number of mediocre writers, mountebanks, and quacks. There have been hack-writers and mediocre poets at all times. Literary culture is advanced *by the good, the great and the original*; it has never been threatened by the bad or the mediocre. Pope's 'dunces', condemned for 250 years among devotees of Pope who have never read the works of his enemies, are no worse than the scribblers of today, or any other day. The idea that men such as Welsted, a passable minor poet, and Cibber, a writer of lively comedies, threatened the future of literature is sheer nonsense. It is nonsense which obscures the true purpose of the *Dunciad* as I have demonstrated it – to pour obloquy on the heads of harmless scribes whom Pope had goaded into attacking him. He made no secret of this. The poem is an elaborate and lengthy exercise in self-glorification. Its justification is that it succeeded. Its purely negative character – the attack on 'Dulness' – is witness to the essential sterility of Pope's imagination.

The poem is, at its best, lively and fluent. Its satirical attacks on individuals are telling. But they do not tell against the victims; they tell of Pope's own energy, cleverness, capacity to turn the writings of others to his own use. The couplet, the false antitheses, the apt and pungent epithets persuade some readers that they are listening to the voice of truth, justice and injured merit. The careful reader knows better. But the *Dunciad* served its purpose. The famous fourth book and the 'seedy grandeur' (in Noel Coward's phrase) of the peroration have provided critical and uncritical readers alike with what some of them prefer to poetry – a brilliant performance. No one can deny the sheer bravura of much of Pope's rhetoric – though, if we are not carried away by its speed and fluency, if we play it, so to speak, in slow motion, it is not difficult to detect very frequent lapses in technique, construction, and argument. It is not a performance to which many poets have accorded unqualified admiration.

Some critics, as I have indicated, have been only too ready to excuse the vulgarity, the injustice, the sheer cruelty of the *Dunciad* by the 'aesthetic' defence: these 'Dunces', it is argued, were not real people; they were fictions of Pope's creative imagination. The 'moral' case against the poem is a Victorian heresy. But do we now, in the last quarter of the twentieth century, make a simple dichotomy of moral and aesthetic criteria? To Pope, for one, the notion of the 'Dunces' as figments of his imagination would certainly have been unacceptable. If he had been writing what was intended to be taken as fiction, he would have proceeded very differently. He would scarcely have taken the trouble to stir up a nest of actual, living 'hornets' to sting him. He provoked their attacks; he revelled in them. He collected their pamphlets against him, and the four bound volumes can be seen in the British Museum. This is perhaps more a matter for psychological than for literary comment. The 'Dunces' were real men, hack-writers, mostly, without Pope's unquestionable talent. They were pilloried, and many suffered. They were pilloried for the greater glory of Alexander Pope. When I call the *Dunciad* an evil poem, therefore, I mean that it is morally ugly, and therefore aesthetically unacceptable. I cannot see how we can take much pleasure in the poem unless we enjoy watching the enactment of evil. Perhaps we do. But let us be honest about it.

Select Bibliography

Books quoted, discussed, and consulted.

The Seventeenth and Eighteenth Centuries

ADDISON, JOSEPH, *The Life and Writings of*, London 1843.
AYRE, WILLIAM, *Memoirs of the Life and Writings of Alexander Pope Esq.*, London, 1745.

CIBBER, COLLEY, *An Apology for the Life of* (ed. R. W. Lowe), London: 1889.

DRYDEN, JOHN, 'The Grounds of Criticism in Tragedy': The Preface to his adaptation of *Troilus and Cressida*, London, 1679.

GAY, JOHN, *Letters* (ed. C. F. Burgess), Oxford, 1966.
GILDON, CHARLES (ascribed to but now regarded as being by Dennis), *A True Character of Mr. Pope*, London, 1716.
GRANVILLE, GEORGE, Lord Lansdowne, *The Genuine Works in Verse and Prose*, London: 1736.
GRAY, THOMAS, Correspondence of (ed. Paget Toynbee & Leonard Whibley), Oxford, 1935.

JOHNSON, SAMUEL, *Lives of the English Poets*, London, 1781.

POEMS ON AFFAIRS OF STATE, *Augustan Satirical Verse*, Vol. I, 1660–1678, Yale, 1963.
POOLE, JOSEPH, *The English Parnassus: or A Help to English Poesy*, London, 1677.
POPE, ALEXANDER, *Poems* (Twickenham Edition, eleven volumes. General Editor: John Butt), London, 1939–1969.
POPE, ALEXANDER, *Correspondence* (ed. George Sherburn), Oxford, 1956.
POPE, ALEXANDER, *The Prose Works*, 1711–1720 (ed. Norman Ault), Vol. I [Vol. II not published], Blackwell, Oxford, 1936.

RUFFHEAD, OWEN, *The Life of Alexander Pope.* Compiled from Original Manuscripts; with a critical essay on his Writings and Genius, London, 1769.

SWIFT, JONATHAN, *Letter of Advice to a Young Poet,* London and Dublin, 1721.
SWIFT, JONATHAN, *The Poems* (ed. Harold Williams), Oxford, 1937.
SWIFT, JONATHAN, *The Correspondence* (ed. Harold Williams), Oxford, 1963–65.

WALPOLE, HORACE, *Notes on the Poems of Alexander Pope,* London, 1871.
WARTON, JOSEPH, *An Essay on the Genius and Writings of Pope,* London, 1756 and 1782. Revised Edition, Farnborough, 1969.
WELSTED, LEONARD, *The Works in verse and Prose* [ed. John Nichols], London, 1787.

The Nineteenth Century

ARNOLD, MATTHEW, *On Translating Homer,* London, 1861.
ARNOLD, MATTHEW, *Essays in Criticism* (Second Series), London, 1888.

BOWLES, WILLIAM LISLE [ed.], *The Works of Alexander Pope Esq. in Verse and Prose,* London, 1806.
BYRON, GEORGE GORDON LORD *Poetical Works* [ed. John Murray], London, 1845.

DENNIS, JOHN, *The Age of Pope,* London, 1894.
D'ISRAELI, ISAAC, *Quarrels of Authors,* London, 1814.

ELWIN, WHITWELL, *Introduction to his edition of Pope's poems,* London, 1871.

HAZLITT, WILLIAM, *Lectures on the English Poets,* London, 1825.

LLOYD, CHARLES, *A Poetical Essay on the Character of Pope, as a Poet and Moralist,* London, 1821.

NICHOLS, JOHN, *Literary Anecdotes of the Eighteenth Century,* London, 1812.

ROBINSON, HENRY CRABB, *On Books and their Writers* (ed. Edith J. Morley), London, 1938.
RUSKIN, JOHN, *Oxford Lectures on Art*, Oxford, 1870.

SAINTSBURY, GEORGE, *A Short History of English Literature*, London, 1898.
SPENCE, JOSEPH, *Anecdotes, Observations, and Characters, of Books and Men*. Collected from the Conversation of Mr. Pope, and other Eminent Persons of his time, London, 1820.
STEPHEN, LESLIE, *Alexander Pope*, London, 1880.
STEPHEN, LESLIE, *Hours in a Library*, Vol. I, London, 1899.

TENNYSON, HALLAM, *A Memoir* (of Lord Tennyson) *by his Son*, London, 1897.
THACKERAY, W. M., *The English Humorists*, London, 1853.

The Twentieth Century

ALLEN, ROBERT J., *The Clubs of Augustan London*, Cambridge, USA, 1933.
AULT, NORMAN, *New Light on Pope*, London, 1949.

BEALES, A.C.F., *Education under Penalty*, London, 1963.
BEATTIE, LESTER M., *John Arbuthnot, Mathematician and Satirist*, Cambridge, USA, 1935.
BELJAME, ALEXANDRE [trans. E. O. Lorimer], *Men of Letters and the English Public in the Eighteenth Century 1660–1744*, London, 1948.
BOWRA, MAURICE, *In General and Particular*, London, 1964.
BREDVOLD, LOUIS, *The Gloom of the Tory Satirists. Pope and his Contemporaries* [ed. Clifford and Landa], Oxford, 1949.
BROWER, REUBEN, *Alexander Pope: the Poetry of Allusion*, Oxford, 1959.
BUTT, JOHN, *The Inspiration of Pope's Poetry. Essays on the Eighteenth Century presented to D. Nicol Smith*, Oxford, 1945.
BUTT, JOHN, *The Augustan Age*, London, 1950.

CAZAMIAN, LOUIS, *A History of English Literature* [Legouis and Cazamian] Part II, London, 1957.
CLARK, A. F. B., *Boileau and the French Classical Critics in England 1660–1830*, Paris, 1925.
CUNNINGHAM, J. S., *Pope: The Rape of the Lock*, London, 1961.

DAVIE, DONALD, *Purity of Diction in English Verse*, London, 1952.
DOBRÉE, BONAMY, chapters on Pope in the *Oxford History of English Literature* Vol. VII: *English Literature in the Early Eighteenth Century 1700–1740* (ed. F. P. Wilson and Bonamy Dobrée), Oxford, 1959.
DOBRÉE, BONAMY, *Alexander Pope*, London, 1951.

ELIOT, T. S., *The Use of Poetry and the Use of Criticism*, London, 1943.
ERSKINE-HILL, HOWARD, *Pope: The Dunciad*, London, 1972.
FOOT, MICHAEL, *The Pen and the Sword*, London, 1951.
FORD, FORD MADOX, *The March of Literature*, London, 1947.

HALLIDAY, G. E., *A Shakespeare Companion, 1564–1964*, London, 1964.
HALSBAND, ROBERT, *The Life of Lady Mary Wortley Montagu*, Oxford, 1956.
HARLAN, EARL, *Elijah Fenton 1683–1730*, Philadelphia, 1937.
HASSALL, ARTHUR, *Life of Viscount Bolingbroke*, Blackwell, Oxford, 1913.
HAVENS, RAYMOND DEXTER, *The Influence of Milton on English Poetry*, Harvard/Oxford, 1922.
HEATH-STUBBS, JOHN, *Selected Poems of Alexander Pope*, London, 1964.
HILLES, FREDERICK W. & BLOOM, HAROLD [ed.], *From Sensibility to Romanticism: Essays Presented to Frederick A. Pottle*, New York, 1965.
HILLHOUSE, JAMES T., *The Grub-Street Journal*, North Carolina, 1928.

ILCHESTER, LORD [ed.], *Lord Hervey and his Friends 1726–1738*, London, 1950.

KETTON-CREMER R. W., *Thomas Gray: A Biography*, Cambridge, 1955.
KNIGHT, G. WILSON, *Laureate of Peace*, London, 1954.
KRUTCH, JOSEPH WOOD, *Pope and our Contemporaries. Pope and his Contemporaries* [ed. Clifford and Landa], Oxford, 1949.

LEAVIS, F. R., *Revaluation*, London, 1936.
LEAVIS, F. R., *The Common Pursuit*, London, 1952.
LEVINE, J. ARNOLD, 'The Status of the Verse Epistle before Pope', *Studies in Philology LIX*, University of North Carolina, 1962.

LEWIS, C. S., *Essays and Studies*, Vol. XIX, Oxford, 1934.

LEWIS, C. S., *The Discarded Image*, Cambridge, 1964.

LEYS, M. D. R., *Catholics in England 1559–1829*, London, 1961.

MACDONALD, W. L., *Pope and his Critics*, London, 1951.

MACK, MAYNARD, 'Wit and Poetry and Pope': Some Observations on his Imagery: Pope and his contemporaries. *Essays presented to George Sherburn*, Oxford, 1949.

MACK, MAYNARD, 'The Muse of Satire', *Yale Review* Vol. XLI, Yale, 1951.

MACKAIL, J. W., *Pope: the Leslie Stephen Lecture*, Cambridge, 1919.

READ, HERBERT, *Collected Essays in Literary Criticism*, London, 1938.

ROGERS, ROBERT W., *The Major Satires of Alexander Pope*, University of Illinois Press, Urbana, 1955.

ROOT, ROBERT KILBURN, *The Poetical Career of Alexander Pope*, Princeton/Oxford, 1941.

SHERBURN, GEORGE, *The Early Career of Alexander Pope*, Oxford, 1934.

NICHOL SMITH, DAVID, *Some Observations on Eighteenth Century Poetry*, London, 1937.

NICHOL SMITH, DAVID [ed.], *The Letters of Thomas Burnet to George Duckett 1712–1722*, Roxburghe Club, Oxford, 1914.

SITWELL, EDITH, *Alexander Pope*, Faber, 1930.

STRAUS, RALPH, *The Unspeakable Curll*, London, 1927.

SUTHERLAND, JAMES, *A Preface to Eighteenth Century Poetry*, Oxford, 1948.

SUTHERLAND, JAMES, *Defoe*, London, 1937.

SYMONDS, E. M. [George Paston], *Lady Mary Wortley Montagu*, London, 1907.

SYMONDS, E. M. [George Paston], *Mr. Pope: His Life and Times*, London, 1909.

TILLOTSON, GEOFFREY, *The Moral Poetry of Pope*, Newcastle-upon-Tyne, 1946.

TILLOTSON, GEOFFREY, *Matthew Arnold and Eighteenth Century Poetry*: Essays presented to D. Nichol Smith, Oxford, 1945.

TILLOTSON, GEOFFREY, *On the Poetry of Pope*, Oxford, 1938, Second edition, 1950.

TILLOTSON, GEOFFREY, Pope's 'Epistle to Harley': an Introduction and Analysis. *Pope and his Contemporaries* [ed. Clifford and Landa], Oxford, 1949.

TIMES LITERARY SUPPLEMENT [anon. review], 29 December 1961, *The Youngest Pope*, London, 1961.

WAIN, JOHN, *Essays on Literature and Ideas*, London, 1963.

WARREN, AUSTIN, *Rage for Order*, Chicago, 1948.

WHITE, R. J., *Dr. Bentley: a Study in Academic Scarlet*, London, 1965.

WILLIAMS, AUBREY L., *Pope's* Dunciad: *a Study of its Meaning*, London, 1955.

WIMSATT, WILLIAM K., *The Portraits of Alexander Pope*, Yale, 1965.

Index

Cicero, (106–43 B.C.), 134
Clark, A. F. B., 95n.
Cleland, William (c. 1674–1741), 238
Cobham, Richard Temple, Viscount (c. 1669–1749), 10, 37, 182, 194
Cockney School, 17
Colepepper, Sir William, 189
Coleridge, Samuel Taylor (1772–1834), 90
  on Pope and his followers, 3
  Byron and, 16n, 17
  and Pope, 20
  and Lloyd, 20
  Mackail on, 46
  Sutherland on, 74
  Knight and *Kubla Khan*, 88, 89
  Pre-Raphaelites and, 100
Congreve, William (1670–1729), 116, 130, 147, 201
Cooke, Thomas (1703–56), 176
Cope, Mrs, 163
Corbet, Bishop Richard (1582–1635), 142
Courthorpe, William John (1842–1917), 31, 34
Coward, Noel, 254
Cowley, Abraham (1618–67), 120, 137, 151
Cowper, Judith, 73
Crabbe, George (1784–1832), 16, 17
Crashaw, Richard (c. 1613–49), 3, 99
Crauford, David (1665–1726), 160
Cromwell, Henry, 116, 231
Crousaz, Jean-Pierre de (1663–1750), 224
Cunningham, J. S.
  and Pope criticism, 40
  and *Rape*, 142–4, 148
  and Arnold, 143
  on Pope's versification, 143–4
Curll, Edmund (1675–1747), 2, 225
  Edith Sitwell and, 49
  Pope and, 108, 155–6, 174, 224, 229
  Town Eclogues, 155
  and Pope's letters, 231–2, 233
  and *Dunciad*, 242, 243
Cutler, Sir John (c. 1608–93), 190

Dacier, André (1651–1722), 175, 176
Daiches, David, 142
Daniel, Samuel (1562–1619), 157
Dante Alighieri (1265–1321), 87
Davenant, Sir William (1606–68), 134, 146
Davies, Sir John (1569–1626), 99
Defoe, Daniel (c. 1660–1731), 28, 36, 37, 81
Denham, Sir John (1615–69), 3, 120, 134, 146

Dennis, John (1654–1734)
  Pope's attacks on, 13, 27, 35, 83, 139
  on poetry, 73, 130, 131
  Dobrée and, 83
  quarrels with Pope, 126–9, 131, 202
  attacks Addison's *Cato*, 128
  as critic, 129–30
  attitude to plagiarism, 130
  The Grounds of Criticism in Poetry, 130
  one of Pope's sources, 134, 146
  and *Rape*, 139, 144
  and *Dunciad*, 147, 242
  and Pope's *Odyssey*, 176
  and *Essay on Man*, 227
Dennis, John (fl. 1890)
  on Pope's standing, 1
  and Pope, 42
Dobrée, Bonamy, 19;
  and Pope, 82–6
  and *Rape*, 140
  on Pope's *Preface* to Shakespeare, 180
  on *Essay on Man*, 228
Dodington, George Bubb, 1st Baron Melcombe (1691–1762), 203
Donne, John (1573–1631), 54, 99, 157, 165
Dorset, Charles Sackville, 6th Earl of (1638–1706), 146
Drayton, Michael (1563–1631), 157
Drummond of Hawthornden, William (1585–1649), 99
Dryden, John (1631–1700), 130, 201, 249
  his influence on poetry, 72, 98, 99
  Pope and, 7, 43, 54, 58, 85, 100, 104, 116, 122–3, 133, 140, 211, 219
  Johnson and, 8
  Byron and, 17
  Arnold and, 39
  Tennyson on, 44
  Nichol Smith and, 57
  Sutherland on, 74
  Knight on, 87
  Brower on, 97, 98, 99, 100
  dedication to *Examen Poeticum*, 97–8
  on Walsh, 116
  and *Pastorals*, 119, 120, 122, 123
  and *Essay on Criticism*, 133, 134, 136, 137
  and *Rape*, 147, 149
  on Ovid, 157
  and *Elegy*, 165
  and Chaucer, 167, 168, 169
  and translations of Homer, 170
  his satire, 211
  Mack on, 219
Dupplin, Thomas Hay, later 8th Earl Kinnoul (d. 1787), 207

Theophrastus (c, 373–286 B.C.), 222
Thomson, James (1700–48), 63, 109
Tibullus, (c. 54–19 B.C.), 157, 162, 163
Tickell, Thomas (1686–1740), 23, 172
Tillotson, Geoffrey, 19, 68
  and Johnson, 8
  on Bowles–Byron controversy, 13
  and Arnold, 40–41
  and Pope, 41, 60–66, 73
  and Edith Sitwell, 47–8
  On the Poetry of Pope, 53, 60
  his personal aesthetic, 60–61
  and eighteenth-century poetry, 74
  supports bio-criticism, 79
  and *Pastorals*, 118
  and *Rape*, 140, 149
  attitude to Pope criticism, 142
  on Pope's and heroic epistle, 158
  and *Eloïsa*, 158, 159, 160–61
  vindicates Pope's 'borrowings', 166
  and *Wife of Bath her Prologue*, 169
  on Pope's letters, 234–5
Times Literary Supplement
  and Pope's personality, 69, 107
  on *Essay on Criticism*, 133–4
Topham, Richard, 186
Tonson, Jacob (1656–1736), 116–17, 125
Toynbee, Philip, 48
Trilling, Lionel, 78
Trumbull, Sir William (1639–1716), 116, 201
Twickenham
  Pope's way of life at, 170
  Pope and the Richardsons at, 225
Twickenham edition of Pope's Works, 31, 32, 67, 72, 142
  definitive, 53
  Butt and, 58
  and Pope as nature poet, 59
  and Pope's sources, 118
  and *Pastorals*, 121, 123–4
  and *Essays*, 135, 183, 220
  and Garth's *Dispensary*, 136
  and *Rape*, 140, 147
  and *Eloïsa*, 156–7
  and *Elegy*, 163
  and Pope's translations of Chaucer, 167, 168, 169
  on Pope's treatment of Broome and Fenton, 174
  and *Iliad*, 177
  on *Odyssey*, 180
  on Theobald, 182
  and *Dunsiad*, 237

Vaughan, Henry (1622–95), 99
Victorians, the
  and disapproval of Pope, 5, 12
  rhetoric, 29
  and Pope criticism, 40, 107, 111
  Pope's popularity among, 67
  and Pope's letters, 230
  and *Dunciad*, 254
Vida, Marco Girolamo (c. 1480–1566)
  and *Essay on Criticism*, 134, 136, 137
  and *Rape*, 139, 146
Villars, Abbé de Montfaucon, 4, 146
Virgil (70–19 B.C.), 123
  and *Pastorals*, 3, 97, 101, 117, 119, 120, 123
  Ruskin on Pope and, 30
  influence on Pope, 60
  and *Rape*, 100, 140, 145, 146, 151
  Windsor Forest and the *Georgics*, 102
  Dryden and, 116, 147
  Walsh on, 118
  Eclogues, 123
  and *Essay on Criticism*, 137
  and *Eloïsa*, 160
Voiture, Vincent (1598–1648), 231
Voltaire, François Marie Arouet de (1694–1778), 214
Vulgate, the, 146

Wain, John, 108–10
Wakefield, Gilbert (1756–1801), 31, 176
Waller, Edmund (1606–87)
  and Augustan poetry, 55
  Pope and, 85, 102
  and *Pastorals*, 120, 121
  and *Essay on Criticism*, 134
  and *Rape*, 146
Walpole, Horace, 4th Earl of Orford (1717–97), 7, 168
Walpole, Sir Robert, 1st Earl of Orford (1676–1745), 37
Walsh, William (1663–1708), 82, 130, 131
  and Pope, 116, 201
  Dryden on, 116
  and *Pastorals*, 120, 123
Warburton, William (1698–1779), 1, 213
  Pope writes to, 91, 183
  on *Rape*, 149
  attitude to women, 150
  Pope's editor, 183
  Spence and, 184
  defends Pope, 224–5
Warren, Austin
  on Augustan poets, 71
  and Pope, 71–2